"Once a Foe, Now a Friend"

*First-Hand Accounts from Civil War
Veterans of Battles Lost & Won*

William Emerson

"ONCE A FOE, NOW A FRIEND"
FIRST-HAND ACCOUNTS FROM CIVIL WAR
VETERANS OF BATTLES LOST & WON

iUniverse books may be ordered through booksellers or by contacting:

iUniverse
1663 Liberty Drive
Bloomington, IN 47403
www.iuniverse.com
844-349-9409

Cover Images (clockwise from top left):
Front:
Major Preston M. Farrington, 1st Rhode Island Cavalry
Major John L. Thompson, 1st Rhode Island Cavalry
Captain Henry C. Lee, 4th Virginia Cavalry
General Thomas T. Munford, Confederate Cavalry Brigade

Rear:
Captain Henry S. Burrage, 36th Massachusetts Volunteers
George N. Bliss, 1st Rhode Island Cavalry
Captain Alexander D. Payne, 4th Virginia Cavalry
Private Hugh Hamilton, 4th Virginia Cavalry

ISBN: 978-1-6632-3707-1 (sc)
ISBN: 978-1-6632-3708-8 (e)

Library of Congress Control Number: 2022904583

Print information available on the last page.

iUniverse rev. date: 04/25/2022

Contents

Acknowledgments

This is the second book related to George N. Bliss, a Rhode Island soldier in the Civil War. Dr. Elizabeth C. Stevens, formerly associate editor of the *Papers of General Nathanael Greene* series at the Rhode Island Historical Society (RIHS), was co-editor on the earlier Bliss volume and shared transcription and annotation efforts on this as well. Her help was invaluable in making this second book a reality, and I thank her.

Most letters herein came from Bliss's papers; however, a number where noted, come from the George N. Bliss Collection (MSS 298) in the Mary Elizabeth Robinson Research Center at the Rhode Island Historical Society. I wish to thank the society and its director, Dr. C. Morgan Grefe, for permitting the publication of these letters. Others come from accounts Bliss published after the war, and from newspaper articles.

This volume would not have been possible without the far-sighted action of my brother, Frederick G. Emerson, and his late wife, Marion Stewart Emerson. After our grandmother's death in 1967, piles of Bliss's papers and artifacts were headed for a dumpster when Fred and Marion stepped in and saved them. The letters herein, from Bliss's Civil War friends, were only a portion of what they saved.

I am grateful to others who made this book more complete. Leo Kennedy graciously provided photographs from his extensive collection of First Rhode Island Cavalry artifacts. Andrew Smith, of the R.I. Judicial Records Archives, shared court records regarding Bliss's cavalry colleague, Preston Farrington. Ken Carlson of the Rhode Island State Archives provided access to the invaluable Descriptive Muster Rolls (DMR) for the First R.I. Regiment. Teresa Roane, Archivist at the American Civil War Museum, provided access to the papers of Confederate Captain Henry C. Lee, a brave soldier who stepped in to save Bliss's life during the war.

Bryson Clevenger of the Alderman Library at the University of Virginia, and Professor Ervin L. Jordan, Jr., of the Albert and Shirley Small Special Collections Library there, helped find sources regarding Dr. John Staige Davis, who cared for Bliss in a Confederate hospital. Dr. John Staige Davis, IV kindly shared family documents that illuminated his very compassionate great-grandfather. Others who significantly contributed their efforts include Marlea Leljedal, at the Army Heritage and Education Center, with access to their MOLLUS Massachusetts Civil War Collection, and Hannah Rich, who skillfully translated the Latin phrases used.

Thanks, too, to Sara Jane Tanner for translating my poorly expressed mental images into a fine cover design.

Introduction

George N. Bliss, the recipient of the first-hand accounts that make up this volume, graduated from law school in June 1861, just as the Civil War had broken out. He soon became a cavalry officer in the Union army and regularly wrote home to a close friend, David V. Gerald. His letters spanned nearly the entire war and chronicled his many battles; his capture by the Confederates; his wounds and treatment by the enemy; and his imprisonment. These letters were featured in the 2018 book, *"Don't Tell Father I have been shot at," The Civil War Letters of Captain George N. Bliss, First Rhode Island Cavalry*, published by McFarland & Company. Letters from that work are occasionally mentioned in this volume. When so, they are referred to as Bliss's "wartime" letters.

After the war, while holding office in the Rhode Island General Assembly and running a private law office, Bliss regularly corresponded with ex-Confederates, some of whom he had wounded, as well as with former Union soldiers. He pressed his friends to give accounts of battles in which they had fought, especially those in which both were involved, often as adversaries. His efforts were rewarded by dozens of accounts with fascinating tales and remarkable coincidences. See biography of Bliss in Chapter 8.

With the fighting concentrated almost exclusively in the South, life there was completely altered for generations; crops had been trampled and livestock run off or killed. Early on Bliss had written in a wartime letter, "Orchards [are] cut down also acres of woodland fences burned. You know nothing about the evils of war in R.I. but the inhabitants of this section fully appreciate it. An army like a flock of geese eat up everything in front and spoil everything in the rear."[1] Inflation had destroyed the value of paper money and economic hardship followed. In several cities, including the

Confederate capital, bread and foodstuffs had been so scarce that women had rioted; vast numbers of homes, barns, factories, roads, bridges and railways had been destroyed. At war's end, the South had lost two-thirds of its assessed wealth, and by 1870, wealth had decreased sixty percent from the decade before.[2] As one of Bliss's Confederate correspondents had written in his diary immediately after the surrender at Appomattox, "[T]oday I became aware that what I have on is all that is left of my 'worldly goods.'"[3]

By contrast, the war created little disturbance of daily life in Union territory. Agricultural production quickly expanded and despite the need to feed vast armies, food was always plentiful. To meet increased demand, new factories had been built and after the conflict ended, production continued supplying products for the whole nation and beyond. Economically, the war was good for Northerners; wealth increased by fifty percent during the decade of the 1860s.[4]

The accounts herein are extraordinarily frank. Heartfelt opinions about politics and life in the post-war country are expressed, and day-to-day events are reported. Bliss and many of his ex-Confederate friends shared intimate details of personal life and financial woes. The severe economic swings in the late 1800s, which led to numerous financial panics and depressions, obviously effected both North and South. Bliss occasionally and tactfully offered to provide loans and even sent seeds needed for planting. The warm relationships that developed lasted for decades and in some cases, for generations.

With the impact of the war so devastating for the South, it is not surprising that the tone of these letters is quite different depending on whether written by former Union or Confederate soldiers. Former Union soldiers were willing to write out careful details about battles. They were generally upbeat even when describing battles in which they were badly beaten. Southern participants, while quite willing to communicate with Bliss, nevertheless required months, even years, of prodding before bringing themselves to rehash old battles. The South, having lost the war, had bitter feelings that persisted for generations. Revisiting this horrendous loss was an unpleasant activity. As one ex-Confederate officer wrote, "You will pardon me too for saying that any retrospect of the war is a sad one with me. I feel as Aeneas felt when Dido asked him to narrate the story of the fall of Troy – 'iubes renovare dolorem' [*you order me to retell grief*]." Many in the South felt alienated from their reunified country until at least 1884, when Grover Cleveland was elected president, the first Democrat since the Civil War. One Bliss southern friend wrote, "[S]ince the election of Cleaveland [Cleveland] there is a feeling of releif [*sic*] among us, and we feel that we will once more be treated as equals in one Common Country. We think from all we can gather of Mr. Cleveland, that he will make a good President. He has a heap to reform, and we think he is capable of doing it. Already business is beginning to improve in the South. The factories that have been closed, are starting up again almost every day, and new enterprises are being started."[5]

Accounts herein came from a variety of sources as diverse as Union Major Preston Farrington, "the bravest officer" Bliss knew, to Thomas T. Munford, an ex-Confederate general, whose brigade participated in the biggest defeat Bliss's 1st R.I. Cavalry suffered in the war.

Regrettably, there are several racist comments in these accounts, from both Southerners and Northerners. Sadly, these reflect the existing prejudices against minorities at the time. To maintain historical accuracy, they have not been removed.

BREAD RIOTS.

Bread riots, which the rebels were so fond of predicting in the early stages of th national crisis, have indeed arrived; but, unhappily for the prophets, they are at their doors and not at ours. In the very capital of the Confederacy, under the eye of Jeff. Davis and his accomplices in mischief, three thousand starving women have raged along the streets, broken open and sacked stores, and supplied themselves with food and clothing wherever they could. A few weeks ago a similar disturbance was reported as taking place at Savannah; and a short time before the women of Atlanta helped themselves in like manner, presenting pistols at the heads of shopkeepers. At Raleigh, N. C., a company of women went to a store and appropriated several barrels of molasses. At Salisbury, in the same State, on the 18th ult., a mob of soldiers' wives armed themselves with hatchets, and visited one store after another, demanding and obtaining flour and molasses. Another riot has since occurred at Petersburg. We may well imagine that these six instances are only a part of the cases which have actually occurred thus far, and only the beginning of what is yet to come. The Raleigh *Standard* says: "Bread riots have commenced, and when they will end God only knows."

Report of Confederate Bread Riots, *Lancaster Examiner & Harald*, May 15, 1863

CHAPTER ONE

Encounter with Captain Alexander
D. Payne, Fourth Virginia Cavalry

In December 1862, General Ambrose Burnside was commanding the Union Army of the Potomac. With his army opposite Fredericksburg, he was preparing to attack Robert E. Lee's well positioned army across the Rappahannock River. The First R.I. Cavalry was guarding the perimeter of Burnside's army near a small crossroads called Hartwood Church, located northeast of Fredericksburg. At the same time, Alexander D. Payne (1837-1893) was in Confederate general Fitzhugh Lee's Cavalry Corps that repeatedly raided behind Union lines.[1]

George Bliss came upon Payne while in command of twelve men on picket duty near Hartwood Church. Payne commanded a larger group of wounded Confederates and Union prisoners and was attempting to pass through Bliss's picket line. Because Bliss had only a few men with him and Payne had only a few in fighting condition, neither was able to accept battle. Both were extremely relieved when conflict was avoided.

Years after the war, quite by accident, Bliss discovered details about the chance meeting while reading a popular book titled, *Annals of the War*. A chapter had been written by Colonel John Scott, titled "The Black Horse Cavalry." Scott had been the first commander of the troop and had described the encounter at Hartwood Church.

Scott's cavalry was an outstanding fighting force. Formed two years before the start of the war, it consisted of "planters" from Fauquier County, Virginia, and had developed many of the difficult skills needed to fight on horseback. For most of the war this cavalry company was incorporated in the 4th Va. Cavalry regiment.[2]

From Scott's chapter, Bliss learned for the first time Payne's name, and immediately contacted him. Payne, from Warrenton, was tall at 6'1," had a fair complexion, light hair and grey eyes. He entered William and Mary College in 1853 and in three years graduated first in his class. Payne then entered the University of Virginia, studied law for a year, and began to practice law in Warrenton. In April 1861, the twenty-four-year-old, who always referred to himself as A. D. Payne, enlisted in the Black Horse Cavalry. By September he was promoted to Second Lieutenant. Promotion to First Lieutenant came in April 1862. He was commended by General Stonewall Jackson for his services during the battles of Second Manassas and Antietam. His promotion to Captain came in September 1863, and he commanded the Black Horse Cavalry troop until the end of the war.[3]

Payne was captured twice; in November 1862 and in April 1863. He was exchanged each time. He had a horse killed under him at Waynesboro, Virginia, in September 1864, minutes before Bliss was captured. Having lost his horse, Payne was not present when Bliss was captured by Payne's men. (During the war, most soldiers in the South supplied their own horses. Payne apparently did, and was eventually paid $3500 by the Confederate government for the loss).[4]

After hostilities ended, A. D. Payne resumed the law profession, becoming prominent in Warrenton. He married in 1867 and had five children, four girls and a boy. In addition to his high-profile law practice which specialized in bankruptcy cases, Payne was a member of the State Legislature several terms, representing Loudoun and Fauquier Counties. He and his family lived in Warrenton at "Mecca," the family home, situated on Culpeper Street. He died in 1893 at the age of fifty-five, of Bright's disease. One of his pallbearers was Hugh Hamilton (see Chapter Five for Hamilton's letters). His obituary noted one of the "floral offerings . . .presented by his comrades. . . a pillow of red roses four feet square, with a pair of crossed sabres and an inscription 'From Manassas to Appomattox,' in white roses."[5]

There is an interesting story about Payne during the war. In a letter to her father Lycurgus Caldwell, Susan Caldwell wrote, "Lieut. Payne rode in town Thursday with a Yankee Lieut., having captured him the other side of the river. On coming to the River they found the river too high to cross, so they would have to swim. Lieut. Payne made the first attempt, and would have been drowned had not the Yankee Lieut. jumped in and saved him (How generous! Noble hearted Yankee he was indeed, one with a soul has been left in our midst). It appeared that the water was higher at that point than lower down but the Lieut. was not aware of it when he attempted to swim. There were 5 of our soldiers in company with Lieut. Payne who could have saved him as well as the Yankee - but the Yankee took no thought, but was ready to save the life of his enemy - Lieut. Payne wrote an account of it to Genl. Lee. I hope he will be released soon." A southern newspaper reported that the "Yankee" was Lieutenant William F. Stone, of the First Maine Cavalry. After J.E.B. Stuart learned of the affair, the newspaper reported, he asked that some consideration be made for Stone. The Confederate Secretary of War ordered Stone's "unconditional discharge from parole or exchange" and he was immediately sent North on the Flag of Truce boat. In a clipping from an unknown newspaper found in Bliss's papers, the story continued. "But the strangest part of the story is yet to come." When Stone arrived in Washington, D.C. a few days later, he found that Lieut. Paine had since been captured and was in the Old Capital Prison. He obtained a pass to visit Payne. By now, the Stone rescue and release was in the newspapers and Stone sent a copy with a cover letter to Gen. Hitchcock, in charge of prisoner exchanges. Hitchcock wrote Payne, "I should have no hesitation in recommending your being placed on parole. . .You will bear with yourself the proper reward of honorable conduct in the consciousness of it. . ." The newspaper continued, "In a few days . . . Lieut. Payne was on his way to his command again."[6]

Five letters from Payne were found in Bliss's papers, written from 1879 through 1882. Two are presented in this volume, one in this chapter and one in Chapter 5. Due to a mix-up, the men did not meet in 1880 when Bliss visited other ex-Confederate friends in Virginia. Another visit by Bliss was aborted due to illness in Payne's household. There is no evidence they ever met after the war.

Alexander Dixon Payne (Library of Congress Prints and Photographs Division, Washington D.C.; LC-DIG-ppmsca-33343)

A. D. Payne, Attorney-at-Law.
March 29, 1879
Bank Building. Warrington, Va.
Capt. Geo. N. Bliss,

My Dear Sir—I desire to acknowledge the very great pleasure yours of the 22d inst. [e.g., March], with enclosure, gave me. I did not know that the officer whose gallantry at Waynesboro' was the theme of admiring comment for a long time in our command, was the officer with whom I had the Hartwood adventure.[7] According to my present recollection, Col. Scott does not give a strictly accurate account of the last-mentioned adventure.[8] I am quite sure that the first body of men I met some two miles from the Falmouth road were quite considerable in number. They were all dismounted and standing to their horses. I hailed them and tried to delude them by pretending to be an officer at the head of a federal troop. I did, I think, deceive them for a few minutes, and thereby gained that much time. I had under my command about six or eight well-mounted and armed troopers; the balance were prisoners, some twenty-five or thirty in number, some mounted and some dismounted. I had also about ten or fifteen confederates, besides those mentioned, who were either wounded, or on wounded horses. You can readily see that I was in no plight either for a fight or an escape, and after having reversed my column and made off as best I could, I was horror-stricken to find in a few minutes that I was pursued. We plunged along in the snow at our best speed, the federal cavalry pursuing us and gaining on us, until I got up near the point where I left the Falmouth road, when I discovered, as I thought, that the sound of firing was receding from the direction of Falmouth, which indicated that we were falling back. Fearing that I would come out in the main road just in the midst of your cavalry, I turned into a road to my left which I then spied, and which from its apparent direction would bring me into the Falmouth road lower down toward Hartwood Church. It was on this road, I think, I must have encountered you, for I had gone a quarter of a mile on it when I suddenly came across, in the woods, a small body of Federal cavalry drawn up across the road upon which I was. I think they were in single rank. My dismay can be imagined, at thus being caught, as I supposed, between two bodies of the enemy's cavalry; but summoning all the composure I could command, I rode to the head of my column, turned its direction to the left again, and rode around your command (I suppose it was), and within fifty or seventy-five yards. I am sure I can readily understand now, and did a few minutes afterwards, the cause of your inaction. You were in precisely the same fix that I was. Our whole force was on the Falmouth road a little in the rear of you, and naturally you supposed that I was an effective and superior confederate force in your front.[9] In a little while I reached the main road, found a confederate regiment, and told the colonel the situation in the woods, and he sent in a part of his command and captured, I suppose, the men you lost.

At the Waynesboro' fight, thought it was my company you struck, I had had my horse killed a few minutes before, and was not at the scene of your gallant and perilous charge.[10] The color-bearer of the regiment whom you sabred, was a man in my company by the name of Hamilton. I happened to meet him a few days ago and showed him your picture and letter. He was doubtless far better pleased to make your acquaintance in this manner than as at your first meeting.[11] I am very happy to say, and I feel that it will not be unpleasing to you to know that there was universal gratification in my command that so gallant an officer as yourself should have escaped the great peril of life you were in.

I am much gratified that you should desire my photograph, but I have not one, nor do I know where I can lay hands just now on one. I shall be in Washington however the latter part of next month, and will take pleasure in having it taken and sending you a copy.

I shall be happy to accept your kind invitation to visit you, if I can make occasion, and I trust you will believe that I and those of the Black Horse who survive, would be greatly pleased to see you at our homes here in Virginia, and promise a reception of a very different character from that at Waynesboro'.

Very truly yours,
A. D. Payne.

A, D. Payne carte-de-visite found in Bliss's papers

CHAPTER TWO

Battle of Kelly's Ford

Kelly's Ford, March 17, 1863, was the first significant cavalry engagement of the war won by Union forces. It set the stage for the battle of Brandy Station and other cavalry encounters of the Gettysburg campaign in the summer of 1863. George Bliss was not at Kelly's Ford, having at the time been on court-martial duty.

Kelly's Ford opened with the Union cavalry attempting to cross a narrow ford on the Rappahannock River. In a published account at the time, largely written by Bliss using accounts gleaned from others, Kelly's ford "was found to be obstructed on both sides by abattis of trees, felled across the road, while the opposite shore was occupied by a large number of dismounted cavalrymen as sharpshooters, strongly protected by rifle pits, from which they poured a brisk fire upon our men. The obstructions above mentioned were found to be so great that but one horse could leap them at a time, and with great difficulty."[1]

Despite the hazards, after a harrowing struggle, a small number of Union cavalry pushed across the river and forced the defenders to retreat. Twenty-one-hundred troops of Brig. Gen. William W. Averell's Union cavalry division then crossed the Rappahannock and proceeded toward Culpeper. Confederate Brig. Gen. Fitzhugh Lee soon counterattacked with a brigade of about eight-hundred men. On the Union left, Col. Alfred N. Duffié disobeyed Averell's orders to hold his position and led a charge. The unexpected charge forced Lee to withdraw his force. Lee then regrouped his men and counterattacked the advancing Union troopers, but once again had to fall back in the face of superior numbers and artillery. Had Averell been more aggressive, he might have had a complete victory.

Instead, he withdrew, re-crossing the Rappahannock before nightfall. Still, the Federal cavalry demonstrated unprecedented spirit, and while Averell failed in his objective of routing Lee's cavalry, this action marked a major turning point in the fortunes of Federal horsemen.[2]

This chapter features correspondence from former members of several regiments: Preston M. Farrington and Emmons D. Guild, of Bliss's First R. I. Cavalry; William A. Moss, Fourth Virginia Cavalry; and Samuel E. Chamberlain, First Massachusetts Cavalry.

Letter of Preston M. Farrington,
former major, First Rhode Island Cavalry

Decades after Preston Metcalf Farrington (1825-1920) participated in the battle of Kelly's Ford, Bliss asked him to describe his part. Farrington's twelve-page response is below.

Farrington was born in Wrentham, Massachusetts; it is not known when he moved to Rhode Island. He lived in Providence after his marriage to Caroline Thayer in 1848. A merchant of "Fancy Goods" at 63 Westminster Street, he served on the Providence Common Council in 1859-61. In January 1861, Farrington, described as a "member of a trading firm," was serving a sentence in debtors' prison in Providence; little is known of the circumstances of his imprisonment. His son, Robert, was born in September 1861, shortly before Farrington enlisted. Farrington was commissioned a captain in the First Rhode Island Cavalry at the beginning of October 1861. The appointment of Alfred Duffié to colonel of the regiment in July 1862 caused a near-mutiny and led to Farrington's promotion to major in September. He was mustered out when his three-year term of service expired in December 1864.[3]

After the war, Farrington became active in veterans' organizations and in 1877 he hosted a picnic at his home in Franklin, Massachusetts, for the First Rhode Island Cavalry Veterans Association. In March 1915, Farrington joined several veterans in Bliss's law office in Providence for the fifty-second anniversary of the battle at Kelly's Ford. A newspaper reported that "Major Farrington is the oldest survivor of the First Rhode Island Cavalry, being 89 years and six months old."[4]

Franklin Mass   January 31ˢᵗ, 1911
Judge George N. Bliss
East Providence R. I.
Late Captain 1ˢᵗ Rhode Island Cavalry.

Dear Captain, Yours of a few days ago at hand. You ask me at this late day to write my recollections of fifty years ago of the Battle of Kelly's ford fought on March 17, 1863. Those recollections will never be erased from memory. See description from First R. I. C[avalry] history from the time we reached the ford, until the 1ˢᵗ R.I. Cavalry was ordered to cross the river.[5] I gave the order to forward and moved across the road, which ran parallel with the river. Reaching the opposite side of the road I found that large buttonwood trees had been fallen on the bank of the river that formed a complete barricade, except that a path had been cut in the tops of the fallen trees, just wide enough to admit one horse at a time and going straight for a few feet, then turn to the left, and then to the right, and then square to the front and more straight for twenty feet or more to the edge of the bank, and slid into the water. This made a slow and tedious passage. And when you remember that sixty men were stationed behind rifle pits, or earth works on the opposite side of the river about two hundred yards away and were sending from their carbines those leaden bullets as fast as they could send them, it was no pleasant point. When I was about half way across the river two of those leaden messengers had passed through the cape of my overcoat, one had struck the pummel of my saddle, and from the middle of the stream to the opposite bank, the water was rushing down with greater force and I found my horse was being carried down-stream. Just at this instant a reb jumped upon the top of the rifle pit and took deliberate aim at my center. I could look the whole way down the hole in that gun barrel. At the same instant I had turned my bridle hand, and my horse turned slightly up-stream. Consequently, the bullet struck the cantle of my saddle instead of striking my center. Arriving safely on the opposite bank I dismounted to tighten my saddle girth and looking back I saw four men at various distances coming across. Sergeant Brown[6] and three or four of the advance guard were up close to the earth works. The next to arrive was Lieutenant James M. Fales.[7] Then Captain Thayer.[8] Lieutenant Fales was the first to leap his horse across a fence that had been made from the earthworks to the edge of the river. This fence had been made from cutting limbs from trees and cutting them in lengths and driving them into the ground and weaving the small brush and twigs in between the sticks or stakes so as to make a tight fence. The Lt's horse smashed the fence down. Consequently, it made an opening, and we all rushed through and the rebs were rushing away as fast as possible, but our boy's horses were too fleet for them as almost the entire force was captured. The remainder of the regiment was straggled across the river and the pioneers had been set to work to cut away the abatises and open the earth works so that the remainder of the force and the artillery could be taken down the bank and across. After capturing the force in the earthworks and while waiting for the remainder of the force to come across, our boys build fires of fence rails and such wood as they could find and dried their clothing [of] the wetting they got while crossing the river and cooked their breakfasts and made themselves as comfortable as possible. About 10 A.M. the bugles blew the assembly; line was formed and we moved off toward Culpepper Court House. As we got fairly straightened out the company of the Sixth Ohio Cavalry[9] and a platoon of the first R. I. C. being advance guard, General Averill[10] commanding the expedition rode up alongside of me and said, "Major, I want you to take the road to Culpepper. Our enemy have their quarters there. I will furnish you a guide. I shall be along and I want you to send me word from time to time. You will probably meet the enemy coming to meet us. Should you meet him charge him at once." I said, "Why general, I thought Colonel Duffié[11] was in command of this brigade." The general said, "Never you mind, I want you at the front, and if you meet the enemy, stick to him as you did this morning and it will be all right."

**Major Preston M. Farrington, of the First Rhode Island Cavalry
(n.d., MOLLUS Mass Civil War Collection, United States
Army Heritage and Education Center, Carlisle, Pa.)**

At this point the general pulled out. We moved on quietly I think a little more than one mile when word came from the advance that the enemy was coming in force at a charge. The head of the column had just reached the road where we were to turn sharp to the left to take the Culpepper road. I halted the column and sent word to General Averill and Colonel Duffié. Col. Duffié came up [and] I said to him, "Colonel let me throw the 1st R.I. left into line in the edge of these woods and I will empty every saddle." "No, no bring up the artillery, bring up the artillery." Just at this moment, the captain of the Sixth Ohio came up and said, "Major, our men drew their carbines and ammunition yesterday, and did not have time to try them, but what shall I do, the enemy is coming in force and we cannot defend ourselves or hurt him as we cannot get one of our old guns [?]." I said, "Draw off your men and I will detail another advance." The captain wheeled his horse and started. Seeing that Col Duffié was bound to wait for the artillery, I started to the front to look after the advance but I was not able to see a man of either the 6th or the First Rhode Island. I was in the road the enemy in the field just the other side of the fence that divided the field from the road. The enemy were moving down in column of fours at a trot, a magnificent sight. At the first set of forces at the right of the line, I saw a man that I believed, and do [now believe], he was a man that three days before while I was in charge of the picket line at Heartwell church. This man claimed to be a doctor and wanted to pass through our lines to see a patient. And after arguing with me for half an hour I let him pass inside our lines, with the promise from him, that he would return within two hours. He did not return while I was on picket and seeing him at the head of this column made me so mad that I threw my bridle reins over my arm and drew from my holsters both my revolvers and I just stood there and plugged away at him. I got in three shots when the rear of the column had passed me, while I was thus firing at this chap how many of the hundred and twenty men or more discharged their pistols at me, I am not able to say. After I had discharged my second shot, I felt a burning sensation in my neck, but had no idea that I was shot. After the rebel column had passed me and gone on towards the point where I left the head of our column, feeling a warm flow passing down my side, I bethought myself that that stinging sensation I felt might have been a bullet wound. Taking off my gauntlet and putting my hand up to my neck, on taking my hand down I found it covered with hot blood. About this time I heard the boom of our artillery. Thinking it best to get the blood stopped I dove into the woods knowing I could cut off a big corner and quite a distance below where the rear of our column was when I left the front. I had gone quite a distance when who should I meet but General Averill and an aide coming from our rear and going toward the front. We each see the other at the same time and both of us was much surprised to meet each other. I saw by the generals looks that he thought I was skulking. When we got within speaking distance the general said, "How is this major?" I answered and said, "I am stung and as my sting is bleeding quite a little, I am going to the hospital to have it dressed." Before I had finished speaking, the aide was off his horse and at my side and said, "Where, where major?" I think neither the general nor his aide thought I was wounded; leaning down quite low I pulled my coat collar down, & the aide said, "Oh I see I see." At that the general said, "Who has got your Regiment?" I said, "Colonel Duffié had when I left," and we each resumed our journeys. Arriving out on the main road, and about half way from where I came out on the road and where the hospital was located, I met the brigade surgeon going towards the front. I said to him, "Doctor I have caught one of those little fellows that are thrown round so carelessly, I wish you would see what it amounts to. It's bleeding considerable. I was on the way to the hospital to see if they could stop the blood." We both dismounted. The doctor pulled down my coat vest and shirt collar and said, "Beautiful thing. Could not have been better. The only place it could pass through and not prove fatal," and taking his left hand little finger with his thumb & fore finger of his right hand and measuring a full eighth of an inch said, "Had it gone so much this way," pointing to my throat, "it would have cut the jugular. Had it gone this much the other way it would have cut the spine; in either case it would have proved fatal, but it's a nice clean cut. Go to hospital and have it dressed, and you will be all right." We both mounted and went our respective ways. Arriving at the hospital the surgeon in charge sponged and syringed the wound and putting a little cotton on each side of the cut said, "Pretty close call, major." I replied, "Close enough I guess." "Well major," he said, "we have no decent accommodations here. The only place we have is that dirty end room in the elc [?]. Perhaps you can stay there. You may find a place to hitch your horse back there by the shed." I went up to my horse and as I was about to mount, the doctor said, "Where are you going major?" I replied, "I am going to the front." He said, "Going to the front?" "Yes, there is nothing for me to do here."[12] The doctor dropped his head but said not another word. Moving along back on the road on which we went in the morning and on which I had just returned, [I] arrived near the front where I had halted the head of the column in the morning. At the side of the road an improvised hospital was established, and there laid stretched on a poncho Lieutenant Bowditch[13] First Massachusetts Cavalry Adjutant General on Colonel Duffié's staff with his clothing all open from his breast and stomach. I saw at a glance he was mortally wounded, and I could not help crying, "Oh My God." The lieutenant looked up and said, "Major are you much hurt?" I said, "Oh not much," but I said, "I would have rather that hurt of yours had been mine instead of you, if either of us had got to have had it." The lieutenant said, "Thank you major, but I have got it." Passing on crossing the road, going through the hole in the wall where our forces with the artillery had gone, I moved down the field. About an eighth of a mile from this point near a little piece of wood, I found four cavalry officers hugging a huge boulder, three of them belonged to the 1st R. I. C. When I asked what they were doing there they [said], "We're trying to keep out of the way of the rebel's shells as we have no places with the regiment." "Where are your horses?" Pointing to the woods said, "in there." I said, "Well mount your horses & come with me. I [will] find you a place & something to do." They made a stir but I saw nothing more of them until I saw them at dusk on the other side of the river. Going on about another eighth of a mile I saw General Averill on a little elevation surrounded by Colonel Duffié and other staff officers. A little way in front of them were the pieces of artillery and off a little to the right of them and a trifle to the rear was the 1st R.I.C. standing in two ranks regimental front, and about six or eight paces to their left and three paces to the rear stood the Sixth Ohio. As I neared the group Colonel Duffié came out to meet me and said, "Major are you much hurt?" I said, "No, I guess not very bad." He said, "Is glad. Are you able to take charge of your regiment?" I said, "I guess so colonel," and the col. repeated again, "Is glad." I rode down in front of the men and talked with them, inquiring if any of them were in the previous charge and if any of them knew who was taken prisoners or wounded &c, &c. Also giving instructions in regard to charging and rallying &c. I had been there for twenty minutes to a half hour when we all saw a body of cavalry coming across the field from our right from the Culpeper road where the rebs had been shooting from [with] their artillery. They came on at a fair trot and in most perfect order every man looked as though he was a part of his horse. Coming to a rail fence dividing the fields from the one our forces were in when they reached that the column halted. Some of the men advanced and pulled down the fence making a wide opening. The column advanced swinging a little to their left. At this point General Averell, who was about fifty yards from our command, sent an aide to me. "The general sends his complements and says the enemy is coming to capture our guns. I expect you to defend them." "Please ask the general," I said, "please ask the general if I shall open on them with carbine or a charge?" In a half minute, the aide was back and said, "The general says you do as you please." With[in] two minutes the order "Charge" rang out. Please see report in History 1st R. I. Cavalry.[14]

X   X   X   X   X   X

[Page was divided using cross-hatched notations]

After the enemy had been killed, wounded or driven from the field we reformed in our previous formation and near the exact situation. After a little while the enemy opened fire with their artillery, and they had close range on us, so that I was obliged to move up and down the field constantly even at that they picked off some of our men.

X   X   X   [A portion of the line is cross-hatched, followed by the words, "Report 1st R.I. History."]

At one time when we came from the lower part of the field from where General [Averill] was stationed by the artillery Colonel Duffié came to me and said, "Major, the general would like to have you take your command through the gap in the fence that the rebs made, and proceed about half way across the field and see if you can draw the enemy out." I done as requested and after going nearly half way across the field I had come to an excavation from twelve to eighteen inches deep on the outskirts, and deeper toward the center. Somebody had been taking off the pond mud and carrying it away. So I gave the order right wheel and like a streak of lightning, the general's aide shot across the field. "Major the General says you will please face your command the other way. If the enemy should get a solid shot on your line this way, he would empty the most of your saddles." My reply was, "I am aware of that and I am aware that should I go into that mud hole I would lose every man and horse." As soon as I got past this excavation I faced to the left and moved on toward where the Rebs artillery was stationed and I could hear them moving their guns toward Culpeper. Not having drawn the enemy out, I headed the column about and returned to nearly our starting point. But the Rebs got the range on us again and I moved down toward the lower part of the field. Here again they got a range on us killing several of our men and horses. All these various movements had taken several hours. As I returned again toward headquarters Colonel Duffié came to me & said, "Major, the general would like to have you charge across that field," pointing to field again, "and see if you can't strike him in the road and capture his guns." Without stopping an instant to think how impudent I was, I said I could not do it. The Colonel looking a good deal surprised he said, "Why Major?" I answered, "My horses have made three distinct charges and have been maneuvering for more than three hours in this soft ground and they are well blown. And should I attempt to go across that swamp on a charge I would probably loose every man and horse." The colonel said, "I will tell the general what you say." In a few minutes the colonel came back and said, "Major, the general says all right. You will please divide your command, putting the best officer you have in charge and form an advance guard. And you will take the other half and form a rear guard and we will re-cross the river in that order." We started off, we had got about half way to the river and a few of the Rebs commenced sending their compliments after us. I think none took effect, but when the last of our forces had slid into the ford, several of them followed down to the bank and gave us a final parting. We moved from the ford to Morrisville and there bivouacked for the night. Sleeping on top of six to eight inches of cold snow did not soften the wound in my neck. When I got up in the morning instead of being front face, my face presented in turning left face, and constantly looked across my left shoulder. After getting breakfast the next morning we started back, arriving at our old camp at about four o'clock P.M.

> Most Respectfully submitted
> P. M. Farrington
> Late Maj'r 1ˢᵗ Rhode Island Cavalry

[Postscript to this letter: Following the Battle of Kelly's Ford, Bliss described Farrington as "the bravest officer I ever saw . . ." Years later, Bliss's opinion of Farrington had not changed. After Bliss received the medal of honor in 1897, he embarked on a two-year-long effort to obtain the same honor for Farrington. He believed that Farrington deserved the medal because after his wounding, he "returned to his regiment at the front, took command of it and led the 1ˢᵗ R.I. Cav. Vols in three successful sabre charges against the enemy."[15] On Farrington's behalf, Bliss wrote to government officials and Rhode Island politicians, and gathered up affidavits from at least four soldiers attesting to Farrington's participation that day. One document illustrated the severity of Farrington's wound. "I was told by one of the hospital stewards that the bullet through the Majors neck passed so close to the jugular vein that the vein could be seen when dressing the wound."[16] Other documents attested to Farrington's participation in the battle, and his leading charges after his injury. At issue was a lack of records that definitively proved that Farrington had performed the deeds contained in the affidavits. The documents needed were "destroyed August 13, 1864 having been captured and [burned] when our headquarters wagon was set on fire by Moseby [Mosby] at Berryville Va."[17]

[Farrington was aware of Bliss's efforts and wrote, "You say you are still keeping up the fight for my medal of honor, I always knew you had grit to the back bone, but I should think you had fought out in this case long ago. I have two occasions since I saw you that I should have been very proud to have worn such honor."[18] The effort ultimately failed and Farrington never got his medal. Of the more than 2,000 men who served in the 1st R.I. Cavalry during the war, Bliss was the only one who received the Medal of Honor.]

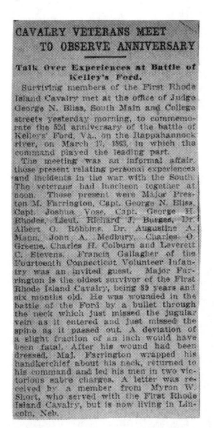

Newspaper article announcing a reunion of Kelly's Ford battle participants. The reunion was held in George Bliss's law office in Providence, on March 17, 1915. Article is from an unknown Providence newspaper, found in Bliss's papers.

Letter of Emmons D. Guild
Former Sergeant Troop "G" First R.I. Cavalry

Emmons D. Guild (1843-1909) was born in Wrentham, Mass. but moved with his family to Attleboro at an early age. He was employed as a jeweler before he joined the First R.I. Cavalry as a private in December 1861 at the age of eighteen. At Kelly's Ford, March 17, 1863, Guild was an acting corporal when his company was ordered to charge across the Rappahannock River and drive the enemy out of firmly entrenched rifle pits. Lieut. Simeon Brown, two men and Corporal Guild were the only men in that initial charge that successfully reached the other side, spearheading the successful action that day. Guild was promoted to sergeant for his bravery. At Warrenton, Virginia, in October 1863, Sergeant Guild was captured along with forty-six others when his detail was cut off by Robert E. Lee's army. He was paroled in February 1865, after being imprisoned for five-hundred days. He was one of only three of the forty-seven men captured who survived the Confederate prisons.[19]

Brattleboro,   Jan 17th 1884[20]
Geo. N. Bliss, Esq.

Dear Comrade

Your letter requesting me to write out my recollections of the Battle of Kelley's Ford March 17th 1863 is received and the following account of the fait [?] of the combat I had an opportunity to witness, but you must remember that twenty two years have passed away since that eventful day and were it not for the many months that I afterwards spent in Southern Prisons I might be able to give you a better account than I can possibly do now. For no man who was unfortunate enough to be confined in one of them for almost seventeen months (as I was) and came out alive, can feel [fail?] to consider his former exploits; and if he does, they will pass into insignificance when he calls to mind those terrible months at Andersonville and Belle Island. However, I will do the best I can.

March 16, 1863, our Brigade, with fo[u]r days rations and one days forage left camp at Potomac Creek Station, and arrived at Morrisville about dark. Here we went into camp for the night but before daylight next morning we received orders "to saddle up and get into line." Following the order "Forward" we had gone but a short distance before we heard fireing [*sic*] in our front and soon came to the bank of the river where we found our skirmishers were <u>exchanging compliments</u> with the Rebel Pickets stationed on the other side. After some sharp skirmishing, the Fourth N. Y. Cav. came past our regiment on a charge to cross the river but instead of taking the Ford they kept on the road that ran parallel to the river.

Our Co. "Duffie" very much excited rode up in front of us and shouted, "My regiment will cross the river." Troop "G" being on the right came first. The Col. rode up to Lieut. Brown and ordered him to take his company and charge across the river and he would follow with the balance of the regiment. Sixteen men and Lieut. Brown started from the right, "myself among the number." We had gone but a short distance when Maj. Chamberlain of the 1st Mass. Cavalry rode up and when nearly opposite me was struck in the face by a bullet. Another bullet struck "Myron Shirt" one of our company disabling him. By this time we had reached the Ford which we found the Rebs had obstructed by felling trees across it. Not stopping for these we jumped our horses over them into the river and started to cross. The current was very strong, the water ice cold and the Rebels were firing at us as fast as they could. You can imagine it was not a very desirable place to be in, but where the 1st R. I. Cavalry were ordered to go they always went.

On reaching the other side I dismounted and as I did so a Reb. jumped up in the rifle pit not more than twenty feet from me and aiming his pistol fired at me point blank. I felt a sharp pain in my side and dropped to the ground, but did not remain there long. Realizing that I was not severely wounded I jumped up and ran for a tree. Lieut. Brown had already posted himself behind one. Then for the first time I saw that but three of us had reached the shore. (Lieut. Brown, John A. Medberry, and myself.) The head of the regiment [w]as in the middle of the river coming on with loud cheers.

Lieut. Brown turned to me and asked for my carbine. I passed it to him. Quick as a flash he raised it and covered a Reb. And the poor fellow['s] troubles were soon over.

By this time the Regiment had reached the shore. The Col's horse had been wounded and threw the Col. into the river but he and the regiment did not stop for that. Every man was anxious to get across. Lieut. Brown['] s horse received two bullets and three or four more passed through the Lieut's clothing.

The one that struck me entered just above the belt on the right side passed through the clothing taking a piece of the skin about two inches long from my side and lodged in the lining of my jacket. I have the ball yet and shall always keep it to remind me how I spent St. Patrick's day 1863.

After the Regt. Reached the shore they deployed and commenced picking up all the prisoners they could. Almost the first man brought in was the man that gave me the pistol ball. I recognized him in an instant and I think he did me for when he saw me, he watched me as though I was one risen from the dead. I have always been sorry that I did not speak to him and tell him that I thought he was a very poor shot for that distance. But at that time I had other business on hand and did not think of it but started out with a comrade to see what we could find. Passing down the river a short distance we came up in the of a line of Rifle Pits and looking in we saw three Rebels laying on their faces waiting to get a shot at some of our men. We covered two of them with our carbines before they saw us but when they did up went their hands. And we marched them in ahead of us. During this time my horse a large and powerful animal had been standing where I left him. Mounting I fell in with the company and we were deployed as skirmishers. I should think we had gone about a mile or more before we came on the Rebs. We first met their skirmishers on whom we opened fire. Very soon we came to a large field with woods on both sides. As we came out of the woods on one side the Reb's came out of the woods on the other side.

We were drawn up in line on the side of the field and the Rebs. advanced at a charge until about half way across where they broke and went up the field to our left. Then Maj. Farrington gave the order to charge and with drawn sabers we started after them. Almost at the same time another Regiment of rebs. came out of the woods and after us. Most of our men saw them and came back into line but a few had gone to[o] far and were taken prisoners. We then charged after this second lot of Rebs. and drove them across the field and through the woods. Here we formed a second line and the Rebs. came on for another charge yelling and shooting. We sat quietly in our saddles awaiting the word. I should think they were within seventy-five yards of us before the word was given. Then it came, Charge! Every man was nerved up and anxious to hear it and such a charge I never saw before or since. Maj. Farrington, with a handkerchief around his wounded neck, led our boys. It was horse to horse and may the best man win. How long it lasted I could not tell. It seemed but an instant befor[e] the Rebs. were retreating and we after them.

Sergt. Fitzjerald [*sic*] singled out a man and was about to cut him down when the Reb. turned in his saddle and shot him through the heart.[21]

It was now quite late in the day and we commenced to fall back so as to cross the river before dark which we and our prisoners did in safety. And arrived in Camp at Potomac Creek Station the following day without any further adventures.

Hoping that the above account will be satisfactory I remain

Yours in F.C.L. Emmons D. Guild
Late Sergt. Troop "G" 1st R. I. Cavalry.

Letters of William A. Moss,
former captain of Fourth Virginia Cavalry

George Bliss encountered William A. Moss (1837-1887) only one day during the war, when he wounded Moss in a saber charge in Waynesboro, Va. in Sept. 1864 (see Chapter Five). Decades after the war, he began correspondence with Moss, and discovered that Moss had also been in the action at Kelly's Ford. He encouraged Moss to forward the details of his involvement there and Moss sent the document below, undated and unsigned, enclosed in a letter to Bliss dated January 1886.

Except during the war, William Moss stayed in Buckingham County, Virginia, his entire life. Located deep within Virginia, the county is seventy miles west of Richmond, and one-hundred seventy-five miles from Washington, D.C. His parents, Thomas and Lucy Moss, had seven children: four girls with William being the oldest of three boys. In 1860, the twenty-three-year-old Moss was a jeweler.[22]

In 1870, five years after the close of hostilities, Moss was working as a dry goods merchant. He had married the former Patty A. Baldwin, who at age twenty-one, was twelve years younger than him. They had a one-year-old son, Albert. Moss must have been doing well, as he reported owning $6000 in real estate and $3500 in personal estate, considerably more than many in his community. In the next ten years, Moss changed professions twice. By his first letter to Bliss in Dec. 1876, he was cashier of the Buckingham County Savings Bank. By 1880 he was Buckingham County Treasurer. At that time, he and his wife had five children, two girls and four boys, aged two to eleven. Moss died in Nov. 1887, at the age of fifty. The cause was said to be "inflammation of stomach and bowels." In 1933, Moss's son William applied to the U.S. War Department for a headstone for Moss's grave. The request was approved.[23]

[Note: At the time of the battle at Kelly's Ford, William Moss was a lieutenant in the Confederate Army. Following Moss's letter is a document he sent Bliss. No salutation or date was given, but it was undoubtedly written circa January 1886.]

Buckingham C. H.,   January 25, 1886

My Dear Captain

Your letter of the 20th is just received and I hasten to reply. As I stated to you some time since I am dependent almost entirely upon memory as to occurrences which took place during the war, having lost all my papers about the time of the surrender at Appomattox C[our]t Ho[use]. My memory now is that I carried with me to Kelley[']s Ford on the morning of the 17[th] of March 1863 about 90 men, that I left as a guard with the horses, in the edge of the woods, about half mile back from the ford, in the Road to Brandy Station five men, taking with me 85 to the Rifle Pits near the ford. Capt. Beckendrige [*sic*], was already in poss[es]sion, giving me no opportunity to find out his force and I do not now remember what number he officially reported, but am sure he must have had sixty men with him, making in all 145 men. Capt Breckenridge stated before the court of inquiry, that he did not fire, being short of ammunition, so all the execution that was done was due to me. I have often wondered how it was that I could have missed the gray horse, as I fired at him more than at his rider, feeling sure, that if I brough[t] him down the rider would be helpless, besides the rider had challenged my admiration by his courrageous [*sic*] bearing, under the trying circumstances.[24] If there are any of the three living who over-took me in the field near the woods where the horses of our squadron were tied, they will remember the circumstances I related in my last letter. The first order to me was to halt! Next was to surrender! And last, do you intend to surrender or not! Twas then that I threw back my cape, and with pistol in hand, ordered my [one illegible word] sharp shooters to fire. The charge on your part was a gallant one, for few Regiments would have undertaken it under the heavy fire that was poured upon them that cold morning.

Many thanks for the kind references to my wife. She is much better, and I hope will be up in a few more days. My kind regards to Mrs Bliss. I hope to see you and her sometime in the near future.

Very truly your friend
W[m]. A. Moss

Send on the book if you can possibly get one, also the Kelley Ford Paper[25]

[Moss's Document]

On the night of 16th March 1863, an orderly called at my tent and said Col W[illiam]. H. Payne, (afterwards Brig Genl) wished me to report at once to him, which I did, he showed me an order from Genl Fitz Lee to send a good Squadron under a reliable and trusted officer to reinforce the picket then on duty at Kelley[']s Ford. That the enemy's cavalry was then at Morrisvill[e] on the opposite side of the Rappahannock and would make an early advance the next day, and that I must be at the ford and in position by day-break, and in order to be certain of Genl Lee[']s wishes I had better report to him as his head-quarters were just in my way. [W]e were then encamped very near to Culpeper Ctho [Court House]. I reported to Gen Lee, who said the enemy are at Morrisville, said to be 4000 strong, and would undertake to carry the ford by light the next morning, that Capt Breckenridge[26] was on picket there and that I must report to him, and say it was his order that he must not fire until the enemy[s]s horses were in the water, and that the senior officer would take command that we must not allow the enemy to pass the ford, as he would be in supporting distance by sunrise the next day. I proceeded to the ford and delivered the order, but before we got well in position, Your Command came up and took position behind what seemed to be a stone wall on the opposite side, which position commanded our pits, [making it?] impossible for us to do much execution, in fact the whole position was untenable. I suppose we resisted your advance about one hour when you crossed and commenced to cut away the barricades, when I ordered my squadron out. I remember there was a gallant fellow on a gray horse who led the charge in the Ford. He seemed to have a charmed life for I fired deliberat[e]ly at him five times without effect and I am a good shot[.] Most of my men were captured, and two or thre[e] killed. I ran across a small field, but was intercepted within two hundred yards of the woods where our horses were left under guard, by three of your men one of them I think was a colonel, who ordered me to surrender. I ordered (in a loud tone) ["]Sharp shooters, fire["], when the three beat a hasty retreat, much to my gratification, as I had but five men with the horses and no load in my pistol. Of the fight during the day, I will not go into, it was fine and well contested on both sides. If you can give me the name of the man on the white horse I will be glad to have it. As

I saw him during the day frequently on the field, almost appearing to be daring the fates. Of the officers who were with me at the ford that morning I think I am the only survivor. Breckenridge fell mortally wounded at Five Forks.[27] My own squadron officers in the twenty years have passed away.

Our forces numbered only a little over 1000 what was yours?

Capt Breckenridge ranked me and charged that I left the Rifle Pits without orders. His charge amounted to nothing as it was shown that it was impossible from our relative positions to communicate with each other.

Samuel E. Chamberlain,
Former General, First Massachusetts Cavalry

Samuel Emery Chamberlain (1829-1908) was born in New Hampshire and raised in Boston. He ran away from home at fifteen, entered the military and soon was fighting in the war with Mexico (1846-48). He became well known for his watercolors; they are considered the most definitive depictions of the Mexican War in existence. A collection of 147 of Chamberlain's watercolors is owned by the San Jacinto Battlefield Museum. Chamberlain also served in the western campaign against the Apache Indians and spent time in California and New Mexico during the 1850s.[28]

In November 1861, Chamberlain was commissioned a captain in the First Massachusetts Cavalry. Thirteen months later, he was promoted to major and then lieutenant colonel in July 1864. At the end of the war he was brevetted a brigadier-general. In his memoir of the Kelly's Ford engagement, William Meyer, a private in the R.I. Cavalry, described "looking back" to view "Major Chamberlain of the First Massachusetts on horseback, full exposed to the enemy's fire: 'No danger, all right,' he cheered us on. We poked our heads over the ridge, such a swarm of bullets whizzed by our ears that I fairly tumbled backward for fright." Chamberlain "received a bullet through the nose, and a ball striking him in the left cheek," while his horse was shot in three places. The major was "fearfully wounded," and quickly removed from the field, Meyer recalled. In his history of the First Massachusetts, Benjamin Crowninshield observed that Chamberlain "came very near losing his life," from his injuries.[29]

Chamberlain's memoir, *My Confession: The Recollections of a Rogue*, was published posthumously in 1956.[30]

General Samuel Emery Chamberlain (https://www.findagrave.com/ memorial/79283463/samuel-emery-chamberlain, accessed 7/31/21)

Concord, [N.H.]   Nov. 10th 1879

My Dear Major

Book, letter and paper at hand.[31] I would be happy to see you here at any time, but there is no way to reach this place on the same day if you leave Providence on the 4.15 P. M. train. You cannot connect at Mansfield, and the last train leaves Boston, Via. B. Fitchbury R. R. at 6.

I would be pleased to have you come and spend a Sunday with me. I have many mementos of the war which would interest you. If you cannot come, I will send you a <u>true</u> statement of the crossing at Kelly Ford.[32] By the way as an old comrade of the cavalry corps, and Ass. Insp. General, I must enter a strong protest against the reversed "Cross Sabres" (points down signifies surrender) on the cover of the book, for though the First R[h]ode Island Cavalry might be overwhelmed, annihilated yet they never surrendered.[33]

Very truly yours
L. C Chamberlain

To
Maj George N. Bliss
Providence

Newton   Jan'y 16th\85.

My Dear Major

Your favor of the 10th is before me. What in the name of the two faced god, does Maj. McClellan and Maj. Bliss want to fight a cavalry out post affair over again for? Will "Stuart Cavalry" never give us a rest? So the doughty Major thinks "so far as he (Averill) was concerned it (Kelly Ford) weak affair." Well compared with the achievements of the Union Cavalry in -64 & 5, I most heart[i]ly agree with him. But it proved of much benefit to our mounted volunteers, yeleped [sic] cavalry! God save the mark! With a few exceptions our cavalry regiments (Vol.) were THUSLY

[here Chamberlain inserted this sketch]:

The cavalry skirmish at Kelly Ford, March 17th 63 has never been understood by parties outside of the gentleman who lead of the dance His Honor, the Master of Ceremony, FitzHugh Lee. (whos[e] monogram like signature, something in this way

is attached to a little bit of paper that he kindly gave me Sep 5th, 62) of Culpepper Va. one of the F.F.V. and W.W. Averill, a very punctilious gentleman of Va. Mr. Averill, with many friends was passing the winter and spring of 63 in cold uncomfortable quarters at Potomac Creek. During this time on several occasions the friends of Mr. Lee, call[ed] on friends of Mr. Averill and with true Southern hospitality extended to them such pressing invitations to visit their capitol, that many accepted, and many left their friend for a still warmer clime. Through these northern guests, Mr. Lee learned with indignation that his class mate Averill was not only suffering with cold, but for want of amusement, he not having a fandango all winter. His generous spirit was at once aroused, and sometime in February, calling on a few of his friends to accompany him, and taking with them materials to give Averill a proper warming, he cross'd the Rappahannock at Elys Ford. Proceeding on to Hartwood Church, Fitz Hugh Lee with much gravity of manner relieved some scores of Averill's attendents [*sic*], who he found out in the cold and so muffled up in their great coats, that they saw nothing until they were on the road to Richmond. It was eight miles yet to his classmates['] quarters and he hurried forward to be in time for dinner, when some verdant youths out a gunning stop[p]ed him and his party because they had no pass! Such impudence to him on his native soil, such base ingratitude and return for favors intended, made him righteously wrath and after by powerful augments trying to convince them of their error, he rode off, leaving some of his friends as his card. Going back to Culpepper the more he thought of his uncivil reception by Averill the less he liked it, and so one day he fast[e]ned a napkin on a pole, and with a waggon [*sic*] and sent a servant with it and a note to Mr. Averill. The note as near as I can remember as follows. "Bill Averill, D – m you. Take your troops out of my State, your Ships from My Ports. Send me by the Flag of Truce the bodies of my men and a bag of sugar and coffee.

From that unco[n]quered, but "pulverized" Rebel, Fitz Hugh Lee."

Mr. Averill's excursion that brought on the Kelly Ford affair was only his attempt to return Mr. Lee['s] visit and if the pig headed fellows stationed by Lee at the Ford to welcome[e] his old friend to the South bank of the Rappahannock, had been less profuse with their compliments (ugh! There a sudden twing in the spinal column, where one of their confounded compliments lodged at that reception[34]) we would [have?] tried and might have dined at Culpepper. As it was Averill took his gruel like a little man at the Ford and then taking his constitutional promenade for a mile or two towards the home of Fitz Hugh Lee, when on seeing that gay and festive cavalier J.E.B. Stuart, coming too [*sic*] the entertainment with his "nigger" playing "on his old Banjo" haste to the wedding. He paid his devoir to "Jeb" in so gallant a manner as to cool the ardor of this rollick some beau saber and he retired in "reserve."

Then Mr. Averill, satisfied that he had carried out in the most punctilious manner all that West Point etiquette demanded, and had reciprocated with interest Fitz Hugh['s] kind intentions in February, gracefully retired to the north bank of the river. Averill's command on leaving camp was not far from 2,100, this includes Tiaball[']s Battery of four guns.

The First Mass. Cavalry about 500 in number, did not cross, they being on picket duty towards Warrenton.

If Maj. McClellan, ex Cheif [*sic*] of Staff to the gallant cavalier J.E.B. Stuart, will on St. Patrick's Day next, at 12.m. drink in all honor to our brave departed, the Blue and the Grey, he will join with ex Cheif of Staff to the Heroic Trooper Wm. W. Averill, though miles apart in doing a soldier[']s respect to the memory of brave men who died for their convictions.

"Whos bodies are dust.

Whos swords are rust, we trust

Whos Souls are with the Saints

Now old fellow, what apology can you mak[e], for awakening old, sad memories and on this blustering day of sleet and rain, despondent and discouraged as I am, to cause me to blush for serving at the front, when I might have been a Government contractor or a sutler, and being rich now enjoy the gratitude of an appreciating and patriotic community, instead of being turned adrift like our old cavalry horses to perish.

I am suffering infernally from my old wounds, and so pardon this hash and believe as ever

Sincerely yours

L C Chamberlain

CHAPTER THREE

Incident of Second Sergeant George A. Earle, First Rhode Island Cavalry

Before he mustered into the First Rhode Island Cavalry as a private in Oct. 1861, George Earle (1838- 1913) was a jeweler in Pawtucket, R.I. Earle eventually attained the rank of sergeant. He was wounded in the arm on May 1, 1863, in an incident described here. Records indicate that Earle was captured at some point during the war. In late 1863, Earle entered the Invalid Reserve Corps, which was made up of soldiers that had been rendered unfit for active field service on account of wounds or disease contracted in the line of duty. These soldiers were used in a military or semi-military capacity as guards, provost duty, cooks, orderlies, nurses, or to police public buildings. It is not clear as to the extent of Earle's disability or whether it was related to the incident described here.[1]

Statement of George A. Earle Former Second Sergeant of Company F, 1st R. I. Cavalry[2]

On the first day of May 1863, I was on the skirmish line fighting dismounted on the North side of the Rapidan River in Virginia. In my opinion the river was about 50 yards wide and the enemy were sheltered by rifle pits and log huts while we had no shelter except such as we could find in the natural inequalities of the ground. It was about two o'clock in the afternoon when we went down to the bank of the river and there was a steady fire whenever the enemy could see one of our men. One of the rebels opposite me attempted to run from a rifle pit to a log hut and I brought him down with a bullet through the leg. Two others came out to take him in and one of these two was hit by a bullet from another of our men but the enemy finally succeeded in getting both the wounded men behind their log huts. There was one rebel in a log hut just opposite me and he fired at me through a little porthole six or seven times and I fired several times at the port hole locating it as well as I could by the smoke from the rebels gun. About four o'clock in the afternoon I wound up my watch and shortly afterwards I noticed a rebel getting over a fence some distance up the hill on the opposite side of the river, I fired at him and while I was looking to see the effect of my shot I exposed myself in full range of my enemy in the log hut and a bullet from his gun passed through my right arm about midway between the wrist and the elbow and struck my watch in the pants watch pocket. The bullet hit the watch on the edge near the stem breaking and twisting the watch so as to entirely destroy it, but the bullet which would have otherwise passed directly through my body was thus turned aside and went whizzing on its way without further damage to me. The first thought that came into my mind was that the rebel should not have the satisfaction of knowing that he hit me, so I looked all around and then slowly sank down out of his sight just as I should have done if the shot had missed me. This closed my fighting for that day but I was obliged to lie there until after sunset and then in the darkness made my way back to the regiment. The surgeon of the regiment William H. Wilbur dressed my wound that night and the next day the regiment moved and as I was not able to go, I was left at the house of Solomon Yagers, a citizen living near Mitchells station on the battle field of Cedar Mountain.[3] I stayed with him twelve days and was treated with great kindness. Mr Yagers told me he had three sons in the rebel army one of whom had been killed at the battle of Cedar Mountain but that after a man had been wounded, he did not look upon him as an enemy. On the thirteenth day of May late in the afternoon a squad of some twenty five or thirty rebel cavalry stopped at the house and the officers came in and found me. They took my sabre, revolver and sabre belt. I was sorry to lose the brass belt plate of my sabre belt because there was the mark of a rebel bullet on it. This bullet struck me on the first of May as I was going down to the river bank turned me half round and went on leaving a mark something like a thimble in my belt plate. These officers were very polite but said they should come for me on their return from their scout and take me to Richmond. After these troops were gone Mr. Yagers told me there was a great deal of hard feeling among the rebels on account of the death of General Jackson and that I had better escape to my own army if I could as he could not tell what the rebels might do.[4] My kind friends filled my haversack with provisions and about sunrise on the fourteenth of May I started out and on nearing Culpepper Court House I made a wide detour fearing to find the enemy there and then coming back to [the] rail road track on the North side of the town pressed fo[r]ward. At Brady Station I met a rebel officer who gave me a written parole which he said he had authority to do and that it would protect me if I met any troops of his army but I thought I would prefer not to meet them. About sunset when I by the route taken had travelled at least twenty five miles I came to the edge of some woods about half a mile from the Rappahannock River and saw the U.S. flag flying from an earth work on the opposite side of the river. I put my white handkerchief on a stick and waved it and a squad of men came over the rail-road bridge and escorted me into camp where I found Battery H. 1st R. I. Light Artillery Capt Jeffrey Hazard commanding and it is needless to say I received every attention and kindness from these brave men.

I leave this watch in trust with the Soldiers and Sailors Historical Society of Rhode Island reserving the privilege of retaking it at any future time if I should think it best for me to do so.

George A Earle

In the City of Providence R. I. on this eleventh day of January 1881 the foregoing narrative was given to me by George A. Earle now residing at No 48 Spring Street Providence and by me reduced to writing in his presence and after the whole statement had been read to him he signed it and stated that the piece of cotton cloth in which the watch was wrapped was spun and woven in the farm house of the afore mentioned Solomon Yagers. I knew Earle well as he was in my regiment, he was a good soldier and I heard of this incident of the watch at the time and am quite sure I saw the watch on the night of May 1st 1863 after Earle had returned from the skirmish line to the main body of the regiment[5]

George N. Bliss
Late Captain Company C. 1st R. I. Cav. Vols

CHAPTER FOUR

Battle at Middleburg, Virginia
(June 17-18, 1863)

In June 1863, Robert E. Lee led his army into the Shenandoah Valley as part of his invasion of Maryland and Pennsylvania that resulted in the battle of Gettysburg. Lee attempted to block the mountain passes to screen his movements so Union forces could not follow. In a poorly conceived mission, Gen. Alfred Pleasonton ordered Alfred Duffié's First Rhode Island Cavalry to ride through Thoroughfare Gap and proceed on to Middleburg. There he was to join Gen. David M. Gregg's division, traveling through Aldie. Unfortunately for the 1st R.I. Cavalry, the order pushed the 400-man regiment into the center of Robert E. Lee's army.

Middleburg was the most calamitous battle ever fought by the First Rhode Island Cavalry. Unknown to Pleasonton or Duffié, Confederate General J.E.B. Stuart had set up a temporary command post in Middleburg. On the afternoon of June 17th, Duffié's troops successfully fought their way through the Confederates at the gap and proceeded toward Middleburg. When they got near the town, the advance guard was ordered to rush the place and completely surprised Stuart who was nearly captured. Stuart's biographer observed, "At four o'clock P.M. [Duffié and his men] struck the pickets which Stuart had established for his own safety outside the town, and drove them in so quickly that Stuart and his staff were compelled to make a retreat more rapid than was consistent with dignity and comfort." Stuart's large army returned a few hours later, however, and surrounded Duffié's much smaller force. Realizing his plight, Duffié ordered Capt. Frank Allan to take an urgent message requesting support to Gen. Greg in Aldie, just five miles to the east. Allan got through, but no support was ever sent. No explanation for this failure was ever given.[1]

Duffié's command was miles behind enemy lines in an extremely precarious position. The regiment was moved into thick woods after nightfall to conceal themselves. In the morning they attempted to retreat down the road they had come on a day earlier. A small Confederate cavalry force soon challenged them, and the demoralized regiment retreated in disorder. Soon, the panicked remnants of the regiment were being hotly pursued. Bliss wrote, "I traveled with the regt about three miles and the rebs were constantly shooting down men at the rear of the column, . . .[I] saw I must soon be shot or be taken prisoner unless I did something for myself with great swiftness so I just dashed off sideways into the woods, a tree swept me from the saddle and I stopped while the horse went on. Some of the men saw my dodge and imitated the same and I have 6 men and 5 horses here with me." Bliss and his six men abandoned the horses and climbed over the Bull Run Mountains to Union lines. While Bliss escaped, some 187 men were killed or captured.[2]

The battles around Aldie and Middleburg were a victory for the Confederates. They successfully shielded Lee's movement into the Shenandoah Valley and delayed the Union pursuit as he invaded the North. Historians blame the disaster at Middleburg on General Alfred Pleasonton. He failed to understand the situation in the area in which he sent Duffié, and he failed to give him adequate flexibility in his orders. Pleasonton complained of Duffié's performance at Middleburg, saying, "I cannot understand Duffié's conduct."[3]

Letters from four participants in this battle are presented here: Major John L. Thompson, First Rhode Island Cavalry and later General, First New Hampshire Cavalry; Major Preston M. Farrington, First Rhode Island Cavalry; General Thomas T. Munford, Division Commander, Confederate Army; and Captain Edward M. Henry, Ninth Virginia Cavalry.

Letter of John L. Thompson,
Major, First Rhode Island Cavalry

John Leverett Thompson (1835-88) was born in Plymouth, New Hampshire. He was the grandson of a U.S. senator from the state; Daniel Webster studied in the law office of Thompson's father, William C. Thompson. John Thompson attended Dartmouth College and Harvard Law School, being admitted to the bar in 1858. He studied abroad in Berlin, Munich and Paris returning to the United States in 1860 and settled in Chicago. Thompson first enlisted in the Union army as a private with the Illinois Light Artillery in April 1861; he resigned just three months later for health reasons. He was commissioned a lieutenant in the New Hampshire battalion by the governor of his state in the fall of 1861 and was promoted to captain in December. Thompson and his New Hampshire men joined the New England Cavalry, a regiment made up of N.H. and R.I. men. That regiment became the 1ˢᵗ Rhode Island in 1862. Thompson served as Captain of Company K before being promoted to Major on July 3, 1862; he was promoted to Lieutenant Colonel on August 15, 1862, under Col. Duffié.[4]

During the Middleburg affair, the twenty-eight-year-old Thompson was second in command under Duffié. During his escape from the Confederates, he brought out eighteen men. When Duffié was promoted and left the regiment in late June 1863, Thompson was in full command. On the 7ᵗʰ of January 1864, Thompson's N.H. battalion permanently separated from the First Rhode Island Cavalry to become the First New Hampshire Cavalry. On March 24, 1864, Thompson resigned from the R.I. regiment to become colonel of the N.H. regiment, which was wholly made up of men from his state. With the New Hampshire regiment Thompson saw action around Petersburg before moving into the Shenandoah Valley with Gen. Phillip Sheridan. Thompson impressed George A. Custer at the battle of Tom's Brook, October 9, 1864, with a timely charge by the New Hampshire troops. He sent an orderly to Thompson telling him "General Custer sends his compliments, and says you, with your regiment have saved the battle." It is said that when Thompson and his New Hampshire cavalrymen were put in charge of escorting 1800 Confederate prisoners after an action at Waynesboro in March 1865, Thompson "selected for this perilous duty his old Rhode Island cavaliers on whom he knew he could depend." Thompson was made brevet Brigadier-General on March 13, 1865. He was mustered out of the Army on July 15, 1865. Thompson declined the offer of a commission in the Regular Army.[5]

Following the war, Thompson returned to Chicago and opened his own Chicago law firm in 1866 with a fellow Civil War veteran. The firm soon became prominent in the city, and counted industrialist George M. Pullman, former United States First lady Mary Todd Lincoln and the Western Union Telegraph Company as clients. From 1876 to 1878 he served the city as Alderman. He was also a member of the Union League Club, The Military Order of the Loyal Legion, and numerous other veterans' organizations. John. L. Thompson died at his home in Chicago on the morning of January 31, 1888, after a stroke. He was fifty-two. He was buried in Graceland Cemetery, Chicago, Illinois.[6] A painting of Thompson hangs today in the New Hampshire State House.

Chicago,   May 19, 1883

Dear Captain:

Your letter of last February has been allowed to remain unanswered on account of a journey which I have been taking in the South. I have suffered severely from pneumonia in the Spring in two seasons, and I thought I would try to avoid our Spring weather. The result I hope has been good. I have been quite well. I was in Florida, Southern Georgia, and the last of April in the mountains of North Carolina. I don't know how I can assist you about your Middleburg history.[7]

Col. [Alfred] Duffié was sometimes communicative and sometimes, and about some matters, very reticent. I remember only in a very general way what he said to me about the affair. I know there was not the most cordial feeling between him and the controlling officers in the cavalry, and his orders to keep so far west of the main body were regarded by him as an effort to get rid of him, by having his regiment captured or lost, or by his own mistakes in executing his very difficult and very remarkable orders.[8] You will, of course, have a copy of these, and a study of them, in view of the then known position of the main body of the Confederate army and the probable position of the cavalry, will show that there must have been some truth in Duffié's surmise. Then, again, I suspected that he was more or less a thorn in the side of the higher officers. He was not companionable with them; did not think as they did; had little in common, and, was perhaps, inclined to be boastful; perhaps solicited such a combination of regiments in brigades as would give him a larger command, and he certainly thought he was entitled to it, and felt injured that he did not receive it. Perhaps he solicited an independent command; my recollection is that he did, and when he received this, he discovered that it was sufficiently independent, and before we were through with it, we discovered that it was too much so. These jarring relations, which I have indicated in such a general way, were the cause of his being sent out. He would say that his orders were an intentional error. They would say that he asked for them and more too. He was very uneasy as soon as we were through the Bull Run Mountains, and his anxiety increased from that time on. Still he was very ambitious as well as proud, and he would not have turned back, except in the presence of an overwhelming force, for anything in the world. He sent Captain Allen dashing into (I have forgotten the name of the town was it Middleburg, or some other at the junction of one road and the Aldie pike?) and came near making splendid captures.[9] He was exceedingly desirous of distinguishing himself, and really hoped to do so, although he knew he was liable at any moment to meet a very much larger force than he had. Still there is little distinction without danger.

I cannot tell you the secrets of his management of the affair after we had our fight[.] After dark, and when we knew we were in the presence of a large force, and they might surround us and overwhelm us at any moment, he was considerably shaken. He could not bear to retreat, and to stay till daylight was perhaps destruction. My recollection is that he wanted to wait before moving, until he could hear from Captain Allen's mission; but the indications of the strength of the enemy were too plain, and his final idea, I think, was to conceal his command until the morning might show him a way to extricate himself. We hid successfully, but the extrication did not come. We can all say what we might have done in view of what we know now, but he was embarrassed by his relations to the cavalry officers. He could not go back to them in a disorganized state, such as would probably follow cutting through a large force in the night. He did not want to go back to them at all, and his sagacity and shrewdness was shown by the fact that he went directly to General Hooker, to whom he told such a story as induced the General to send him at once to Washington endorsed for a Brigadier-General. Duffié had no idea of returning to [Alfred] Pleasanton with his command gone.[10]

Now, I have given only impressions. I have referred to no book or letters, and I may be wrong, but I think not. Duffié was in many respects an excellent soldier. His command was very fond of him, and he liked his command, but everything was subordinate to his personal ambition and his ambition and the generally discordant relations between him and the controlling spirits of the cavalry all combined to sacrifice the regiment that day. The regiment should not have been there alone; should not have had such orders, and Duffié should have thought less of himself and more of his command and the good of the service. It demoralizes a command to skulk and hide. This was the cause of the only exception to the splendid bearing of the regiment throughout the whole expedition.

The truth is, we disgraced ourselves by fleeing from a comparatively small force as we emerged from our hiding-place. A larger force came upon us later in the morning, but at first it was small. In all other respects the men acquitted themselves gallantly, and they were justified to some extent, at least, in being at first demoralized by the hiding, and the consciousness of a great danger.

I have only given you a few rambling impressions of my own and not historical facts, and have not helped you at all. I shall be very glad to see your paper, for everything relating to the history of our regiment is very interesting to me. I have within a week passed through Andersonville, Ga., and Salisbury, North Carolina.

There is no appearance of a prison. Scrub pines cover the ground and have obliterated all traces of the confinement and misery of our soldiers, but the sight of the places brought up memories and accounts of experiences which will last as long as life.

I have tried to give you accurate impressions, but they are hastily written, and I should not consent to have my name mentioned as authority for anything without an opportunity for more careful expression and an examination into documents.

Very truly,
John L. Thompson.

Capt. Geo. N. Bliss, Providence, R. I.

John L. Thompson as colonel of the First New Hampshire Cavalry
(n.d., carte de visite image courtesy of Leo Kennedy)

Letter of Preston Farrington,
Major, First Rhode Island Cavalry

Note: See biography of Farrington in Chapter Two, above. This letter was not dated but was written circa February 28, 1911; it comes from the George N. Bliss Collection (MSS 298) in the Mary Elizabeth Robinson Research Center at the Rhode Island Historical Society.

Rem[embrances] of Battle of Middleburg Va. of June 17th, 1863

Captain George N. Bliss
Providence R. I.

Dear Captain

You want me to give my recollections of the battle of Middleburg as I remember them. Those scenes are burned indelibly in memory and will probably remain as long as life lasts. The General Orders [for the expedition are] in [Denison's] History 1st R. I. Calvary page 232.

When about half way from Manassas to Thoroughfare Gap, Lieutenant Col. [John] Thompson, who had been riding in front of the regiment with the colonel [Duffié], stepped out and as I came along said, "The colonel wants to see you." Of course, I shot forward expecting orders; the colonel said, "Come in here," pointing to the place by his side and as we moved along the colonel commenced to talk on religion, a subject which he never had mentioned before, I soon saw that he was ill at ease, and was not at all satisfied with his own beliefs. And we rode on for an hour or more continually talking on the subject, although I could give him but a little information. And as we came to a pause I reined out. I said, "I will let Lt Thompson come back." The colonel said, "Come in here," meaning for me to keep my place. As we reached the Gap and got about half way through, our advance guard commenced firing. I started and pushed as fast as my horse could go. Arriving at the entrance of the Gap on the further side I found our advance having quite a skirmish with quite a force of cavalry. It was evident that the Rebs did not like our boy's society for they were retreating as fast as possible. On looking the matter over we found that 3 horses had been killed and some wounded, but the Rebs had passed out of sight.

We then turned short to the right and took an inside road toward Middleburg coming out on the main road, here small parties kept scouting all firing upon our rear. Coming near Middleburg we detailed a strong advance and ordered them to charge through the place. [We] placed strong pickets at the 4 corners of the road [while] holding the balance of their men in reserve. At the same time, we sent pickets out at our rear upon the road we had come. When our advance charged through the town, they found quite a force of cavalry at the hotel at the corner of the roads and our boys pursued for some distance but their horses being fresh or well rested they got away. It was afterwards learned that the party was General Lee and his staff with a strong body guard.[11] The remainder of the regiment held an elevated position from 3/8 to a 1/2 mile from the town just off of the main road we had come from the Gap on. At this time, it was just past sun down. Colonel Duffié & Lt Col Thompson were seated on the ground looking down the road, and all seemed quiet when our pickets at the point were attacked by quite a force. The force coming around and down the upper side of the Aldie road, the enemy came so quickly that our men had not time to fire upon them. Consequently, the Rebs knocked down the barricades and were upon our men as it was in a minute, our men came back a little way towards the main camp & then wheeled [and] charged the foe shooting and finally drove them back out of sight. When the shooting was at the fieriest, the colonel said to me, "Major, Why don't you go and see what to do." Without answering, I mounted my horse and was there as soon [as] my horse [could] carry me, when I reached there the boys was just returning from there chase, and a part of them dismounted and began to replace the barricades. We gathered more rails and made all four of the barricades much stronger then had before been, and all seemed quiet and no enemy in sight.

I then returned to camp & found Lt Colonel Thompson sitting in the same spot as when I left. I asked where Colonel Duffié was. Col Thompson said, "I don't know, he went off a few minutes ago." I said to Col Thompson, "Colonel, I am tired, thirsty and hungry; I am going to have some bread & milk, will you have some?" And I took from my saddle bag two small cups & 2 spouge [?] a small can of condensed milk & some hard tack and I had a canteen of fresh water and thinning the condensed milk with water commenced to break in the hard tack. The colonel messed but a very little, & I think broke into the milk but ate one hard tack. I tried to chafe the colonel some telling him I did not believe he was brought up on milk &c. Then I asked him, "Colonel, what is the situation?" He answered, "Major it looks bad." I said, "Is that so?" He said, "Yes, I think we are surrounded by large forces, and I think we will all be shot or taken prisoners." He then said, "The colonel could save the regiment if he would move back right away, but he is so stuffy about obeying his orders to remain here for the night." At this [he] dropped his cup of milk not having taken as I believe but two spoonfuls, went back, mounted his horse and rode away and I did not see him again until I met him in Centerville. At about this moment Colonel Duffié came up and asked, "Where is Thompson?" I replied, "He has just gone to the rear." At that moment the pickets commenced firing again and it was evident that the force was larger than ever. The colonel said, "Major, if you take your battalion down in the hollow there by the road & dismount them by the stone wall you will stop the charge should the enemy charge down." I immediately moved as directed, dismounting, telling the man to tie their horses securely to the young trees and where they could find them even in the dark. This being done, the men were posted along the stone wall with instructions not to fire until they got the word, but at the word to all fire at once but be sure they did not shoot over, but try to get the horse or his rider. Our pickets were now falling back fast, and although it was quite dark, we could see that they were all in by the space between them and the coming force. When the charging column got nearly opposite our left, the word "fire" was given, and every one of the 80 carbines were discharged [and] down went the leading horses & their riders. How many men or horses fell in the rear of course we could not see. See account page 234 History 1st R.I. Cavalry.[12] The front horses falling some of those in the rear coming so rapidly stumbled over those that had fallen in front. I have always thought that a few went on two or three perhaps, but the bulk mounted and dismounted hurried back. Captain Wyman[13] who had come down and stood beside me said he wanted to see the effect and went over the wall, he returned in two or three minutes and [reported?] three men and three horses lay dead in the front, one man was an officer. Again they came thundering down and received the same reception and as quickly rallied and retreated and then I heard a force go down in the field the other side of the road. I called Lt. [James M.] Fales and told him to follow the cart road on which we came in and at the edge of the woods he would find Colonel Duffié tell him the above facts which I had given him. Hardly had I given this order before the Rebs came down the third time on a charge and met the same fuselage from our carbineers and were hurled back. Very soon Lt. Fales returned and said he could not find Colonel Duffié or any of the command. I said, "Why you must have missed him, he is right at the edge of the woods at the left of this cart path." The Lt was quite vexed as I was and said, "I assure you major I went up and down in front of these woods and out where we stopped when we first came up." Believing the colonel was there as described for the last words he said to me was, "Fight as long as you think it any use and then draw off your men and join me, I will wait for you at the edge of the woods." Mounting my horse I shot through the cart path about as the bullets from our carbines had gone into the charging column and sure enough there was no colonel or headquarters to be found. I could hear considerable confusion up on the road quite a little way back from where we halted when we first came up. Not finding the colonel I immediately returned to the dismounted carbineers and finding Captain Chase[14] I said, "Captain, call off and mount your men as quietly as you can form in column, take this cart path back to the front of the woods. Remain at the front yourself and leave your men be in the path and wait there until I come. I will call off the rest of the men and join you as quick as I can." I went back to call off the balance of the men and could hear a dismounted force coming into the field in which we were in, and but a short distance away. The men being mounted we moved quietly along, took the cart path, moved out to the open, found no Chase, or anyone else, wasting no time we moved across the fields in a southeasterly direction until we struck a road which I had seen in the morning, presuming that probably the colonel had taken that road, I followed down for some more than a half mile. Hearing a little babbling brook at my left and a big growth of timber I turned head of column to the left, got into the woods, dismounted, [and] led our horses back about one hundred yards. Finding a comparatively level place (for a side hill) I bade the boys to tie their horses securely, unsaddle, make no lights, or fires, & make themselves as comfortable as possible.

Of course my spare horse & pack horse with all my food, blankets & bedding with my servant was with headquarters, that is if there was any headquarters. But taking my saddle for a pillow, my poncho for a mattress, my saddle blanket for a caverte [?] we went to bed. If I slept at all, I slept with one eye & both ears open. At the first streak of day, I rose in a sitting posture and I could look over camp & see that every[thing?] seemed peaceful. As soon as it was fairly daylight, I was up, as soon as the horses saw me each began to ask for their breakfast. I walked down towards the road that we came from last night, in order to view it and see if the water in the little brook was fit for men and horses. I got within seventy [feet?] or a little nearer the road. I looked up and saw a brigade of Infantry moving rapidly past down towards Aldie. They were moving in the middle of the road and as noisily as a cat moves. I moved about the same gate and as quietly as possible back to the bivouac. Captain Gould[15] had gotten up and was a couple of rods from his bed. I went up to him and said, "Captain do you see that Rebel force going down the road?" He had not, I said, "Hurry, wake up every man, hush him as soon as he opens his eyes, tell him to get up quick, gather up all his things, take his saddle with his other things and his arm and lead his horse right back up the hill, keeping a little to the right to avoid the opening." But I had shaken quite a number awake before the captain got there. I shook the men quite roughly retching [?] them where I could. As soon as the man opened his eyes, I said she [shush?] and repeated the above order. I think within five minutes we were all on the summit. On gaining the summit we found the hill sloped off and descended so sharply that within two hundred feet there was a swale where quite a stream of water was flowing. But immediately over the ridge there was a little hollow as handsome as a hand bowl. Into this hollow the men led and saddled their horses and was seu [set?] to mount at the word. I went out on the ridge of the hill about two hundred feet, the hill dropped off as square as so it had been cut away leaving a bald bluff. Peeking through the underbrush I could see that there was as much as a squadron of cavalry if not more. Returning I took a man and placed him behind a heavy growth of young chestnut sprouts as a picket and sent another picket to guard the way we came in. Thus we waited. The men bore themselves superbly they all had rations but could neither cook or make coffee. Some of the men became so thirsty that they would take a couple of canteens and crawl snake fashion down to the brook and get water. The horses not having anything to eat or drink would grab every green leaf er how [?] within and chomp it down ravenously. In pulling up the growing bushes the ground was so dry the dust would fly up [in] their noses and then they would snort or blow so our picket on the bluff said that the rebs under the bluff heard it and would come up to find out where the noise came from. At one time a man came so near he could have shoved his carbine through the bushes and reached him, but as the man heard nothing more, he retreated down the bluff. So we had to either tie the horses up so high or stand and hold them up so they could not get them to the ground.

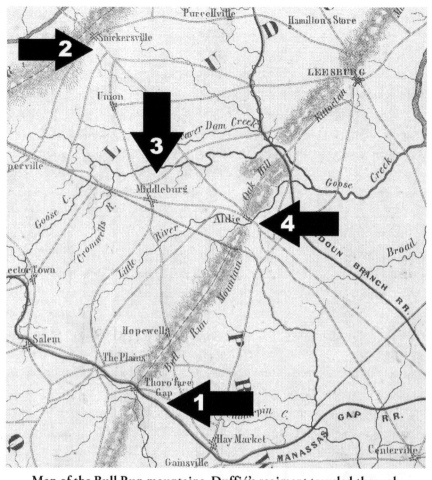

Map of the Bull Run mountains. Duffié's regiment traveled through Thoroughfare (Thoro'fare) Gap #1, with orders to proceed to Snickersville, #2. En route they were nearly annihilated at Middleburg, #3. Union Gen. David Gregg's division was in #4, Aldie. (Library of Congress, Geography and Map Division, Dwyer, *Map of the Manassas Gap Railroad*.)

Thus we remained until about one o'clock pm when some of the men complained. They could [not] see why they should remain there without making some effort to get away. I said to them, "Mount your horses men." They mounted. I said to them, "Now men you seem to be dissatisfied having remained here so long. I have remained here as I did not want to see any of you either shot or taken prisoner. I thought it better to wait for a change. As that will come, and when it does there may be a chance to escape. To move now or to have moved before will be certain death or capture. Thus far myself I prefer death to capture but if you want to go, I am ready. All I ask is that you stick together and obey commands." At this point someone said, "I doubt there are any of us that want to be shot." I showed how foolish it was to expect anything else, but said, "If you want to go, I am ready. I will leave it all to you. All those that want to go now raise your right hands," not a hand came up. "All those that are willing to wait until there is a prospect of making an escape, raise their right hands," every hand went up. Gentlemen, dismount, tie your horses as they were tied before and make yourself as comfortable as possible."

Thus we remained until about three o'clock p.m. when the picket from the bluff came in and said the cavalry force under the bluff was moving out. The word was given, "Mount your horses gentlemen," dispatching a currier for the remaining picket. As quickly as possible we moved out onto the road on which we came last night. Turning to the left [we] moved right under the bluff which we had just been above and the cavalry force had moved from. There rear had just passed around the point to the left as we came down the main road running parallel with the Aldie Pike which ran from Middleburg to Aldie and the johnnies had swung around to cut across to the Aldie Pike.

A mile or two from our starting point over a high knoll off the road we discovered a picket but as we could not descend [discern?] upon his color we did not molest him or neither did he molest us, we were not in a waiting or pausing mood. So we pushed on as fast as our horses could walk. About three or four miles of course we had no way of telling distances except by the gate of our horses, we came to a large square farm house with large barns and out buildings everything, land and all, bespoke of a well to do or rich farmer. As we neared the house in the garden near the [*missing word*] was a colored boy I should think about twenty years old. I asked him the name of the parties who lived there and asked if the man was at home. And the boy said he was not at home and further questioning said that his master and one son and one servant had gone to the fight. Asking him about the roads to Centerville he gave us the way over the mountain telling to keep the straight when we got to the top of the mountain, we would find a road running right across this road. "Don't take none of them roads. If you goes to your right you goes to where you don't want to. If you

46

goes to your left you goes right into Stewart's Cavalry. Jest keep straight ahead." I said, "Well my boy go to stable and get a horse and go show me the road." "There no hoss in the barn only a two-year old colt masses jest took one hos young muster got one and the servant took one to go to the fight width." Well, I said, "You can walk over can't you?" "I is willing to go and show you the way, but you must command me to go." well I said then, "I command you all right." Dropping his hoe he started & led the way. We soon struck the mountain road which proved to be quite a smooth and hard-faced road, though steep, arriving at the top and crossing the road that run exactly across this road, the boy said, "Now me just keep this road straight down, I can't go another step." I asked, "Why can't you go further," and he said, "Because if I go a step further, I shall be shot, and I doesn't want to [be] shot. I know you will be all right." And he turned back. As he passed down along the line the boys all spoke cheerily to him as we passed along. About two miles further down the road we came to a small weather-beaten frame house standing close to the road, with the front door on the back side which faced the south east with a little wood shed and a small hen house. Going in, in search of information, we found a man and woman I should think about sixty-five years old. Inquiring if members of either armies had been around there, they said a few of each army had been past there. I asked the man if he knew anything about the fight at Aldie, he said some of the soldiers said that Stuart had been driven back and that the Union Army [was in] possession of the place. The man said, "I am known as a Union man and should I go out much I should be shot as quick as the <u>Secesh</u>[16] <u>would shot one of yourselves</u>." But the women had been talking and hustling around to get the boys something to eat. She brought out some cold chicken and corn pone and everything she could pick up, and said, "I have not got much and don't know when we can get any more, for all the rich farmers about here are all Secesh and will not sell us anything so we have to go a long way to get what we need." I said to her, "My good women, our men have all got some rations keep what you have we shall soon be where we can cook our rations and our men will not starve. Her reply was, "I had rather starve than to see any man that fights to save the union go hungry."

Believing the women would give away every morsel of food she had I ordered an advance. We moved rapidly on. Nothing more occurring until we struck the village of Centerville. The road that we had come on struck about the center of the village, and as we came out to the main street an officer halted us and asked, "What regiment do you belong to." On being told, he said, pointing a little south of east, "You will find some of your men over there." Moving in the direction designated by the officer we soon found Colonel Thompson and a few men and you may be sure we tried to make ourselves comfortable, remaining there through the night. Lt. Col. Thompson having gotten such of our men as had been previously detailed to various general's quarters, about eighty men, we started the next morning for Alexandria where we arrived in the afternoon. Arriving in Alexandria we found a camp had been lain out, a headquarter tent pitched, our band and a few men there in charge of Lieutenant [Otis C.] Wyatt.[17] When Lt. Wyatt saw us coming, he mounted that fine horse of his and hat in hand rode out to meet us, in his hearty and enthusiastic meeting. Lt. colonel said with his incarace [?] grant God. See Pages 237, 238, 239 History 1ˢᵗ R. I. Cavalry for list of casualties.[18]

Most Respectfully Yours
P.M. Farrington late Major
1ˢᵗ R.I. Cavalry Vol[unteers]

Thomas T. Munford Letters
Former General in the Confederate Army

Thomas T. Munford (1831-1918) graduated from the Virginia Military Institute in Lexington, in 1852. While at VMI, Munford had close proximity to Thomas J. Jackson, later known as "Stonewall" Jackson. Munford once confided, "I very much doubt if there was a man at the Institute at any time who had been thrown more directly with him [Jackson] or who knew him personally better than I did." While his father and grandfather had been lawyers, after graduation from VMI, Munford bypassed that profession and become a farmer. By 1860, the twenty-nine-year-old Munford had a very productive farm in Bedford County, Virginia, with a large house, eighteen-horse stable, and slave quarters for six. The U.S. Census that year showed he had $33,000 of real estate and personal property of $63,500. His father, though, was concerned, "He has incurred a heavy debt . . ." he wrote in a letter.[19]

In May 1861, the thirty-year-old Munford joined the Confederate army. He left behind his pregnant wife and four young children. Munford became lieutenant-colonel of the Thirtieth Virginia Mounted Infantry (later renamed Second Regiment of Cavalry). Organized at Lynchburg, the regiment was mustered in by Col. Jubal A. Early. At the battle of Bull Run, Munford had command of three squadrons composed of the Black Horse, Chesterfield, and Wise troops, the Franklin rangers, and three independent companies. His command pursued the enemy further than any other, capturing many prisoners and ten rifled guns which he turned over to President Davis at Manassas.[20]

In 1862, Munford served with Stonewall Jackson in the Shenandoah Valley. He participated in the battle of Cross Keys, the Chickahominy campaign, and at White Oak swamp. Munford received two saber wounds at Second Manassas. He was actively engaged in the Maryland campaign that resulted in the battle of Antietam. His regiment fought at Poolesville, Monocacy Church, Sugar Loaf Mountain, Burkittsville and Crampton's gap. During the Antietam battle on the 17th and 18th of September 1862, on Lee's right wing, he guarded the lower fords of Antietam Creek. During the retreat back into Virginia following the battle, Munford's unit crossed the Potomac in the presence of the enemy and defended the movement from Boteler's Ford.[21]

Fitzhugh Lee fell ill with inflammatory rheumatism shortly after Chancellorsville and Munford assumed command of the brigade. He commanded the brigade at Beverly's Ford and Aldie. He took part in the Gettysburg campaign, the Bristoe campaign, and cavalry operations in the spring of 1864. Under Gen. Fitzhugh Lee, Munford participated in the Shenandoah Valley campaign with Jubal Early in late summer of 1864. He was again in command of the brigade in Waynesboro where he observed George Bliss after Bliss's charge into Munford's forces (see Chapter Five). In November 1864, Munford was promoted to brigadier-general although that promotion, coming very late in the war, was never confirmed by the Confederate Congress. With this promotion, Munford was assigned to the command of Fitzhugh Lee's division.[22]

Lee commanded a division late in the war, fighting at Five Forks. On the retreat from Richmond his division assisted General Thomas Rosser in the defeat of the Federals at High Bridge, where 780 Union prisoners were captured. He fought in the battle of April 7th, when the Union General David Gregg was captured. At Appomattox, at daybreak April 9th, he commanded the cavalry on the right of the Confederate line. His division was not among the units surrendered by Lee that day, and Munford moved toward Lynchburg, collecting scattered Confederate units in an attempt to join with Joseph E. Johnston's army in North Carolina. After Johnston surrendered, Munford followed suit late in April.[23]

With the close of the war, Munford retired to his home in Lynchburg and again engaged in agricultural interests in both Virginia and Alabama. He also served two terms as president of the board of visitors of the Virginia Military Institute.

Munford and Bliss became friends in about 1880. Of twelve Munford letters found in Bliss's papers, three relate to the fight at Middleburg and are included in this chapter. In these, Munford contributed his unique viewpoint regarding the battle at Aldie. Munford's brigade, five miles to the east of Middleburg, was firmly positioned between Bliss's regiment and the Union forces they hoped would come to their support at Middleburg. When Stuart was initially pushed out of Middleburg, he hastily recalled Munford, who reluctantly withdrew from his very strong position at Aldie. His exit left an opening for Union forces to proceed through Aldie to Middleburg and relieve the 1st R.I. Cavalry. Union troops, however, made no move to do so. (Denison, *Sabres and Spurs*, 241-42)

Thomas Munford during the Civil War (n.d., courtesy of Virginia Museum of History & Culture

Munford visited Bliss at his home in East Providence, R.I. at least once, in 1897. Bliss, with a lifelong love of sailing, owned a two-masted sailboat named *Fanchon*. Munford, likely ill at ease aboard *Fanchion*, wrote Bliss, "I remember your hospitality and my nice visit to your home, the sweet girls, and your gentleman[l]y sons, all contributed to my pleasure whither at your home or in your gallant little boat which skimmed along in the water like a summer duck and bore us as smoothly as it was possible to glide on the "Briny Deep." [Munford to Bliss, May 8th, 1903] Bliss and Munford met again in July 1913, at the fiftieth anniversary of the Battle of Gettysburg. Munford died February 27, 1918, in Uniontown Alabama, at aged 86.[24]

George Bliss aboard his sailboat *Fanchion*. Munford was aboard for a sail in 1897. (Photograph found in Bliss's papers)

Lynchburg Va   April 26th, 1884
Major Geo N. Bliss

Dear Sir:[25] I was in command of Fitz Lee's Brigade at Aldie, June 17. Gen. Fitz Lee had been kicked by a mule or horse in passing a wagon, & was compelled to take an ambulance until nearly at Gettysburg.[26] My Command was composed of the 2d Va Cav. my own Regiment, and the 1st and 3d. [Thomas] Rosser had been sent off to the Right, com[man]ding his regim[en]t, the 5[th] [Va.], & [Williams] Wickham his 4[th] Va., had been sent off, but both were sent to report to me at Aldie. The 2d Va & 3d Va. and 1[st], were feeding their horses at Carter's, about a mile and a half from Aldie, when I was notified of the advance of the enemy. Rosser arrived just before my reserve Regiments got up & had a short Skirmish. When I arrived, I put the 1st Va. on the Upperville Pike, with the sharp shooters dismounted behind the two stone walls. The triangular or V shaped land between the two pikes <u>rises</u> to the <u>west</u>. [A]t the apex was a meadow with some stacks of hay. My position was an extremely strong one. The enemy did not try to go up the Upperville road but once, but they charged <u>repeatedly</u> up the Snicker Gap road. The sharp <u>shooters</u> behind the stone wall & stake fence to their right gave them a splendid position. The Federals could not turn it, they would charge up the lane and <u>receive</u> a <u>galling fire</u>. My mounted regiments <u>would counter</u> charge & <u>drive</u> them <u>back</u> down the lane & they would get a <u>second volley</u>. This was done six or eight time[s] by different squadrons & regiments, but they had not dislodged me. I never saw men show <u>better spirit</u> than the Federals did, and they <u>should</u> have run over me if two or three regiments or a Brigade had been thrown in [at one time]. I was ordered to retire by a staff officer from Gen Stuart. I would have preferred to attempt to <u>hold on</u> to leaving, as my men had gained confidence and we believed we could keep him off. I did retire up the Snickers Gap road but <u>was not pressed</u>. I never saw as many dead & wounded men & horses in the same space before or after as we had before us. I do not wish to try at this late day to write a description of the battle. I made a report at the time, <u>&</u> sent in the reports of all the col[onel]s. We captured about 130 men and officers. Rosser lost heavily. I was the ranking officer. Genl Stuart had been held in check & kept out of Middleburg, by a very inferior force <u>compared</u> to his command and <u>we never had the credit</u> from <u>our side</u> for what was <u>done by us.</u>[27] My command was like the R.I. Regiment, fighting with 5 times <u>its numbers</u>. I believe Major McClellan, who was Genl Stuarts adj[utan]t will write a fair account of that battle in his <u>narrative</u> of Stuarts Campaigns now in progress.[28] I do not send you this as a report & do not care to appear in print but I am responsible for the <u>truth</u> of what is said, & I don't care how you use it. You can get full extracts from the Reports from Major McClellan. His address is Lexington

Kentucky. He is a <u>gentleman</u> & can be relied upon & will I have no doubt cheerfully respond to any enquiry you may make of him.

We see so much of garbled history I feel disgusted with a great many accounts. I have sent a review of Genl Ropers Papers to the Phila book <u>9</u> times. Which he will <u>print one of these days.</u>

I feel no disposition to go into print- hope you will excuse a hurriedly written letter & a very slight sketch of Aldie as I remember it.

Very truly yours,
Thomas T. Munford.

P. S. I was not a West Pointer. I graduated at the Virginia Military Institute, and had seventeen graduates of that school in my regiment, and I had one of the finest regiments in the army. I knew all of my men, served with them four years. I do not say this unkindly, but our army had to supply places for graduates of West Point of the old army, and some of them had better been at home.[29]

T. T. M.

I did not receive the paper you refer to Prison life by Lt. James Fales. I shall be glad to see it.[30]

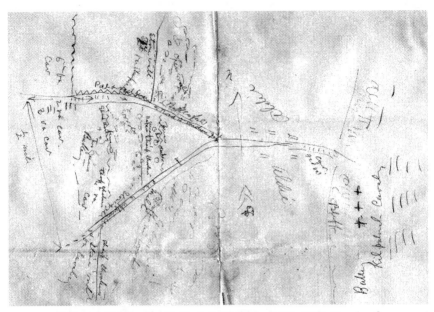

Thomas T. Munford's Sketch of the June 17, 1863, Battle of Aldie. Aldie is to the right. The Snicker Gap Road is the top branch; the Upperville Road, which led to Middleburg, is the left branch. (From Munford's April 26, 1884 letter)

Lynchburg Virginia   April 30, 1884
Major Geo N Bliss

Dear Sir

Immediately after I received your letter asking me about the Fight at Aldie 17th June 1863, I addressed the enclosed letter to Capt Frank S Robertson resides in Washington County, Virginia, thinking he could recall the circumstances connected with the Order. His reply is enclosed. Capt. Robertson was A.A.D.C on Genl Stuarts Staff - This should settle the point as to whether I was <u>ordered</u> <u>off</u> or <u>driven off</u>, – It matters very little to me. I <u>left</u> <u>there</u> and as I had a strong position, would have preferred to hold it to having a fight with a largely superior force when I did not & could not have the advantage of the strong position I had taken at – [Aldie?] I was not <u>pursued</u> or hampered to any extent when I did fall back

54

and I certainly carried off all of my prisoners and did not leave any of my wounded that could be moved. –

> I am major very truly y[ours]
> Respectfully
> Thomas T Munford

If you will do me the kindness to enclose Capt Frank S Robinson['] s letter to Major H. B. McClellan's address Lexington Kentucky after <u>satisfying</u> yourself – it will be an introduction to Major McClellan who will be better able to give you information than I can. The Captain[']s reply was not received until today did not wish to delay my reply to your letter – hence I did not send it in my hurried letter a few days since - Yours

> T T M

[The Enclosure]

Lynchburg April 22, 1884,
Capt Frank Robertson
A.A D C. Late A N. Va.

Dear Capt -

I enclose you a letter from a gallant Federal Officer, Major Geo N Bliss. He asks some information at my hands about the battle at Aldie, 17 June 1863. Remembering that you came in person & delivered an order to me from Genl J. E. B. Stuart to fall back from my position at Aldie; will you please state that fact on the other side of the page of this letter. A good many reports have been made on this fight and the Federals claim that <u>we</u> were driven off. – I reported that I was ordered by Genl Stuart to fall back <u>through</u> you as his A. D. C ["aide-de-camp"]. I will thank you to state as far as you can what order you delivered to me

> Your friend –
> Thomas T. Munford

[Written on same piece of paper]

The Meadows near Abingdon Va   April 26, 84
Gen Thos T Munford

Dear Sir – In reply to yrs, will state that the orders I carried you from
Gen J. E. B. Stuart, were delivered under difficulties that vividly recall
them – He & Staff were very unceremoniously driven out of Middleburg
by the sudden & unexpected approach of a large body of Federal Cavalry.
Shortly afterwards general Stuart called me & gave the following orders.
"Go back & find Munford about Aldie – explain matters, & order him
to fall back immediately, & join me as best he can at Riders Cross Roads
to night" – Less than an hour afterwards these orders were given you at
Aldie, and as I remember, quite late in the evening –

I found you sharply engaged, but recall no impression of the enemy's
pressing or having any thing to do with your falling back which of course
immediately followed my orders from Stuart.

Yrs' very Truly
Frank S. Robertson

205 Harrison St   Sept 27, 1884
Lynchburg Va
Major Geo N Bliss

My dear Sir

Please accept my thanks for your remembrance in sending me a copy
of your very readable narrative – It was my fond fortune never to have been
captured nor to have visited prison, – I packed many a good fellow off,
with a sigh when he saw the inevitable – I was four years in the conflict.
My regiment & brigade was always active. – and I am sure I saw as <u>hard</u>
service as any man in the A. N. V. [Army of Northern Virginia]

For two years Wickham was a Confederate Congressman & <u>retained</u>
both commissions so I did <u>his</u> work & he got the credit of what <u>Wickhams</u>
Brigade did when he was nary on hand with it – Our Brigades took

the name of its commander. [A]s he had the <u>Brigade</u> & did not <u>resign</u>, I could only stand to my post until he did resign, which was after our fight at Waynesboro, he was not there.[31] Genl Fitz-Lee was wounded at Winchester. Wickham had the Div[ison] & I his Brigade in all of the fights including the Battle of Winchester –

Can you tell me of any work I can get containing the reports of the Federal Cavalry officers in Sheridan's Valley Campaigns?

Thanking you again,
I am very respectfully
Thomas T. Munford

Edward M. Henry Letter
Former Captain 9th Virginia Cavalry

Edward Moore Henry (ca 1832-1905) was born and raised in Stafford County, Virginia. He enlisted as a lieutenant in Company A of the 9th Virginia Cavalry in April 1861, just days after the bombardment of Fort Sumter. A farmer before the war, Henry was twenty-nine years old. He was absent due to a broken arm, Nov.-Dec. 1861. In June 1863, his company commander, Thomas Towson, was killed at the battle of Brandy Station, and Henry was immediately promoted to fill the position, just eight days before his encounter with Bliss's First Rhode Island Cavalry regiment at Middleburg. Henry described that encounter in this letter.

Henry was wounded in October 1864, a severe enough wound that he was absent for two months. Apparently captured very near the end of the war, he was paroled at Ashland, Virginia, on April 30th, 1865, having served the Confederate cause nearly four years.[32]

After the war, Henry became a well-respected businessman in Norfolk and was mayor of the city in 1890. He was active in the Picket-Buchanan Camp of Confederate Veterans. Although he was a captain in the service, he received the title of General from his rank in the Confederate Veterans organization. In the mid-1890's, Henry was a founding member of a large and influential group, the Norfolk Business Men's Association, in which he was president for many years. Among other activities, the group worked to lobby congress for such business deals as the building of two battleships at the Newport News Shipbuilding company. He died June 20, 1905.[33]

Norfolk, Va.,   Oct 13th 1888[34]
Maj. Geo N Bliss

Yours of 8th requesting me to send you my recollections of the Cavalry fight between your Regiment 1st RI Cavalry & our Regiment 9th Va Cavalry recd.

It was on the morning of the 17th June I think, tho the exact date I don't recollect, that our Regiment passed to the right of Warrenton in to the Plains, & sent a small Pickett in advance to Thoroughfare Gap. [B]efore they had gotten posted, only a few having gotten through the Gap, your Regiment drove them back. [T]hey reported to our Col that your Regiment had come through the Gap & turned to the right towards Middleburg. [A]s we were under orders to cover the flank of Genl Lee's Army, there moving up the Valley, we could not follow you, till we had reported to Gen Stuart, who had passed on another road with some N[orth] Carolina Cav. towards Middleburg, but sent word near night that we must follow you, we started late that evening & marched during the night to Middleburg, but heard nothing of your Regiment, till we got to Middleburg, where we were halted by one of the N.C. Cav Pickets, who said they had had a fight with you, & that you had retired, but where to they did not know.

We then went into camp, without fires. Early next morning a corn detail was sent out to get forage for the horses. On their return to camp they found your Regiment between there & our camp & charged through you, the Bugle Blew Mount & the Regiment mounted quickly & sent in pursuit, the squadrons taking different roads, the one who got on the Road you were retreating in was if I recollect rightly Co.s G & H, who captured some of your regiment & killed & wounded several. There must have been a Maine Battalion with you, for I think we captured an Irishman who had the surgeon[']s instruments, medicines &c along in hennies [?] on a mule, among the medicines some good liquor (Brandy) which was very refreshing to many suffering (thirsty) patients. As to our force in numbers I don't remember, but we were small, as we had lost pretty heavily in the fight of 9th June at Brandy Station (my Captain killed)[35] & many horses disabled & we only had effective men & horses & consequently small in numbers, the cavalry of Genl Stuart was marching on Lee's flank by different roads, so I can form no idea of the forces. Captain Haynes, a gallant fellow, I think led the charge that pursued your Regiment, he commanded Co. H. He was badly wounded 2 days afterwards in a charge near Paris Gap & was paralyzed by the wound & never recovered.[36] Your Regiment captured two of my company who were sent with dispatches to Middleburg, one rode a very fine spirited iron grey mare, he said the Major (I think) took her from him & in the retreat made good his escape from capture by her fleetness. Is my friend Maj. Bliss that gallant major?[37] We never encountered your Regiment afterwards & heard it had been assigned to other duty. I am sorry I cannot give you more of the details from our side, as to numbers &c.

I am so busy just now, with so many interruptions, could not give you a graphic description as I could, with time to bring back to memory many of the details long since forgotten. I hope you have a pleasant evening & would like to be present to hear your paper on the fighting of 17 & 18 of June & hope you will send me a copy & wishing the major may live to give his comrades many pleasant evenings by his war papers, & recollections

I am yrs Resp
E M Henry

[I] was Capt Co. A 9th Va Cav in the days mentioned, & have the honor now to be Commander of the Grand Camp C.V., Department of V[a].

CHAPTER FIVE

Encounter at Waynesboro, Virginia (Sept 28, 1864)

George Bliss's days on the battlefield ended abruptly the afternoon of Sept. 28, 1864, when he rode eight miles from his regiment in Staunton, Virginia to deliver an order in the small town of Waynesboro (known at the time as "Waynesborough"). In a postwar memoir he wrote, "My negro servant, Winson Gaskins, was engaged in frying a chicken, and as I reluctantly turned away from the scene of his promising labors, I assured him that I would soon return. It was five months before I saw Winson again, and my first question was, 'What did you do with that chicken;' to which he replied, 'I thought you was never coming back Massa, so I done eat it myself.'"[1]

The order Bliss carried, to prevent looting, instructed officers in Waynesboro to keep their men from entering the houses in the captured town. Bliss was about to return to Staunton when his attention was drawn to soldiers tearing down the railroad trestle that carried the Virginia Central (sometimes incorrectly referred to as the Chesapeake & Ohio) over the South Fork of the Shenandoah. Suddenly hearing gunfire that he first thought was a minor skirmish, he soon realized that a surprise attack by a determined Confederate cavalry brigade was underway. The attack soon routed the unprepared Union troops guarding the eastern approaches to Waynesboro, pushing them back through the town. Bliss, at the suggestion of Col. Charles Lowell, Jr., led a saber charge to stop the Confederate advance. In the charge, Bliss was wounded, and his horse was shot from under him. He narrowly escaped death at the hands of

Confederate soldiers before being taken prisoner. Eventually arriving at Libby Prison in Richmond, Bliss wrote to his friend, David V. Gerald:

"I often wonder, however at my escape from death at the time of my capture, I was leading a charge of a squadron of the 3rd N Jersey Cavalry, and was some 40 yards ahead of everything (I had a very swift horse) when the Capt Com[manding] [Captain Daniel R. Boice] the squadron saw that he was flanked and was obliged to wheel his men with great celerity and fall back to prevent the destruction of his command; I did not see the rebels on our flank and did not hear the Capt shout for me to come back (which he says he did, for strange to say he is also confined as a hostage in the next cell, having been taken later in the day) so I charged all alone into a brigade of rebel cavalry who were at the time running away having been routed by the moral effect of seeing our men sweeping down upon them at the charge; by the time I got among the rebels I became aware of my dangerous situation but my horse was so much excited that I could not pull him up quickly and presently found myself so deep among the rebels that it was safer to go forward than back. I expected to die and resolved to sell my life as dearly as possible, and so made vigorous use of my knowledge of the sabre practice. This was in the Main st[reet] of Waynesboro Va so the rebels were in columns of fours and I rode down between their files and since the rebels had their backs towards me, I went by them like the wind before they knew they had a yank in the regiment. I wounded a Lieut, the color bearer of the 4th Va Cav. and two others total four while behind me the rebels were yelling, "Kill that d—d s—n of a b—h," not an elegant but a very forcible expression, I struck six blows but two rebels dodged and escaped. At this interesting juncture I thought I saw a chance to escape by a side street and darted into it but at this time one of the bullets that had been whistling about me so merrily, struck my horse and down he went and spread me out on the ground, before I got upon my feet a sabre struck me across the forehead and I parried about the same time another blow, while a gentleman with a Colt's revolver was trying to get a good aim at me. I jumped upon my feet and said, "For God's sake do not kill a prisoner" the reb said, surrender then. I replied I do surrender and del[ivered] up my arms. About this time something hit me in the back and pushed me forward a step, looking quickly around I saw that a reb had stabbed me with a sabre and another gentleman was bringing his pistol to bear. I called out, "is there a mason here, I am a mason" someone said, "are you a mason" I replied, "I am" he said, "I will protect you" and he ordered a man to take me to the rear which was done after I had been robbed of my watch & money but this was done before the man who was to take me back got to me. The wound in the back was from a quarte point, and would have been fatal (probably) if the rebel had turned the wrist, *a la* tactics, but his ignorance saved me since the sabre jammed between two ribs instead of passing soomthly [smoothly] between them. I suffered no pain at all when I was wounded but had some difficulty in breathing during the first night, since the point of the sabre had slightly injured the lower part of the left lung. When I had a good opportunity to look into my military condition, I found five sabre marks on my person one on the forehead over the right eye, one on the end of my nose, one on the body, one (scratch) on the left wrist, one (very slight) on the top of my head. I was very kindly treated in the hospital and found myself on exhibition as "the bravest Yank you ever saw," I began to think myself one of the most remarkable heroes of modern times, but have now so far recovered as to look on the ground occasionally and talk with my fellow victims as though I was an ordinary mortal. Once a week we are allowed to go out into the cellar and wash our clothes which would be a very good thing if I had any clothes."[2]

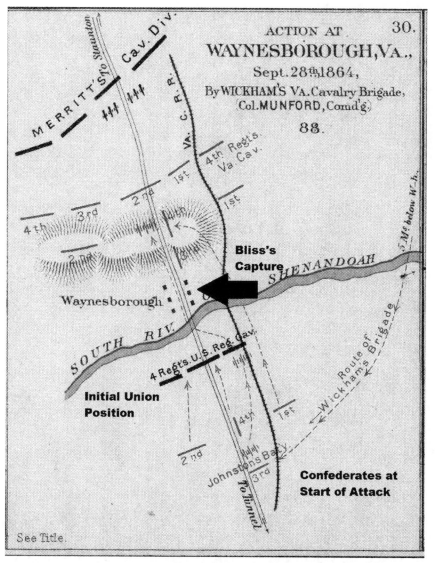

Arrow indicates where Bliss was captured by members of the 4th
Virginia Cavalry. He was in the town of Waynesboro (then spelled
Waynesborough) when Williams C. Wickham's brigade unexpectedly
attacked in full force. (Calvin D. Cowles, comp., *Atlas to Accompany
the Official Records of the Union and Confederate Armies* [Washington,
D.C.: Government Printing Office, 1891-1895], plate LXXXV.)

Long after the war, Bliss began to learn of the Confederates he battled in Waynesboro. By the 1880s Bliss knew the names of most: Thomas T. Munford, the brigade commander; Captain Henry C. Lee, the officer who stepped in to save his life; and two of the four men he had wounded, Captain William A. Moss and Private Hugh Hamilton. Not until 1902 did he learn the names of the final two men he wounded, Corporal Robert L. Baber and Private Thomas W. Garnett. Postwar letters from all these men and another Confederate soldier at Waynesboro, Captain Alexander D. Payne, are presented here.

Letter of Thomas T. Munford,
Commander of Confederate cavalry at Waynesboro

[See biography of Thomas T. Munford (1831-1918) in Chapter Four, above. This letter, from Bliss's papers, was transcribed by him and included in his memoir, *How I Lost My Sabre in War, and Found it in Peace*, pages 51-55.]

Lynchburg, Va.,   March 4, 1882.
Captain George N Bliss, 1ˢᵗ R. I. Cav., late of U. S. A.:

Dear Sir:

I am in receipt of your letter by this evening's mail, asking me to give you an account, from a Confederate standpoint, of the action on the 28ᵗʰ of September 1864, at Waynesboro, Augusta County, Virginia, between the cavalry under my command and the Federal cavalry, commanded by General Torbert. I very much regret that I have no data at hand in the shape of a report from the commanding officers of either of the four regiments, or from Captain Johnston, commanding the battery attached to my brigade. So much time has elapsed since those scenes occurred, my memory cannot be trusted. Reading your narrative has recalled to my mind many points, but it is impossible for me to particularize lest I may do injustice to some of the noble and glorious spirits who so generously sustained me upon all occasions when their best efforts were required. My brigade was composed of the First, Second, Third and Fourth Virginia Cavalry, A. N. V., and Captain Johnston, of the Horse Artillery, with two guns, was serving with me that day, when we left our camp near Weyer's cave.[3]

My orders from General Early, commanding the Valley District, were to move at once to Waynesboro, and attack the Federal cavalry who had gone there to cut the Chesapeake and Ohio Railroad and to destroy the iron bridge over the Shenandoah river between Waynesboro and the mouth of the tunnel at the Blue Ridge. I was notified that we would be supported by the infantry. Having the advantage of a company in my command whose homes were in that county, (Captain MeCluny, First Virginia Cavalry,) instead of taking the most direct road to Waynesboro, which I knew was heavily picketed by the Federal cavalry, I secured a guide who carried me by a blind road through the "old coaling," along the foot-hills of the Blue Ridge, which had not been used for years, but with the assistance of a few axes we soon made it so that the artillery could accompany us; indeed, their indomitable spirit was such that they would go wherever we could go. Coming out by this blind road, where we were least expected, I found the Federal cavalry hard at work endeavoring to destroy the railroad bridge. I crossed the main road half a mile from the mouth of the tunnel which was guarded by a militia force, consisting of the reserves from Staunton and Waynesboro, under Colonel Leo, but who had withdrawn to the top of the mountain. From this point I could see the Federal picket. Dismounting the First, Second and Third Regiments, I ordered the Fourth Regiment, Colonel William B. Wooldridge[4] commanding, to charge this picket, mounted, and deploying the three dismounted regiments, moved rapidly to the attack. Captain Johnston's guns were pushed up at a swift trot to a commanding position and used most effectively. Perceiving that my attack from that unexpected quarter was a surprise, I was not slow to push my advantage, and pushing steadily forward, I drove the force from the bridge and saved it. Meeting a stout resistance at the river, where we lost some good men, I soon cleared my approach to it with my artillery, driving the Federals through the town of Waynesboro. General Early, by this time, had arrived with the infantry via regular road on the northwest of the town, and a few artillery shots from General John Pegram's command started General Torbert to change his base. I more than regret that I cannot here give a detailed account of this fight; no record has ever been made of it;

we were so constantly engaged during those stirring times, no opportunity was afforded us for elaborate reports. I well remember the good services of Captain Henry C. Lee, A. & I. G ;[5] Major J W. Taylor, A. A. A. G. ; Rev. Randolph McKim, Chaplain of Second Regiment Regular Cavalry, acting A. D. C.; Colonel Cary Breckenridge, Second Virginia Cavalry; Colonel William B. Woolridge, Fourth Virginia Cavalry; Colonel W A. Morgan, First Virginia Cavalry, and Lieutenant-Colonel Field, Third Virginia Cavalry, were never wanting upon any field, and gave me their best efforts and support upon that occasion.

In fighting over our battles, as all good soldiers love to do with those who went hand in hand together, I have frequently had the incidents you recalled in your letter, mentioned by those of us who witnessed it, and it affords me pleasure to say it was worthy of a better support than you received from the ranking officer ordering the charge, or the men who should have followed.[6] A little dare-deviltry in a cavalry officer sometimes acts like magic; a few dashing fellows, well led, have turned a victory from one side to a rout on the other, without any cause. As we are strangers, neither being able to recognize the other were we to meet, I can only say your courage will never be doubted by any Confederate who saw your manly bravery in the fight, and you may thank a kind Providence that you are now alive to tell your own story in your own way. You have spoken in a manly and generous way of what passed in our lines. When I saw you at night, sitting behind a Confederate cavalryman, with the blood streaming down your face, going to the rear, a prisoner, I said to Doctor Randolph, brigade surgeon, that you were one of the "widow's son party." He being one of the elder brothers, replied, "I'll see your mother's son well taken care of this night," and as most of the staff officers were of the clan, they did the best they could for a brother in trouble.[7]

I am not a mason, but most of my staff were masons, and I know they frequently did many things that seemed to give them extra pleasure, for the unfortunate on the other side. I was sure the institution was full of good works, and, although I was only a poor soldier who tried to do his duty, without being a mason, I believed the organization was based upon Christian principles, and was always in sympathy with the work of the fraternity.

I can only add that every true and generous soldier, on either side, was willing to extend the healing balm to friend or foe, after the battle was over.

Thanking you for your kind letter, and wishing you prosperity, I am, with much respect,

Thomas T. Munford,
Brig.-Gen. Cav., A. N. V. Late War.

P S.—Should you ever come to Lynchburg again, I should be glad to meet you, and if I can give you any information connected with the operations of our cavalry during the war, will do so with pleasure. I was four years with the Army of N. V.[8]

Letters of Robert L. Baber,
Former Corporal, Fourth Virginia Cavalry

Robert L. Baber (1826-1917) was one of four men Bliss wounded. Until Baber wrote in 1903, Bliss did not know his name or that of Thomas Garnett.

Before the war, Baber was a farmer. He joined the 4th Virginia Cavalry in August 1864, relatively late in the war. He was thirty-eight years old, much older than most in his regiment, and he had left his wife of eighteen years, Elizabeth, at home with six children. A corporal in Company K, he served under Captain William Moss.[9]

After the war, Baber owned and operated a farm of some 268 acres and a mill, known as Baber Mill. Located on Rock Island Creek in Buckingham County, it was both a grist and sawmill. He and Elizabeth had a total of fifteen children. Bliss travelled to Virginia and visited Baber sometime between May 1902 and March 1904, and they exchanged many very friendly letters. Three that most pertain to the war are included here. Baber lived ninety-one years, the same number as Bliss.[10]

Rock Island Va.,[11]   March 24, 1902.
George N. Bliss, Providence, R. I.[12]

Dear Sir:-

Having seen in the Richmond Dispatch a very interesting war incident, speaking of your wounding at Waynesboro, Va., four men with a sabre, and as I received three sabre wounds on my head and believing that you were the man that wounded me, I respectfully request you to send me your photograph. I was a member of Capt. Wm. A. Moss' company, Buckingham county troops, Fourth Virginia cavalry, Company K. Wickham's brigade, Lee's division, and also a Mason.[13]

Please let me hear from you and oblige.

Yours fraternally,
Robert L. Baber.

Judge George N. Bliss
Providence R. I.   Rock Island
Buckingham Co, Vᵃ   April 29ᵗʰ 1902

Dear Bliss: Yours of recent date was duly received & was highly gratified to learn of the man who gave me such an awful drubbing, but proud to know that it did not seriously injure me, it only gave me six weeks furlough. You say that three of the four men that you wounded after 37 years were still living which is correct. Mr Thomas Garnett[14] is the man if I mistake not, whose name you had not learned, who is living, whose P. O. is Arcanum, Buckingham Co. Vᵃ but Capt. Wm A. Moss has been dead 12 or 14 years I suppose. As we have been giving a short history of our lives, I will go a little farther but do not know that it will interest you but however will give you a little anyway. I am nearly seventy six years of age have been a member of the Methodist Church nearly sixty years, a Mason nearly forty two years, was Justice of the Peace for twenty five years, & a Notary Public now, and have been, for about 28 years. You desired me to give you an account of the fight, but having been so long I think it would be difficult to give a correct account of the same. I would like to learn a little more of your history if it will not tire or weary you too much, as I have right much interest in the person who wounded me, and should you ever find it convenient I should be glad for you to visit me

Yours Truly
Robert L. Baber

Judge Geo. N. Bliss   Rock Island V[a]
19 College Street   Feb 6th 1903
Providence R. I.

Dear friend Bliss:

Yours of 2nd inst came duly to hand, and was truly glad to hear from you again, and truly hope that you will continue to write me occasionally as long [as] we live. You said that you wished my picture which I will send you with the request that you return as soon as you can, as it is the only one I have, and I have no opportunity to have another taken living nearly 90 miles from Richmond Va, where I might have them taken[15] – I am as ever Yours Truly

Robert L. Baber

Letters of Thomas W. Garnett,
Former Corporal, Fourth Virginia Cavalry

Thomas W. Garnett (1842-1928), too, was wounded by Bliss in Waynesboro. According to a 1916 pension application, Garnett had lived in Buckingham County, Virginia "all my life," and his occupation was "farming in a small way." Garnett gave his address as "Andersonville RFD [Rural Free Delivery] No. 2." He joined the 4th Virginia in August 1861 and served in Company K, under "Col. Woolridge" and "Captain William A. Moss." Garnett had entered the army at "Richmond, Va.," and remained until "Lees surrender at Appomatox [*sic*] Co[urt] Ho[use] 1865."

His justification for a pension, he wrote, was for "nothing more than I faithfully discharged my duty in the Civil War."[16]

An undated note from Garnett's wife Ann was found in Bliss's papers. The note, a short biography of Garnett, read, "Thomas Wm. Garnett, only son of Thomas Henry and Ann Eldridge Garnett - all of Buckingham Co. Va. Was born June 5, 1842. Photograph taken by Hunt of Farmville Va. February 13, 1911. Height 5 feet, 10 ½ inches, weight 175 lbs (not positive). Enlisted in war of Southern Confederacy August 1861 – served four years. Only severe wound received during conflict was a sabre cut on the back of his head, given by Capt. George N. Bliss in a charge at Waynesboro Va. in 1864. (Capt Bliss-once a foe-now a highly esteemed friend.) Mrs. Tho[s]. W. Garnett"

Bliss learned Garnett's name from Robert Baber in 1902. Bliss wrote Garnett immediately. In April 1903, Bliss visited Garnett at his home in Arcanum, Virginia. All four Garnett letters sent to Bliss are presented here.

Captain Bliss: Arcanum, VA., May 14th, 1902.[17]

Dear Sir: I am agreeably surprised to hear from you. I was at Waynesborough, Va., on the 28th of September, 1864. I was wounded by the same man who wounded Capt. William A. Moss and Robert L. Baber.[18] (His name I have forgotten.)

I received a sabre wound on my head. He or you gave me a right cut and passed on. I followed you to a left hand street. I shot at you and your horse fell. Just then Captain Moss called me to his assistance. I went and did not see you again until that night at the hospital. I was the first man you wounded in the fight.

I got your sabre from Thad Sheppard, and carried it the balance of the war, and buried it on my return home after the surrender.[19]

I never knew Hamilton. Captain Moss has been dead about twelve years. I know Baber. He lives about thirty miles from here. I heard yesterday that he is dead; don't know that it is true.[20]

I am glad we are both still living. Write again.

Yours truly,
Thomas W. Garnett.[21]

[Bliss's reply to Garnett's Letter[22]]

East Providence, R. I.   July 21, 1902[23]
Thomas W. Garnett Esq

Dear Sir

Your letter about the sabre is received. I should like to have the sabre together with its broken scabbard but if I cannot have it I should be glad to have it hang in your home for of right it belongs to you.

I have received the Congressional Medal of Honor for gallantry Sept 28, 1864 at Waynesborough Virginia which was the last time the sabre was in my hands.

I do not much care for the sabre for myself but my boys two of whom served their country in the U. S. Navy in the War with Spain would be delighted to have it.[24]

Hugh Hamilton the Color Bearer I wounded at Waynesborough has promised to visit me this summer and I expect him to be present at the reunion of the 1st R. I. Cav. Vols August 9, 1902. I should be delighted to have you come here at the same time and you would have no expenses while here.

Yours Truly George N. Bliss

George Bliss' July 21, 1902 letter to Thomas Garnett (found in Bliss's papers)

Arcanum, Va.
July 27- 1902.

Judge Bliss,

Dear Sir:−

I am glad to say I have been getting a daily mail from you for several days.

Your picture looks like you are just in your prime, you look like you might stand another campaign.

I had to make the second trip to see Mr. B. F. Shepherd before I saw him. He said I was welcome to the sabre, but if sent to you five dollars must be paid for it.

I put the sabre under the fence April 11th 1865 and Shephard found it in 1874 − nine years under the fence−. The leather on the hilt had rotted off and the scabbard nearly eaten up by rust. Shepherd put a wood hilt on in place of the leather, and used it to kill rats with and cut off a part of the guard to make it handy. There is but one thing about it I can recognize and that is the dent place in the blade, which was in it when I got it.

Thad Shepperd has been dead for many years. I don't know that Thad Sheppard was the man to whom you surrendered but I suppose he was as he had your sabre.

I have heard nothing more from Baber since I wrote you of his death.

I will express the sabre to you from Farmville Pr. Edward Co. July 28 and hope it may reach you by Aug 9

Many thanks for your cordial invitation to visit you, but it is out of my power to do so. We would be glad to see you.

I carried your letter to Shepherd yesterday you will see on the back of it what he says.[25]

Hoping to hear from you again I am
Yours very truly, Thos. W. Garnett.

**Thomas Garnett's photograph was published in Bliss article, *How I
Lost My Sabre in War and Found It in Peace*, opposite page 37.**

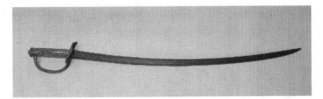

**Bliss later wrote, "The sabre came a few days later and was on
exhibition at the annual reunion of the First Rhode Island Cavalry
Aug. 9, 1902 . . ." It is in the possession of Bliss descendants.**

Arcanum, Virginia,   Jan. 11, 1911.
Judge George N. Bliss,
Providence, R. I.

Dear Sir:-

I'll write you my recollections of the battle of Waynesboro, Sept.
28-1864-only the part that concerns you. When you led the charge into
Waynesboro up to a barricade across the street your horse jumped the

obstruction. At the time you ordered your men to forward up, they fired several shots; wheeled and went back. I was the first man of four whom you wounded in that charge, (The other three men you know as you have found them, and made personal friends of them).

Capt. Wm. A. Moss and Robert Baber of Buckingham, and Hugh Hamilton of Warrenton, Va.[26] You gave me a right cut with your sabre and passed on through a part of the 4th Va. Cavalry under command of Capt. Strother of Madison Co., Va.[27] The blow knocked me over on my horses' neck, and came near giving me a mortal wound on the back of my head – the scar still shows plainly – I rallied, and ran my horse down the sidewalk till I got opposite you, then I ran in three feet of you with my pistol in hand aiming to shoot you when you made a rear cut with your sabre and I had to dodge to keep from being cut in the face. Then you made the circle to escape, and I shot at you with my pistol, but missed you and the ball struck your horse on the skull right between the ears. I was told that your horse lay on the ground about thirty minutes, and got up not seriously hurt, and was taken by one of the Black Horse Cavalrymen. I saw Thad Shepard and a Black Horse man going towards you, and Capt. Lee was on his horse near by; just then Capt. Moss asked me to stop his horse which I did. I asked him what was the matter, and he said "I am shot in my arm and side, and sabred."[28] I carried him to the Doctor at an old house near the mountain, and it was not long before you were brought up – as "bloody as a butcher" - Dr. Hickey (our surgeon,) told me the next morning to leave for home, which I did. When I returned after an absence of about thirty days, Thad Shepard told me he had the sword of the man who wounded me, and I ought to have it. I took it, and gave him mine. The history of which I have given you in former letters, and also talked with you personally in my own home when you visited me April 21, 1903. I was told that you gave the Masonic sign which Lee recognized and saved you from being killed by our men after you had fallen from your horse.

I assure you I am glad we are yet living, and can talk over the horrors of war as friends instead of as foes. I wish you great joy the remainder of your life. Accept many thanks for your kind invitation to visit you, and also for your generous offer, but it is not convenient for me to leave home, and I do not expect over [ever?] to get so far away. Would much rather you and Mrs. Bliss or any of your family would come to see us. I hope Mrs. Bliss is well also yourself and family.

> With kindest regards, I am
> Very truly yours,
> Thos. W. Garnett

Waynesboro   February 11/1923
Judge G. N. Bliss
East Providence R. I.

Dear Sir

I was glad to hear from you and to know you are well. I should have written to you long ago, but I am a good hand to put off. I am now living in Waynesboro. Just four blocks from where you gave me that love lick with your sabre.[29] I think of you every time I pass the place. The Capt. that charged up with you saved my life. Four of his men shot at me and he said, "don't shoot that man" and he was ordered to fall back. I followed you down to the corner shot at you and your horse fell, if that Capt. is living, I would like to shake hands with him. Can you put me on track of him?[30]

I got to this place 19 Dec/1919 I have been here a little past three years.

I like very well you would not know the country now it has improved wonderfully. Fine roads, no mud nor dust, ground lime stone and tar makes a first class road. The Rebels get together every year at Tinkling Spring about five miles from here, and have a big dinner & smoke and tell war tales that never was heard of before. I have been three times. I was in Charlottsvill[e] some time ago I met with a man that belonged to the black horse Co he told me Hugh Hamilton was too feeble to get about much. I expect you hear from him sometimes.

This leaves me with good wishes for you and yours

Tho⁵. W. Garnett

Thomas W. Garnett at age sixty-nine. The photograph was undoubtedly sent by Ann Garnett. On the back was written, "Photo taken February, 1911."

Letters of Hugh Hamilton,
Private Co. H, Fourth Virginia Cavalry

George Bliss fought Hugh Hamilton, Jr. (1841-1928) in Waynesboro. Hamilton was from Warrenton, the county seat of Fauquier County, Virginia, and its most important town. It was located about fifty miles west of Washington, D.C.

With its proximity to the Union capital, much of the fighting in Virginia occurred in that area. Hamilton's father, Hugh Hamilton Sr., was a physician. The 1850 U.S. Census showed five Hamilton children ranging in age from six to twenty, living in the "Ashby District" of the county; the younger Hugh Hamilton was nine years old.[31]

Hamilton was nineteen when the Civil War began but did not join the Confederate Army until nearly a year later, on March 15, 1862. He joined "H" Company of the 4th Virginia Cavalry as a private and stayed with the company for the remainder of the war. The company was in Thomas Mumford's Brigade, Fitzhugh Lee's Division, Army of Northern Virginia. In September 1863, Hamilton was detailed with the Provost Marshal for a period. A year later, he was color bearer for his regiment when he was wounded by Bliss at Waynesboro. The Black Horse Cavalry Company in which Hamilton served participated in the Battle of Williamsburg, the Seven Days' Battles, 2ⁿᵈ Manassas, Maryland campaigns, Fredericksburg, Kelly's Ford, Chancellorsville, Brandy Station, Upperville, Gettysburg, Bristoe, Mine Run, The Wilderness, Todd's Tavern, Spotsylvania, Haw's Shop, Bethesda Church, and the Shenandoah Valley campaign. They were at Appomattox at the close of the war.[32]

After the conflict, the twenty-four-year-old Hamilton became a farmer. In 1870, he married Isabella Roberts Vass; she was sister to three other members of the Black Horse Troop: Pvt. George Fitzhugh Vass (killed In action at Meadows Bridges, Va.), Private Townsend Daniel Vass (killed at Kennon's Farm, Charles City County, Va.), and Pvt. James A. Vass (who survived the war). The couple had three girls, Susan, Betty, and Janet. By 1880, Hamilton's farm covered more than one-hundred-fifty acres and was valued at $4100. While listed in census reports as a farmer as late as 1900, he also had a thirty-six-year career as Treasurer of Fauquier County, although he was not listed as such until the 1910 census. He was seventy-eight in 1920 and still employed at that job.[33]

Hamilton and Bliss met at least once after the war. Hamilton travelled to East Providence to visit Bliss in August 1902 and was present at a reunion of the First Rhode Island Cavalry that month. Proudly on display that year was Bliss's saber, with which he had once wounded Hamilton, and which had recently been returned to him.

Apparently, Bliss's wife Fannie visited the Hamilton household in Warrenton, Va. in the spring of 1903. She suffered with severe rheumatism, and Hamilton had recommended she visit and drink the waters of a nearby spring, said to help with a cure.

Hugh Hamilton (n.d., from Find-a-Grave.com)

Hamilton died in February 1928, at age eighty-six, six months before Bliss. His death certificate indicated that he was a widower, had worked as "County Treasurer for 36 years and then retired for 4 years." Cause of death was "bronchitis of old age" and "loss of wife."[34]

Starting in February 1897, Hamilton wrote Bliss at least six letters. His last was in September 1913. Two of Hamilton's letters are presented here.

Hugh Hamilton.

Late private. Company H.
4th Virginia
C.S.A. Cavalry.
known as
"The Black Horse Cavalry."

George N. Bliss.

Born at Tiverton. R. I.
July 22 1837.
Late Captain. Company C.
1st. R I. Cavalry Vols.

Picture taken August 1902.

In a charge at Waynesborough.Va. Sept. 28 1864. Hamilton while holding
the colors (State of Virginia) received a sabre cut on the head from the sabre
of Capt. Bliss.
Once foes, for many years past and for all the years to come friends.

Bliss with Hugh Hamilton. Photograph taken in August 1902.

Warrenton, V^a   Feb 4th 1897
Capt George N. Bliss

Dear Sir

Yours of the 1st inst to hand this A. M. I enclose you the affidavit which I hope you will find satisfactory. The Clerk Mr Bartenstein thought that the bare statement of the facts only should appear in an affidavit. I have often heard your great gallantry on the occasion spoken of by our officers & men. Remember me kindly to Mr Guild, Ray & Kenyon. With best wishes

I am yours truly
Hugh Hamilton

[Hamilton's] General Affidavit.

State of Virginia, County of Fauquier, ON THIS 5th DAY of July, A.D. 1882. Personally, appeared before me, a Clerk of Fauquier Circuit Court V^a, Hugh Hamilton, aged 40 years, a resident of Fauquier County, Virginia, whose Post Office address is Rappahannock Station Fauquier County Va. as follows

That on the 28th day of Sept 1864 in an engagement at Waynesboro, Augusta County Va between a detachment of United States Cavalry and a troop of Confederate Cavalry, Capt Geo N Bliss of Rhode Island who was an officer in said United States Cavalry force was wounded by a sabre stroke over the head and a wound in the side. That he the said Hamilton who was color bearer of the 4th Regiment of Va Cavalry was wounded at the same time by the said Capt Bliss, and that he saw the said Captain Bliss after the engagement who was taken prisoner by the Confederate force and taken to a field hospital that his wounds might be attended to.

[Signed] Hugh Hamilton, Late C. H. S
[Counter Signed] Jno R. Turner Clerk of Fauquier Circuit Court Va.

Warrenton, V^a   Sept 23, 1899

Dear Capt Bliss

I am very sorry to have to write that it will not be possible for me to get to see you this fall, I highly appreciate your kind invitation & I had looked forward to my visit to you with so much pleasure. I had quite an attack of something like rheumatism this summer which disabled me for three weeks or more & I have not been able yet to make up the lost time. Remember me kindly to Mr Ray & the other two friends that I have met (Mr. Guild & Kenyon) & express to them my regrets & with best wishes for yourself & family

I am most truly yours
Hugh Hamilton

Letters of William A. Moss
Former Captain in the Fourth Virginia Cavalry

Note: See biography of Moss in Chapter 2.

George Bliss wounded William A. Moss (1837-1887) in Waynesboro in the charge in which Bliss was captured. At the time, Moss was a lieutenant in Company K of the Fourth Virginia Cavalry.

Buckingham C. H, Va.,   Decr 12, 1876
Geo N. Bliss, Esqr

Dear Sir

Your favor of the 16th Nov. came, I understand duly to this office, but on account of my absence from home, was layed away & I only got it today, and hasten to reply.

Have remembered you with pleasure, and can assure you that nothing would give me more pleasure than to meet with you again, not as we met at Waynesboro – but as <u>friends</u> – beneath the old stars & stripes.

Come down here next summer and lets talk the matter over, I always loved a gallant and honorable foe – we met on the bloody field and crossed sabers – you got the best of it, and I have nothing more to say on that score. You proved yourself to be an honorable gentleman and I mark you down as a friend from this date.

I introduce my humble self as per card enclosed.

Yours very truly
W. A. Moss

I write in a great hurry. Write again and I will try and be more deliberate in my answer.

Moss's "card" or, more accurately, cart-de-visite. On the back Bliss wrote Moss's name and address, and "Wounded at Waynesboro, Va by George N. Bliss September 28, 1864. Received December 16, 1876." (Found in Bliss's papers)

**Portion of William A. Moss's December 12, 1876,
letter to Bliss (Found in Bliss's papers)**

Buckingham Court House, Va   Nov. 17th 1879.
Maj. G. N. Bliss
Providence, R.I.

My Dear Maj

Truly, procrastination is the thief of time. A hundred times I have determined to answer your very kind letter of a year or more ago, but as often neglected the duty and even now I have only time to say that all you wrote refer[r]ing to the engagement at Waynesboro is true, we were brought of[f] the field in the same ambulance, and you correctly detailed all that happened.[35] I made all arrangements to go to see you last winter, but sickness prevented. Hope the <u>new arrival</u> you were expecting is now one of the ornamental responsibilities [*sic*] of the house you so kindly said

I should be welcomed at, and that you can now spare the time to come to see me.[36] Assuring you that I will do all in my power to make your visit agreeable in old Va – Saw Maj Henry C. Lee a short time since, he always speaks in kind terms of the "gallant Road [*sic*] Islander.[37] Wm. T. Allen of the 1st National Bank of Richmond, often speaks too in kind terms of you.[38] I have a family of five a wife and five children, with no present prospect of any new arrivals, so when you come, there will be no obstacles in the way of our giving you as pleasant time as this remote locality can afford, will be glad to send to Farmville on the a. m & o Road if you will say when you will be here.[39] I am sorry I cannot write a longer letter, as I would like to give you my recollections of the Waynesboro fight, but if you will answer this I will be more prompt in my answer

Very truly your friend
Wm. A. Moss

Have sent you some papers today, and hope they may go safe to hand[40]

Buckingham C. H.,   May 17, 1880
Maj. Geo. N. Bliss
Charlotte[e]sville Va[41]

My Dear Friend

Your card was received on Saturday, but owing to our imperfect mail facilities, I could not answer 'till today. The sweet corn had already been received and planted. You have my hearty thanks for it.

Am truly glad you and Mrs Bliss are spending your time so pleasantly – which brings to my mind again to my great sorrow at not being able to entertain you and her this summer at my home, but it is well you did not come, my wife is very seldom out of bed and one of my children, a little girl about 5 years old, is quite ill, and I have been in bed myself almost the whole time since I left Richmond and am still on the sick list.[42] Write me when you will be at home, I have a fine pair of Game Chickens to send you and also a small package of old "apple whiskey," which I will not send 'till you arrive at home. The game chickens, a compliment to your gallantry at

Waynesboro, and the Brandy to remind you of the curious way in which we became acquainted.[43]

Hoping to hear from you again soon, and that your visit may continue agreeable I am

Very truly your friend
W. A. Moss

Buckingham C. H.,   Nov 4th 1881

Dear Captain

Your kind letter of the 1st inst is received and I was delighted to hear from you and to learn that you had extracted yourself from the financial difficulties you were in. I assure you that while I apparently seemed to neglect you, yet you had my deepest sympathies in you[r] troubles, and I knew how to feel for you, because I was in the same boat with you, but the crushing weight upon me caused me to lose sight of all else in my effort to extricate myself from the tangled web I had fallen into. On tobacco speculations I lost $7000. As security on the bond of the Post Master at Richmond I had to pay $1300. By my deputies in office I have been compelled to make good about $1700. By the Piedmont and Arlington Life Co I lost $300. Besides these there were other smaller losses which have taken everything I had but my house and lot in the town here. My property is not yet sold, and there is a rail road projected to this place, and as some of my lands are mineral lands, I have a hope yet that they may sell for enough to extricate me, and leave something to put us on foot again. $7000 is about the amount of my indebtedness, but my real estate ought in a prosperous community double that amount.

The death of your little baby boy must have been a heavy blow upon Mrs Bliss and yourself.[44] Truly hope your family are not seriously sick, and that they are now entirely recovered. We have been generally blessed with good health, and have not yet had a death in our family. Our youngest child is sixteen month[s] old, and all now in good health, and my wife being of a cheerful temperament, has stood my failure remarkably well, which has been a great comfort to me. Am still Treasurer of the County, the pay of which gives us a tolerable good living.

Our state election comes off on Tuesday next after that is over will write you a short account of the Waynesboro fight.

Remember me kindly to Mrs Bliss, say to her that we will be glad to see her in our home now at any time, and if you will bring her on, we will do all in our power to make you both hap[p]y. I send no better words from my wife – because I have not seen her since I received your letter but I know she joins me in the invitation. Promising to behave better in the future, and hoping to have another letter soon, I am

Very Truly
Your friend
Wm. A. Moss

Buckingham C. H., May 9th 1882
Capt Geo N. Bliss
Providence R.I.

My Dear Captain

I have just gotten home from a business trip to Petersburg, and found your letter. A thousand thanks for all your kindness and good wishes. My children had already credited you with "The Youths Companion" they value it very much, and ask to be remembered to you.[45] My wife will plant the flower seeds, and requests me to say she will take special care of their cultivation. I am really ashamed to allude to my promised Waynesboro letter, but I have been so incessantly occupied with official duties, that I have really not had time. In order to reduce expenses I have discharged my clerk, and am now and have been for twelve months doing all of the clerical labor of this office, but you will have the Reminissences [*sic*] of Wayn[es] boro by the middle of next week. Give my kindest remembrances to your wife, and wishing you and yours a prosperous future I am

Very Truly Your friend
W. A. Moss

Buckingham C. H.,   June 21, 1884

My Dear Capt Bliss

Find enclosed a second note about the Waynesboro fight. I am sorry I have not done my duty in this matter sooner, but my time was [one illegible word] and I am not so much in fault as you may think. I have been in great financial trouble, which has taxed me almost beyond the power of an honorable gentleman to endure and I have in many instances ignored those when I could not hope to give such recognition as they deserved.

> Very Truly Your friend
> W. A. Moss

[Moss's Enclosure]

Buckingham C. H. Va.,   June 21st, 1884
Capt Geo N. Bliss
2 College St
Providence R. I.

My Dear Captain

I regret exceedingly that so much time has elapsed, and that I should have delayed you so much in your publication of the Waynesborough[46] fight, but my time has not been my own, and I am a poor hand in the descriptive line, <u>albeit</u> it is about the late war, in which you and I took so active a part. I think it was in the afternoon of the 28th day of Sept 1864, when we first met; it has been so long my memory may fail me, (and I have not visited the ground since the war) but I am sure I state the prominent facts. I made a charge with my squadron and met you with a regiment near a house on the right of the street near the top of a hill in Waynesborough.[47] Your regiment came in good order until within one hundred yards of my command, when it deserted you with the exception of two men, who followed you. Your men had placed a barricade across the street which you and one of your men leaped and at that point I engaged you with the sabre, and was at once put on the defensive by your superior swordsmanship, which kept me active to prevent a thrust from you. At this juncture I received a pistol wound from the man who followed on your right, which so disabled me that I had to abandon the fight; my horse reared and plunged to the rear, my bridle hand being disabled by the wound referred to above, when you spurred up and struck me with your sabre on the back of the head. I tried to draw my pistol, but having my sabre knot over my wrist and being disabled in the bridle hand I could not do so, and you passed me, striking two of my men just in front of me. Capt. H. C. Lee has told me that he met you afterwards, and that you had requested him to give you his recollections of the affair.[48] At that point my memory ceases until a later hour, about dark, when I became conscious and was laying in an ambulance, and someone said there was a "Yankee officer," badly wounded, and would I let him ride in the ambulance. I said, "Certainly, bring him in," you took the seat with the driver, but becoming faint, said you must lie down. The surgeon had given me some apple brandy, and I gave you some, which revived you, and we had a conversation which satisfied me that you were the officer who wounded me. My brother, Beverly T. Moss, now of Surry County, Va., who in that day's fight had gotten his leg shattered, but who with unusual fortitude, had forgotten himself in his effort to take care of me (I was shot thru the left breast), said he would go and give you some breakfast if his leg was well enough, and did hobble away, and came back and said you could not eat, and said if he could he would search the man up who had stolen your boots, but he was not able to walk.

I have stated little incidents connected with the Waynesboro fight, and will thank you to put me right where I may be [at] fault as to dates.

Very truly your fd
W. A. Moss, Late Capt Co. K. Fourth Va Cavalry

Buckingham C. H., Sept 9th 1887

My Dear Capt Bliss

Your letter of the 8th inst is received. I shall be greatly obliged by the rect [receipt] of a copy of your Paper. I was traveling between Harrisonburg and Stanton Va when I lost the copy you sent me.[49] Judge Jno Paul of the U. S. Dist Court[50] who is a warm personal friend came on this train and I laid the paper down to talk with him and could never find it again.

I want you to meet me in Richmond on the 27th of October. I will have you inviteded [*sic*] and will bring you prominently before the public at this time. The included will indicate the reason.[51] By todays mail I have written to have you invited.

I am greatly disturbed by Mrs Bliss ill health it will be certainly agreeable if you will bring her on some days before the 27th of October. Ours is a splendid climate and her health I am sure will be benefited by a trip in this mountain country. Your kindly expressed letters to me have captivated my wife, and she feels anxious to see you and Mrs Bliss

Very truly your friend, W. A. Moss[52]

RICHMOND, VA., Aug. 30th, 1887.

To the Survivors of the Fourth Regt. Va. Cavalry:

At a meeting of the Hanover Troop Association, held at Ashland Park, August 23d, 1887, the following resolutions were adopted :

Regarding the occasion of the laying of the Lee Monument corner-stone as a grand event in the history of our State, and believing that it is the sense, pleasure, and pride, as well as the duty of the survivors of Company G, Fourth Virginia Cavalry, to contribute to the success of the forthcoming demonstration ; therefore,

Be it Resolved, That the members of Co. G, Fourth Virginia Cavalry, will participate in the aforesaid laying of the corner-stone of the Lee Monument, and that all members present will exert themselves to encourage and ensure a full turn-out of the association worthy of the occasion.

2. *Resolved,* That the president appoint a committee to confer with like organizations of the First, Second, Third and Fourth regiments of cavalry, which composed Wickham's Brigade, and request them to join with us on that occasion.

3. *Resolved,* That the press of the State be requested to publish these resolutions.

The undersigned were appointed to communicate with you and enlist your co-operation in the object specified.

The corner-stone of the Monument to be erected to the memory of General Robert E. Lee will be laid with appropriate ceremonies in this city on October 27th, 1887.

It is the earnest desire of General Fitzhugh Lee and General Wickham that you be present on that occasion to do honor to the memory of our illustrious chieftain.

It is hoped there will be a fair delegation of the old Fourth present, who will be accorded a prominent position in the parade. To this end we trust that you will be with us, and induce as many of your old comrades to join us as possible. The Regiment will be mounted and in citizen's dress, with the old badge, a red diamond, displayed on the hat.

In view of the great demand for horses in this city on the occasion, you are requested to provide your own mounts. Stable-room will be furnished free of charge.

It is important that we be advised as early as practicable in advance as to the probable number who will be present. Please address communications to L. B. Vaughan, care Vaughan & Sarvey, Crenshaw Warehouse, Richmond, Va., to whom, also, members will report on arrival for assignment to stables.

C. A. TAYLOR,
L. B. VAUGHAN,
T. W. SYDNOR,
A. R. ELLERSON,
E. A. CATLIN,
Committee.

Invitation sent by William Moss to Bliss, to join in the celebration for the laying of a cornerstone for the Robert E. Lee monument in Richmond, which took place October 27, 1887. (Found in Bliss's papers)

[Patti Moss to Bliss]

Buckingham C. H.   May 22 [1888]

Capt Bliss

Your letter received. I am so glad that you did not send the money. After long and hard work we got the Securities to come to gather [*sic*] and the Board made a compromise with us. They let me off with 15.00 $ which was so much bet[t]er than I expected at the time I wrote you. Then I was under the impression that I would be striped of home and all. But the good Lord did not suffer that to be. I still have my home, and I will do all I can to raise my children up to be smart men and women. Please accept many thanks for your kind interest in us.

Very respectful[l]y
Pattie Moss

I am sorry to know that you are a Polititon [politician] for that will ruin any man.[53] [I]t may be different in your State, but a Polititon in Va. had just as well go to the Poor House at once.

Henry Carter Lee
Former Captain in the Fourth Virginia Cavalry

Captain Henry C. Lee (1842-1889) saved George N. Bliss from near certain death on September 28, 1864, in Waynesboro, Virginia. Wounded, unhorsed and surrounded, Bliss had surrendered when he realized he was about to be shot. In desperation, he called out for protection as a Freemason. Lee, also a Mason, by chance passing the scene, heard Bliss's plea and took charge of the situation, thus sparing Bliss' life.

Lee was from a distinguished Virginia family. His grandfather, "Light Horse Harry Lee," was a hero of the Revolutionary War, receiving the thanks of congress. The Lee family was living in Washington, D.C. in 1860, shortly before the Civil War. Henry Lee's father, Sidney Smith Lee, was a commander in the U.S. Navy. Henry Lee's twenty-four years old brother, Fitzhugh, was a promising cavalry officer, and Lee's uncle, Robert E. Lee, was a highly regarded graduate of West Point.[54]

Henry Lee was a student at the University of Virginia when war broke out. In June 1861, at age nineteen, he left the school and enlisted with the Richmond Howitzers, an artillery company. He was promoted to 1st lieutenant in August 1862, and to captain soon after, and was subsequently placed on General Williams C. Wickham's staff. At the time of his encounter with Bliss in Waynesboro, Lee was Adjutant and Inspector-General of Wickham's Cavalry Brigade in his brother Fitzhugh Lee's cavalry division. This brigade was composed of the first, second, third and fourth regiments of Virginia Cavalry. It was Company H of the Fourth Virginia Cavalry Regiment, the famed "Black Horse Cavalry," that Bliss charged into that day in Waynesboro. Henry Lee served for the remainder of the war, retreating from Richmond in April 1965.[55]

Bliss and Lee corresponded for eleven years prior to Lee's death in 1889. In his postwar letters, Lee described for Bliss the Confederate action that day in Waynesboro, his own role, and his memory of Bliss's charge. The two met at least once, at Richmond, in 1880.

Volumes have been written about Henry Lee's uncle, Robert E. Lee, General-in-chief of Confederate forces. Much has also been written about Henry Lee's older brother, Fitzhugh, a cavalry general in the war, and later governor of Virginia. Yet, despite serving bravely and honorably throughout the conflict, almost nothing is known of Lee's four years of wartime activities. Most of what is known is revealed in these letters to Bliss.

As with many ex-Confederate soldiers, times may have been difficult for Henry Lee after the war. Most of the Civil War was fought in the South, and destruction of both infrastructure and personal property had been extensive. Soon after the surrender at Appomattox Court House, Henry Lee wrote, "[T]oday I became aware that what I have on is all that is left of my 'worldly goods.'"[56]

In September 1868, Henry Lee married twenty-year-old Sallie Johnston (1848-1925). Sallie Lee came from a wealthy and politically powerful family in Abingdon, Virginia. Her father, John W. Johnston, was a judge and later a U.S. senator. By 1870 Lee, his wife Sallie, and their infant son John were living with Lee's brother Fitzhugh, in Aquia, Virginia. Both brothers were farmers. Brothers Daniel Murray Lee, John M. Lee, and Robert C. Lee also resided there; all fought for the Confederacy during the war.[57]

Sallie and Henry Lee had a total of four children, three boys followed by a daughter. Sometime in the 1870s, Lee briefly formed an insurance agency with Confederate General Dabney H. Maury. By 1880, Sallie and the children were living with her parents in Abingdon while Lee was usually in Richmond, living at 114 Grace St. West. He was employed in Richmond as a coal agent for the Chesapeake and Ohio Railroad.[58] In his letters to Bliss, Lee explained that he travelled back and forth to Richmond from Abingdon. Lee held the post of coal agent for the C&O until his death from a stroke in 1889. He was forty-seven.[59]

Ten letters from Lee to Bliss have been found and are transcribed here.[60]

Richmond Va.   January 25, 1879[61]
Capt. Geo. N. Bliss
Providence R.I.

Dear Sir-

In looking over some papers not long since I came across your letter of the 16th of Nov 1876, and I am sorry it should have been so long unanswered, but I put it away with my papers, and could not remember your address- I enclose you a photograph copied from one taken in the War. I was at that time a captain, and the Adjutant General of a Cavalry Brigade – I am very much obliged to you for your kind expressions – I hope we may be able to meet some day, in the mean time I shall be very glad to receive your Photograph taken when you were in the army if you have one of that kind, if not – one in citizens dress will be very acceptable – I see Capt Moss every now & then – He always mentions you most kindly – I shall be very glad to see you when you come to Richmond, or at my home near Abingdon. Please let me hear from you, and with kind regards,

Very Truly Yrs Henry C. Lee

Henry C. Lee in uniform during the war. Lee sent this photograph in his January 25, 1879 letter to Bliss (found in Bliss's papers).

Henry C. Lee, presumably after the war (from Find-a-Grave.com)

CHESAPEAKE AND OHIO RAILWAY,
Abingdon,[62] Va.   April 12, 1879
Capt. Geo. N. Bliss
Providence - R.I.

My dear Sir-

Your letter of the 8th ult; was sent to me from Richmond to this place, where I have been for nearly three months with a broken leg – I came out here to see my family, and as I was going into town to take the train for Richmond, my horse fell into a hole – it was just before day – catching my leg against the frozen edges of the hole, and literally mashing both bones for three inches just above the ankle, breaking a small bone in the foot, and cracking the front bone a little below the knee – I am over it now enough to hobble about my room, with a plaster bandage on, but I fear I'll need my crutches for some time yet – the leg will be about an inch short – I think I can return to my duties this month.

But for this accident I should have thanked you sooner for your letter and the pamphlets, and photographs – I read the sketch with much interest – The photographs I did not recognize, for my recollection of how you looked "upon that momentous occasion" as you expressed it, the only time I ever saw you, and only then for a very brief moment, is very indistinct – I was on my way up that very road or street you expected to retreat by, when your horse was shot, to see after some of our men – I saw you as you passed down by our men, I was on the opposite side, of our men, to you, I knew you would be either killed or captured, and did not catch anything then but a passing glance, and very little more when I came upon you at the forks of the road.

I was in a hurry then, as we did not know how soon your men might come on those of ours in the town, drive them back, and cut off those that had gone up the road to the right – I was on my way to bring them back for our men were not well up. Every now and then I meet some of our Cavalry in Richmond, and we have been talking of putting our heads together and writing out what we can. To me the war was a kind of passing thing – I find it very hard to separate the different events – We were so much on the go – day ran into night and night into day.

When I see some who were at Waynesboro', I'll write you an account of what was done -My papers were captured all of them, I was the Adjutant General of the brigade and it is only by talking with participants I can send you what you want which I will do as soon as I can. The Brigade was then Munford's (formerly) Wickham[']s, (our Brigades, Divisions & corps were called after their Generals) and consisted then of the 1st 2nd 3rd & 4th Va. Cavalry, and a battery of Stuart's Horse Artillery (Johnsons battery, I think Capt Johnson was <u>then</u> the captain). I don't think our battery was alone at Waynesboro'-

I should be very glad to avail myself of your kind invitation but my time is not my own now – Yes, I am married and like yourself have four children, three boys and one girl – I would be very glad to hear from you when you can find the time to write.

> *Very Truly Yrs*
> *Henry. C. Lee.*
> Direct to C. & O. Railway office, Richmond Va.

Alexandria, Va.   May 19th 1879
Capt: Geo. N. Bliss
Providence R. I.

Dear Sir-

Yours of the 15th was sent to me from the office (Richmond) yesterday. I understand the book you kindly sent me is there. Much obliged to you. I came down here with my wife some two weeks ago, and hope to get back to Richmond this week. My leg is not yet well enough for me to go on duty, but I walk a little on it with my crutches. Thank you for your sympathy. As soon as I can after I get to R. [Richmond] I will get some of our old cavalry men & send you what I can. I will deliver Moss your message when he comes down. I'll try & write soon.

> Very Truly Yrs
> Henry C. Lee

Richmond, Va.,   May 21st, 1880[63]
Capt. G. N. Bliss-
Univ of Va -[64]

My dear Sir -

Just after I wrote you this morning your letter came, and I enclose you
a pass for yourself, leave the other for your wife to come on. Gen Wickham
very kindly asked for a pass for you over the Richmond & Petersburg
road, which will be here on your arrival. The General will not be here on
Monday, but Tuesday or Wednesday he will be in his office, and would be
very glad to see you. I am going as I wrote you this a.m., up the Trevbad
[?] road, but will be back Monday.

                                                    Truly yrs
                                                    Henry. C. Lee.

Richmond, Va.,   May 29st, 1880
Capt Geo. N. Bliss

Providence, R. I.

My dear Sir, I regret exceedingly I did not see Mrs Bliss and yourself
before your departure. But that night, about the time you had gone to the
train, I laid down and asked the waiter to wake me, which he failed to do.
As I had been up for so many nights I slept soundly, and when I did awake
it was so late I went to bed, and not having been put upon the call list I was
not called in time to see you off. Please tell Mrs Bliss I am extremely sorry
I did not see her again. I wish you had knocked at my door a little loud. As
I am outside the Hotel, you might imagine I get accustomed to noises, and
so not for much of the floor servants, who look out for my room, as well
as the floor above. I am very sorry, but when I lie down in the evening, I
generally fall asleep. I hope Mrs Bliss has improved from her trip. We had
a fine rain this evening, which has cooled the air. Please give my kindest

regards to her. I hope you found your Family well, and will soon come down again to see us. I'll try and see more of you next time.

Very Truly Yrs,
Henry C. Lee

114 West Grace Street   July 20th, 1884
Richmond, Va.
Captain George N. Bliss
Providence
R.I.:

My Dear Captain

I found your letter of the 18th inst. here when I came up from the office last night, and in reply will say that it is so long since the event occurred that I can't give you many details. The war to me now is like a panorama. With us in the Cavalry, marching night and day as we were constantly doing, the events ran into each other, and it is hard to get hold of dates; but as you have kindly furnished me with this one, I shall begin, only hoping that Mrs. Bliss and the little Blisses may think I did right. I was at that time, the 28th of September, 1864, the day of the fight at Waynesborough, Va, the Adjutant and Inspector General of Wickham's Cavalry Brigade, Fitzhugh (Fitz) Lee's Cavalry Division, Stuart's Cavalry Corps, Army of Northern Virginia. Our brigade was then composed of the 1st, 2nd, 3rd and 4th Regiments of Virginia Cavalry, and we generally had a battery of Stuart's Horse Artillery with us, at that time I think we had Johnston's Battery of the S. H. A. [Stuart Horse Artillery]. As you have probably learned, our Corps, Divisions, Brigades and Batteries were called after their commanders. You tell me you have heard from some others of our command, and among them, Gen Munford, then the Colonel of the 2nd Regiment, so I shall merely begin at the fight. As you are probably aware, we were sent to prevent the destruction of the R. R. bridge over the river, near Waynesborough, where the Virginia Central (now Chesapeake & Ohio) Railroad, crossed. We were informed that you were destroying that bridge. From our marching on the blind road on the side of the Blue Ridge

Mountain we were not very well closed up when we struck the turnpike near Waynesborough, and it was from this fact that I had the opportunity of serving you. When we struck the turnpike we were between your forces and your pickets, which we captured, and you did not know of our coming.

As we neared the town, our advanced guard reported a regiment of cavalry watering at the stream just east of town. Orders were sent to our Regiments to close up as rapidly as possible, but being strung out so badly it was hard to do. Our order of marching was the order of Regiments: thus, on one day the 1st Regiment would be in front, next the 2nd, next the 3rd, &c., and our Horse Artillery in rear, so you see if the 1st was in front the 4th would be in the rear, and if the 4th was in front, the 3rd would be in the rear, the order marching, 4th, 1st, 2nd & 3rd & Battery. On this day the 1st was in front, and was dismounted and sent down the Railroad. The 2nd and 3rd Regiments were also dismounted when they came up, and sent down the dirt road. The 4th was sent forward Mounted, and Johnston's Battery was placed on a knoll between the road and the railroad, from which point they did, as they generally did, some pretty good work. The first squadron of the 4th, Capt Hill's, I think, was ordered to Charge, which they did gallantly, and some prisoners were taken by them, for I had the pleasure, having gone ahead with orders, of taking two of your men in this charge, for I needed a horse, (but neither of them was worth much.) This squadron was met with a volley from the enemy, and were somewhat scattered, then the next squadron, Capt Moss', was sent forward, and they charged up into the town, the remainder of the 4th supported it. Just as Capt Moss got into town, owing to the 3rd not being up, and the 2nd not well in position, I was sent forward by Col Munford, who was then commanding our Brigade, to halt the squadrons of the 4th, and as I was galloping up one side (the right) of these squadrons - we were in columns of fours- I saw you galloping down on the other side. Knowing you would be looked after, particularly as you were alone, I kept on and halted the head of the troops, and then I saw your men going in the opposite direction, these are the ones you told me when I first saw you after the war, you expected to lead in the charge against us, and thought were following you, I think you called them the "Butterflies."[65] My orders were also to bring our troops back that had been sent up on the road to the right, the 1st Regiment, for we were nearly into Sheridan's camp, and were fearful that your Troops might sweep down this street & cut this party off, and it was as I was returning, and had gotten to this corner that I saw your horse fall, and three or four of our men with you. As I passed you, you called out for relief as a mason, and making a sign, which I recognized, I ordered our men to let you alone, take you to the rear, and see that you were attended to, as you seemed to be wounded. I had to go on to bring our troops back and, although you said something to me, I had no time to stop. One of our men was about to kill you when I got to you, and informed me that you had badly wounded Capt Moss, and had struck somebody else, I have forgotten now who, and though it was wrong for me to interfere. When I came back of course you were gone, and the horse too, I think, and I never saw you again until you came down to see me here in 1880. I heard that you and Capt Moss were carried back in the same ambulance, and Moss, having some "Apple Jack," - our national drink, - you took a drink together. The next I heard of you, you had been sent to Richmond. I did not have an opportunity of seeing you when you were sent to the rear. I was tired, besides I had been struck on the inside of the right leg by a carbine ball and had my horse wounded at the same time, when your men fired from the creek, and my leg was sore. My horse was a fine grey one, captured from your people by one of [Major John S.] Mosby's men, and I got him from him. After he was struck, he bled pretty freely, the ball struck him in the right front shoulder just above his U.S. mark. As I rode back on the knoll where the artillery was, Lieut Willie Hoxton, of the S.H.A., seeing the pants torn from my leg where I had been struck, thought the horse's blood was mine. I shall never forget the look on his young and handsome face when he asked me if I had been that badly hurt, and the relief he seemed to feel when I showed him where the horse was struck.[66] This horse was afterwards shot in one of the skirmishes on the Retreat from Richmond, when I was riding him. I then sent him back to the wagon train. There he was Captured by your Cavalry in some dash on the train. I was sorry to lose "Pip," which had been with me in some right tight places.[67] I would have liked to have had him in peace, instead of the miserable glass-eyed little yankee poney [*sic*] on which I was paroled. Neither of the horses I got at Waynesborough were worth much. I turned one over with the prisoners, and had one kept for me, a large iron-grey, which I afterwards traded off with one of our Division Head Quarters Couriers, and got a right good horse in return.

I enclose you a memorandum by Major W. F. Graves, (who commanded the 2nd Regiment at that time), written last winter, when he was here as a member of the Legislature. Maybe this may be of service to you. I made this a "heap" longer than I intended when I sat down. You can cull out from it what you want. With kind regards to Mrs. Bliss and yourself, from Mrs. Lee & myself, I am

Very Truly Yours,
Henry C. Lee.[68] (Late Capt: & a. a. & I. g. - P. A. C. S)[69]

[Major W. F. Graves' Memorandum].

At the battle of Waynesboro, in September 28, 1864, the Second Regiment of Virginia Cavalry was dismounted and took position on a ridge just to the left of the turnpike leading from Charlottesville to Waynesboro, said ridge overlooking said town. When the charge was made by the Confederate forces, the Second Regiment pushed forward, supported by the Fourth Regiment, Virginia Cavalry, which was mounted, driving the enemy back. When the Federal forces fell back, there was a Federal quartermaster, by the name of Bliss, who volunteered to lead a charge to counteract the advance of the Confederate cavalry. The charge was made by the said officer solitary and alone, without his companions following and supporting him, cutting right and left with his sabre, until he reached a point, as well as I can remember, near the centre of the town, when his horse was shot down. Several Confederate soldiers had their guns and pistols raised to fire upon said officer, when he gave the masonic sign of distress, which was recognized by Captain Henry C. Lee, as he was a free mason, thus saving the life of as brave a soldier as ever drew a sabre in the Federal cavalry. I was an eye witness to the foregoing, and was not more than fifteen or twenty paces from him when his horse was shot down.

Richmond, Va.,   Sept 28th, 1884[70]
Capt Geo. N. Bliss-
Providence, R. I.

Dear Capt -

The book was received. I would rather you had taken out of my letter
such facts as were pertinent, and published them. That's what I thought
you would do, from our conversations. I could have written a much shorter
letter.[71] Major Graves lives in the County of Bradford, and I do not know
his P.O., he will be down here soon, as the legislature will meet again
in October and I will give him the copy, if you will send it to me. He
expressed a desire to have a copy, and so did some others, whom I had told
at various times, that you were going to publish an account of your capture
at Waynesboro', and they had a curiosity to see what you had to say. So I
am sorry you had so few copies printed.[72] You give a pretty bad account of
your treatment.[73] It is dry and warm here, but <u>nothing</u> like as hot as when
Capt. Addiman was here.[74]

Goodbye - with kind regards to Mrs Bliss.

Very Truly Yrs,
Henry. C. Lee.

Richmond,   January 15th 1885[75]
Capt Geo. N. Bliss -
Providence - R. I.

Dear Captain

Yours recd, and am much obliged to you. I thought I answered all the
letters I got from you, but very often I put off writing a long time, that
was because nights and Sundays were the only time I had for writing, and
generally at nights I felt tired, and Sundays somehow were bad days for
writing. I will send you the papers now and then, especially since Moss
sends you the [Richmond] Whig, you <u>ought</u> to see the "other side"- That
is a scurrilous sheet, is owned by the Va. outcast – Mahane[76] – and is

seldom seen, or read, by what John S. Wise called, on the stump, "the best people" – Bill Asp, the Georgia humorist, uttered a truism when he said that he "noticed when a Virginian fell, he fell far & heavy" – And if you lived among us you would see it – Moss has repeatedly told me that he had no more use for Mahane, than we had, so I suppose being a County Officer he takes the paper on account of the official advertisements, but I am surprised he should send it to any one – There is a marked difference between a Republican, and a Mahonsite, although Mahane sets his gang up now for <u>the</u> Republican Party. The Republicans had principles, these others had none. Anything for an office, and an office for plunder. "We are for [Chester A.] Arthur because Arthur is for us" they said. The loaves and fishes are all they know, and they felt so confident that the Republican nominee would be elected, that that very army of office holders could not be overcome, they called themselves "Republicans"– And thank God they have been beaten, for they were mostly composed of ignorant negroes and disreputable whites. We have always felt that if we could govern our State we did not care so much about the Presidents, but these Presidents, from Grant to Arthur, would never recognize any but the worst element in the South, so of course we could not feel as if [we] were considered fully back in the Union, but now since the election of [Grover] Cleaveland [*sic*] there is a feeling of releif [*sic*] among us, and we feel that we will once more be treated as equals in one Common Country. We think from all we can gather of Mr. Cleveland, that he will make a good President. He has a heap to reform, and we think he is capable of doing it. Already business is beginning to improve in the South. The factories that have been closed, are starting up again almost every day, and new enterprises are being started. Altogether we are feeling very well, Captain, and I think even your R. I. Journal, will acknowledge a vast improvement in the condition of affairs next New Year. A Northerner has only to live in the South to get rid of a great many erroneous ideas regarding us. It is a well known fact, that so nearly <u>all</u> that I might say <u>all</u>, who settle among us very soon vote the Democratic ticket in all State elections, if they should vote the Republican ticket in National Affairs. And another thing you will notice that a great many negros will <u>hereafter</u> vote with us, they will find out they have been lied to all the way through, started by the carpet baggers and kept up by the Mahane Scalawags. Some have found this out and voted with us, pretty largely lately. They have been doing the same for some time in the other Southern States, but Mahaneism delayed it here. They will divide now–

The Banks are loaning money on short time, and soon all will be, not well again but, better. I knew you were crippled, but I thought you all not feeling the war as we did, did not feel the hard times we were having in the South and that your monied men had some to invest, or that you <u>had monied</u> men.[77] I hope you will not get put out with the length of this letter, I had no idea of making it so long, but your mentioning the Whig started me on politics, for I hate to hear of any man's seeing the Whig unless he knows what a concern it represents. I will always be glad to hear from you whenever you choose to write. With kind regards to Mrs Bliss & yourself–

Yos very truly
Henry C. Lee

114 West Grace St.

114 West Grace St.
Richmond, Va.   Febru. 8th 1'85
Capt. Geo. N. Bliss
Providence R. I.

My dear Captain–

Your letter duly recd. I am glad you enjoyed the papers. That about sending negroes to fill political places in the north was of course meant as facetious. Out of many reasons, if such a thing <u>could</u> be <u>done</u>, two will suffice for not doing such a thing. First we believe this to be a white man's Country, and however long we have had to bear such inflictions, we are not revengeful, and would not put a negro over a white person; and secondly there are white democrats in the North, who have been steadfast to their faith in all the dark hours, with no hope or desire for reward, these are the men who will fill the offices. You seemed to have treated the matter seriously, and say thus "nothing would please the Republicans better than to appoint negroes to U.S. offices in the North, as it would tear the Democracy then to tatters." We know thus when the thing is brought home to you, you can't any more stomach the negro than we who have had it to do. The negro is not by any means a bad person, on the conntrary [*sic*] he is just the opposite when his head is not kept filled with all kind of stuff by unscrupulous & designing white men. They are still ignorant and can't understand what freedom means. They have an idea that freedom means they can do anything. They can't realize the fact that the laws are for the protection of all, they look upon them as their enemies. Of course, I do not intend this as a sweeping firet [?], but for a general one. On the contrary I have seen a good many intelligent negroes, and have seen them in offices in the South, as the enclosed from the Boston Herald, you sent me, says, and have been told by parties who helped to place them there, that they were far preferable to mean white men (Mahanites).[78] You say party lines are not so "harsh" with you as with us. That is easily explained, you have not such an ignorant and disrespectable lot to deal with. You know who the ignorant are, and the disreputable part is the white who toady up to them for office. Your parties have principles to contend with. Here it is more to keep these creatures out of office. Good government is what we contend for, and down here "the people" are not those meant in vox populi, vox dei [*the voice of the people is the voice of God*] every time. But enough of this, I see you are beginning to understand us better.

I do not know whether you take the Southern Historical Magazine now, so I send you the last numbers – three in one – Gen Munford has an account of the Waynesboro fight, and you will see on page 458 a complimentary notice of yourself.[79] Let me know if you receive the book. I have some other letters to write so must close.

We have had very nice pleasant weather here lately, different from what the papers report they are having out West. Excuse this pen. Hoping you and yours are well, I am

Very Truly yrs
Henry C. Lee

I never was a democrat, none of my people were or very, <u>very</u> few, we were Whigs. And there are very many in the South, for I have been through it a heap, just like us. We could <u>not</u> be Republicans as they are here-

I have seen also negro policemen (Democrats) in Jacksonville, Florida.

#519 North 5th St Feb 15th /88
Richmond, Va

Dear Capt –

I have not heard from you for a long time, and is [it] strikes me you owe me a letter, but I write now to ask if you are, like some others in the North, interested in the removal of Libby Prison to Chicago, it seems it has stirred up some opposition to its removal by some of its former inmates, and if you would like I will send you the papers with the letters from the Union Officers.[80] Did you get a paper telling you of our friend Capt Moss' death? - Moss was a good man and a good friend – I hope you & yours have kept well – All well here except myself – Am sick as a bore [?] – With kind regards to Mrs Bliss & your family –

> Very Truly Yrs
> Henry C. Lee-[81]
> Capt g. n. Bliss
> Providence – R. I.

Letter from Captain Alexander D. Payne,
Fourth Virginia Cavalry

[Note: See Chapter 1 for a biography of A.D. Payne]

A. D. Payne,
Attorney at Law,
Bank Building,
Warrenton, Va.   Jan 31st 1882

Capt Geo. N. Bliss
My dear Sir

At last and after a long delay I send you a sketch of the Waynesboro' affair with some introductory matter. I have no good excuse to offer for my tardiness except laziness if that is an excuse and a reluctance I have had ever since the termination of the war to talk or write about it. I am afraid you will be much disappointed both in the matter of the sketch and the manner of telling my story – the truth is that the 17 years that have elapsed since the war have been busy ones to me, and I have been so engrossed with the work they furnished to the exclusion of thoughts even of the past, that much of the vividness of the events of the war has gone from my recollection. It is quite possible I have made mistakes in the narration if so and you deem them material don[']t hesitate to make corrections.

I cordially reciprocate the wish that we may meet some of these days – what length of time does it take to get from New York City to Providence. I am sometimes in N.Y. & may have the time on some of these visit[s] to run over to y[ou]r city for a little while.

Very Truly Y[ou]rs

A D Payne

[Payne's Enclosure]

A narrative of a part of the operations of the Confederate cavalry in the valley of Va. during the fall of 1864

After the disastrous day at Winchester on the 19[th] Sept 1864 the Cavalry force attached to Gen'l Earlys command, consisting of one division (Fitz Lee's) composed of Lomax's Brigade commanded by Gen [Wm. H.] Payne and Wickham[']s Brigade under the command of Col [Thomas T.] Munford – all commanded by General [Williams C.] Wickham, Fritz Lee having been wounded & disabled at Winchester, fell back to Front Royal and attempted to guard the fords of the Shenandoah river at that point. They were pursued by a superior force of the enemy, who by masking their real design by a feint upon the front of the river line occupied by the Confederate Cavalry, succeeded in crossing at an unguarded ford and compelled an abandonment of the position by the Confederates. It will be observed, that the army of Gen'l Early at this time [was] retreating on two parallel lines, the infantry down the Shenandoah Valley proper and the cavalry down what is called the Page Valley, formed by the Blue Ridge Mountains & the Massanutten Mountains, a span of the Blue Ridge. It was evidently the object of the Union Cavalry by this flank movement to get in rear of Gen'l Early's main army and thus enclose him between two forces – Gen'l Sheridan with his infantry force & part of his cavalry being in his front. The Confederate Cavalry endeavored to prevent this by retarding and obstructing the advance of the Union Cavalry force in their front, till Gen'l Early could reach a place where this purpose could not be accomplished. Gen Wickham in furtherance of this design fell back slowly with his division down the Page Valley disrupting the advance of the enemy and reached Browns gap a pass in the Blue Ridge in Augusta County on the 26th day of September. Early by this time had reached what was supposed to be a defensible position from a flank and rear attack. Whilst Wickham was encamped at Brown's gap information was received by the Confederates that a small Union Cavalry force was outlying at or near the village of Waynesboro in Augusta county situated on the road from Charlottesville to Staunton and near the mouth of Rockfish Gap. It was believed that this force was unsupported by infantry, and by a swift and bold attack by the Confederates could be captured or severely crippled. Accordingly on the morning of the 28th Sept, Wickham's Brigade of Cavalry commanded by Col Munford consisting of the 1st 2nd 3d & 4th Regiments of Va Cavalry with a section of horse artillery moved upon Waynesboro, and at the same time Gen Breckinridge's division of infantry was put in motion down the valley pike to strike the road from Waynesboro to Staunton at some point that would intercept the retreat of the Union Cavalry from Waynesboro. Col Munford with his cavalry wound along the base of the Blue Ridge on the west side by obscure mountain roads as noiselessly & swiftly as possible and reaching the Charlottesville & Waynesboro road about one mile from the village about 4 or 5 oclock of the afternoon of the 28th. As was expected the enemy were completely surprised – many of their horses were unbridled and grazing on a piece of meadow land lying between the highway leading to the village and a small stream a tributary of South River, one of the branches of the Shenandoah. Col Munford as soon as he saw the situation quietly disposed his forces for an attack – the 1st Regiment, commanded by Col Wilby Carter, was dismounted as sharpshooters and formed on either side of the road leading to Waynesboro and the remaining three regiments advanced quickly upon the village mounted. The enemy immediately began to bestir themselves and in a few minutes their cavalry made its appearance in front of the village between it & the Confederates. A sharp engagement at once ensued, charges and counter charges were made by the opposing forces, but the Union Cavalry was forced steadily back into and through the village until the western edge was reached, where the Confederates found some obstruction across the street doubtless put there to retard their advance. The 4th Va Regiment was at this point in the front and Capt Morgan Strother, its commander, when he discovered the barricade ordered some of his men to dismount with a view of removing the obstructions. Whilst this was being done he suddenly gave the order for the dismounted men to mount – this was immediately done – and just at this juncture an incident occurred worthy of mention as exhibiting a deed of individual heroism rarely witnessed; just as the men of the 4th Reg were well in the saddle after the order of their commanding officer, a single soldier coming from the direction of the enemy, with sword in hand, dashed into the Black Horse troop, which composed one of the squadrons of the 4th Va Cav. and on that occasion was the color squadron, and commenced sabering the men right and left and wounded one or two, one of them was Corporal Hugh Hamilton a gallant soldier and the color bearer – the boldness and suddenness of the attack paralyzed for a moment or two the Confederates and in that interval this bold assailant succeeded in forcing his way through the Confederate column and might possibly have escaped but a shot fired by a Confederate killed his horse and he fell with it. He was immediately surrounded but refused to surrender and while defending himself with his sabre received a sabre thrust and was knocked down with the butt end of a carbine and would in all probability have been slain on the spot, but for the timely interference of Capt Henry Lee, an aid of Col Munford, who seeing the struggle, rode up and put an end to it. It is said that Capt Lee recognized in the prostrate man a brother mason through some sign or cry used by that order in times of destress or danger. The hero of this affair, which sounds like a romance, turned out to be Capt. Geo N Bliss of the United States Army at that time commanding the Provost guard of Gen'l Talbert, who was in command of this force at Waynesboro. He was of course captured, and his explanation of his rash and desperate enterprise was that he was ordered with a part of his cavalry to charge the Confederate Cavalry, that he dashed ahead supposing that he was followed by his command when too near the enemy to retreat, he discovered that he was unsupported and alone – rather than surrender he determined upon the bold project of attempting to break through the Confederate column and to escape from the other side, it came near being a success and at the same time his escape from death was almost a miracle – this adventure ended the work of the day. Immediately after it Capt Strother advanced with his Regiment but found that the Union force had retreated, it was near dark and pursuit impossible – beyond driving the Union force from Waynesboro and inflicting some damage to it the results of the enterprise to the Confederates were not very important – by some mischance Gen'l Breckenridge's division of infantry did not get up in time to intercept the Federal force in the Stanton road.[82]

CHAPTER SIX
Charlottesville General Hospital

At Waynesboro, Virginia, Bliss had received a deep cut on his forehead over his right eye and a few smaller cuts. His most serious wound, however, was a saber thrust in his lower back that injured his left lung. He had lost much blood and if the wound became infected, he would surely die. Fortunately, he was well treated, and along with an officer he had just wounded, Bliss was carted off to a Confederate field hospital near the top of the nearby mountain where his wounds were dressed. The next day Bliss was transported by train to a hospital in Charlottesville.

The Charlottesville General Hospital was located on the campus of the University of Virginia and included buildings in the surrounding town. In a memoir published in 1884, Bliss recalled, "Late at night, on the twenty-ninth of September, the wounded were all landed by the cars in Charlottesville, where I was placed in the officers' hospital and passed two pleasant weeks, for a prisoner, thanks to the kindness and courtesy of the officers and attendants, and especially that of the surgeon in charge, J. S. Davis, M. D., Professor in the University of Virginia." Following the war, Bliss developed a close, personal friendship with Davis, his wife and their son, John Staige Davis, Jr., also a doctor.[1]

While only one letter from the elder Davis has survived, letters from his wife and son, plus family photographs and Christmas cards, were found in Bliss's papers. Also found were photographs of John Staige Davis, Jr. on a visit to the Bliss home in East Providence. Only the single letter from the elder Davis is included in this chapter.

Bliss had given his word of honor to Dr. Davis that he would make no effort to escape the hospital and was given remarkable freedom there.

He was once allowed to attend the funeral of a Union officer he had met there. Bliss remembered:

"[The officer was] Captain Farr, of a New York regiment, wounded at Waynesborough, by a bullet through the lung, [and who] was placed in the same room with me. He had received a bullet, piercing the body from front to rear, at Gettysburg, and his recovery from that terrible wound seemed to make him confident that he should survive this wound also, and at his dictation I wrote a cheerful and manly letter to his sister. But the inflammation of the wounded lung steadily increased, and, at the end of a week, Doctor Davis told me that he could not live; and yet he was very strong. At supper-time of the last day of his life he rose from his bed, sat down at the table and ate a large bowl of bread, milk and roasted apples; an hour afterwards he died while apparently in a quiet sleep. I was allowed to attend his funeral . . ."[2]

Letter of John Staige Davis,
Surgeon, Charlottesville General Hospital

When the Civil War began, John Staige Davis (1824-1885) was one of three doctors at the University of Virginia given permission to serve as Confederate surgeons in the neighboring hospitals that became known as the Charlottesville General Hospital. Davis's son later wrote, "These were indeed hard times: the country was desolate, the State Treasury empty; but the heroic spirits of the faculty enabled them to serve virtually without pay, and even to replace personally the glass in the shattered windows of their lecture rooms."[3]

Davis's father, John Anthony Gardner Davis, was a lawyer who attended the University of Virginia during its first session in 1825. He became Professor of Law at the university in 1830. In 1841, in his role as Chairman of the Faculty, the elder Davis attempted to stop two students who were causing a disturbance. One of the students shot Professor Davis, and he died three days later. A year before this incident, at age fifteen, John Staige Davis had received his diploma, signed by his father. In 1847, Davis joined the faculty at the university as "Demonstrator of Practical Anatomy," and required each medical student to do individual dissections. He went on to become Professor of Anatomy and Materia Medica, Therapeutics and Botany at the school. As he was thwarted by a Virginia law that prohibited the disinterment of dead bodies, he resorted to grave robbing. Most of the bodies came from African American and pauper cemeteries, others from executed convicts. In 1859, Davis requested the bodies of men sentenced to be hanged after John Brown's raid on Harpers Ferry but received none. Davis died in 1885 at the age of sixty.[4]

John Staige Davis (n.d., found in Bliss's papers)

take place to-morrow at the Central Chuch, in
Fifty-seventh-street, near Broadway.

DR. JOHN STAIGE DAVIS DEAD.

Dr. John Staige Davis, Professor of
Anatomy and Materia Medica at the University
of Virginia, died last evening of paralysis at
Charlottesville after an illness of six weeks. He
was born Oct. 1, 1824, in Albemarle County,
Va., and was educated at the University of
Virginia, from which he was graduated
and received his diploma of M. D. in
1841. In December of the following year he
went to Jefferson County, West Va., and in January, 1845, he moved to his native place. In the
latter part of 1849 he went to the University of
Virginia and became a member of the Virginia
Medical Society. On June 10, 1847, he married
Lucy Handon Blackford, who died about 12
years later, and then the doctor married Caroline H. Hill.

SAVED FROM THE UNDERTOW.

While the little inmates of the Health
Home for Children, at the west end of

Obituary for John S. Davis in *New York Times* of July 18, 1885

Dr. John Staige Davis IV, in Charlottesville in 2006, flanked by brothers Fred (left) and Bill Emerson. Davis's great-grandfather cared for the Emerson's great-grandfather during the Civil War.

University of Va.   Nov: 23rd 1865

Dear Sir,

Your letter of the 28th ult: reached me day before yesterday – Our intercourse at the Hospital having inspired me with a sincere respect & good will for you, I had remembered you kindly, and often felt anxious to know that you had passed safely through the war. Permit me to thank you for relieving this solicitude, & to assure you that I duly appreciate your grateful acknowledgments of the treatment you received at my hands. My recollections of the Struggle are not embittered by the consciousness of inhumanity toward any of the wounded prisoners entrusted to my care, but I think it highly probable that the reputation you had acquired among our people & which accompanied you to Charlottesville, of kindness to them when they were helpless, & of courage in action, procured for you a larger measure of consideration than perhaps you might otherwise have received[5] –

My brother concerning whom you expressed an interest, was held at Elmira until the 1st of March when he was paroled & returned home – And his exchange not having been consummated when general Lee surrendered, he did not re-enter the field.[6] It is not likely that Dr: Moses ever got your answer to his letter. For as soon as communication with the North was fully restored (i.e. about the 1st of July) he went to New Hampshire where his parents reside, and at the last advices was still with them[7] –

Mr: [Thomas] Johnson & his sister Molly are here and well – Dr: Dinwiddie, whose Ward you entered when you first arrived, lost his wife three or four months after your departure, and replaced her recently with a very handsome & blooming girl of about twenty. He has settled in the Village, and is doing a very large business as Dentist.

Renewing the expression of my cordial esteem & respect, I am, dear Sir.

Very truly yours,
J. S. Davis
G. N. Bliss, Esq.

University of Va. Nov: 23rd
1865

Dear Sir,

Your letter of the
28th ult: reached me day before
yesterday — Our intercourse at the
Hospital having inspired me with
a sincere respect & good will for you.
I had remembered you kindly,
and often felt anxious to know
that you had passed safely through
the War — Permit me to thank
you for relieving this solicitude,
& to assure you that I duly appreciate your graceful acknowledgments
of the treatment you received at
my hands — My recollections of the
Struggle are not embittered by the

John S. Davis's letter to George N. Bliss (found in Bliss's papers)

117

CHAPTER SEVEN
Libby Prison

In mid-October 1864, still a prisoner, Bliss was removed from the Charlottesville General Hospital. He wrote his father, "I was then sent to Lynchburg and from thence to Richmond where I arrived Oct. 17ᵗʰ and was sent to hospital since one of my wounds had got into bad condition from the exposure of the journey." Bliss had arrived at the notorious Libby Prison. Housing mostly Union officers, conditions were somewhat better than at most Confederate prisons.[1]

Bliss, ever resourceful, did relatively well there. Even though a prisoner he was able to raise sufficient money to buy extra food for himself and some of his fellow prisoners. On one occasion he wrote his father, "I have just received $250 in Confederate money so that I can buy such articles of food as I need beyond the prison ration." On another he wrote, "I have just received $200 in Confederate money from William F. White Private Co. F. 3ʳᵈ Va Cavalry in return for which you will please send $20 Twenty dollars in Greenbacks to Bernard Schmidt 8ᵗʰ C. S. Cavalry Hospital Fort Deleware [sic] Del."[2]

While in the prison hospital Bliss carved a chess set from an old broom handle. In early December he was well enough to return to the general prison population, housed in an open room on the third floor. Almost immediately he was selected as a hostage. "I am held in close confinement [i.e., in a small cell with a sentry immediately outside] as a hostage and am depending on the efforts of my friends to secure my release." The reason for his situation began in the summer of 1864 when Union forces, under General Ambrose Burnside, arrested six Confederates. Dressed as civilians, these men were "[T]ried by court martial and sentenced to be hung for recruiting men for the rebel army within the Union lines in East Tennessee," Bliss recounted in 1884.

Libby Prison, Richmond, Va., April 1865. Andrew J. Russell, photographer. (Library of Congress Prints and Photographs Division, LC-B8184-10215.)

Two officers were hung and the four enlisted Confederates were being held in "close confinement." Their death sentences were eventually commuted.[3]

Chess figures carved by Bliss from a broom handle while he was in Libby Prison hospital. The set is in the possession of Bliss descendants.

Released from the cells in late January, Bliss was paroled a week later. He signed a paper, "promising to do no harm to the Confederacy until duly exchanged" and "passed out of Libby prison into the streets of Richmond." He and other prisoners boarded a small vessel and sailed a few miles down the James River, marched across a neck of land at Dutch Gap, and boarded the side-wheel steamer *New York*. By February 7th Bliss was recovering in a military hospital in Annapolis, Maryland. His military duty continued there as president of a court martial until his discharge in mid-May 1865. By then, the war was over, and he was told, "The end of the war renders your services no longer necessary."[4]

Among the inmates Bliss joined in Libby Prison was Henry S. Burrage, an old college friend. After the war, Burrage and Bliss exchanged letters. Four of Burrage's seven letters to Bliss are presented in this chapter.

Letters of Henry S. Burrage, fellow prisoner
at Libby Prison, Richmond, Virginia

Henry Sweetser Burrage (1837-1926) was born in Fitchburg, Massachusetts. He prepared for college at Pierce Academy, then attended Brown University, where he met Bliss, who was a fraternity brother (Delta Kappa Epsilon) and in the class one year ahead. Burrage graduated in 1861, then spent a year at Newton Theological Seminary. He enlisted in the 36th Massachusetts Volunteer Infantry as a private in 1862, the second year of the war, and rose quickly through the ranks. He was appointed sergeant, and then sergeant-major, before the end of August. By May of the following year, he was a second lieutenant, and was appointed first lieutenant in November 1863. Burrage was wounded in the shoulder by a mini ball at Cold Harbor, Va., in June 1864, and was promoted to captain the next month. He was taken prisoner in Nov. 1864, at Petersburg, Va.[5]

The circumstances surrounding Burrage's capture at Petersburg are unusual. On duty with instructions allowing him to exchange newspapers with enemy forces, Burrage met a Confederate officer on a road through the woods where such exchanges had taken place almost daily for some time. The Confederate gave Burrage three Richmond papers; Burrage had only a single Washington paper and promised to bring another later in the day. When he returned, he was taken prisoner. In retaliation, Union forces soon captured Confederate general Roger A. Pryer when he, too, attempted a newspaper exchange. Pryor was incarcerated at Fort Lafayette, in New York harbor, while Burrage was sent to Richmond's Libby Prison, where he met fellow prisoner George Bliss. Negotiations for an exchange of Burrage for Pryer immediately began. Meanwhile, in December, Burrage was initially selected as a hostage for Confederates captured by General Ambrose Burnside in Tennessee and under threat of being hanged. Burrage convinced the prison commandant to select someone else, lest the ongoing exchange efforts be further complicated. Ironically, the new man selected to take his place was George Bliss. Burrage discussed this incident in his first letter to Bliss. In February 1865, after lengthy negotiations, Burrage and Pryer were exchanged.[6]

Burrage returned to duty in April 1865 as Acting A.A.G. (assistant adjutant general), 1st Brigade. 2d Division, 9th Army Corps. He was brevetted major, U.S. Volunteers "for gallant and meritorious services in the campaign from the Rapidan to the James, March 13, 1865." He mustered out with the regiment on June 8, 1865.[7]

Burrage soon resumed his studies at Newton, graduating in 1867. His first and only pastorate was at the First Baptist Church in Waterville, Maine, from 1869 to 1873. For the next thirty-two years he was the editor of *Zion's Advocate*, a statewide Baptist weekly newspaper which was based in Portland. Highly thought of in education circles, Burrage was a trustee of Colby College from 1881 to 1906, Newton Theological Seminary from 1881 to 1906, and Brown University from 1889 to 1901. Active in veterans' organizations, he served as chaplain of Togus, the Civil War veterans' home in Chelsea, Maine, from 1905 to 1912. A well-respected researcher and writer of history publications, Burrage became president of the Maine Historical Society. In 1907, Governor William T. Cobb appointed him Maine's first State Historian, a position he held until his death on March 9, 1926, at the age of eighty-nine.[8]

Portland   Oct. 29, 1879

My Dear Bliss:

I do not think I can add anything to what you already know concerning that episode in our Libby life.[9] The date was Dec. 9, 1874 [1864]. In the forenoon Capt. Boise and Lt. Huff were sent to the cell. A little while after Maj. Phillips, Lt. Towle and myself were called for and taken down to Maj. Turner's[10] office. He said he was very sorry to inform us that we were to be held as hostages for some Confederate soldiers at the west who had been captured. Four men were sentenced to be hung – bushwhackers[was] inferred, and Maj. Turner read to us the order he had received from Commissioner Ould.[11] I asked him if he remembered not Roger A. Pryor had been captured in retaliation for my capture and was held as a hostage for me according to the Richmond papers.

"Are you the officer" he asked, "captured while exchanging papers, and who was taken and held [at] headquarters several days?" I replied, "Yes." "Then I can't take you," he said, and looking over his list of prisoners he selected Captain _____ the name I have forgotten. On enquiring, however, finding that this captain was a German, he looked for another Massachusetts officer, but not being successful in his search, he said, "I will take Capt. Bliss, 1ˢᵗ R.I. Cavalry." And so I was returned to the room above, and you were sent down in my place. I was sorry then, and am still that I opened my mouth on that occasion; and on this account I do not wish to send a letter to print but you are at liberty to use the facts in your paper, which I have no doubt will be one of interest. Please send me a copy.

Very Truly yours
Henry S. Burrage

Portland, Me.,   Dec. 16, 1879.

My Dear Bliss:

You ask me to give an account of my interview with Major Turner on the day you were sent to the cells in the Libby. It was December 9, 1864;

you came up from the hospital in the Libby, December 7, and it gave me much pleasure to greet an old college friend, even in such a place. During the following day, though, we were interrupted by the visit of a committee of the Confederate Congress, who came to inquire into the condition of the prison, we recited our army experiences, and made ourselves as comfortable as the situation allowed. On Friday, December 9th, early in the forenoon, Captain Boice and Lieutenant Huff were sent to the cells. Not long after, Dick Turner came up stairs and called for Major Phillips, Lieutenant Towle and myself. Following him down stairs, we were shown into Major Turner's office, and were informed by the Major himself that we were to be sent to the cells and held as hostages for some men, bushwhackers, I inferred, who had been captured by our forces in the West, and sentenced to be hung. He then read an order from Commissioner Ould in reference to the matter. Only a day or two before, I had found in a Richmond paper the following: "Roger A. Pryor has been sent to Fort Lafayette. A Washington telegram says: 'Roger A. Pryor arrived here this morning and leaves to-night for Fort Lafayette. He attracted much attention as he was escorted down the avenue to the old Capitol, under guard, and was recognized by many of his former acquaintances here.' It is probable that he will soon be returned, as it is understood that Captain Burrage, for whose capture he was taken, in retaliation, is to be returned." I called the attention of Major Turner to this announcement, and remarked that I thought he was complicating matters. He said that the fact in reference to Pryor had escaped his attention, and added, "I cannot take you." Then he turned to his list and said, "I will take Captain, — Massachusetts Volunteers," the name I have forgotten; it was a German name, and Turner asked if the officer he had selected was American born. When informed that he was a German, he ran his eye again over his list, saying, "I must have a Massachusetts officer." But finding none, he turned to Dick Turner, and said, "Bring down Captain Bliss, First Rhode Island Cavalry." I went upstairs with a sad heart, but remember well the bold face you put on as you packed up your things and followed Dick Turner down stairs. There was nothing I would not have given could I have recalled the suggestion which secured my own release at your expense. I had only one more day at the Libby before I was sent with other prisoners to Danville, and we did not meet again until after the close of the war, but I was glad to learn that you were relieved and exchanged even before I was.

Always truly yours,
Henry S. Burrage,
Captain Thirty-sixth Massachusetts Volunteers.

P S.—The regiments of Captain Boice, Lieutenant Huff, Major Phillips and Lieutenant Towle I cannot give. I enclose a scrap of paper which you sent to me during the first night, I think, you were in the cells; you sent it up by the officer of the guard. Upon the enclosed scrap of paper the following appears written with a lead pencil: "Captain Burrage:—Please deliver my money to Lieutenant Adams, who will give it to me. We are all 5 in one cell, 8 ft. by 12 ft.; the floor is of wood, raised about 12 inches above the ground; we have a fire, but find it cold nights. Tell Trippe, C. S., to send down the articles we sent out for. We do not know yet for whom we are held.

"Yours truly, G. N. Bliss.
P. S.—We are all well. G.N B."

Portland   Sept. 24, 1884

My Dear Bliss:

Your narrative[12] came this morning, and I devoured it at once. You have made a most interesting story, doubly interesting to me from my connection with it. The letters from the Confederate officers which you append to the narrative add to the value of narrative, and are in good spirit. You have done a good [*one illegible word*] in putting your reminisces in record.

The story of my capture and events connected with it I have written out but it is so personal that I hesitate about publishing.

Henry S. Burrage in his chaplain's uniform during the years he served Togus, the Civil War veterans' home in Chelsea, Maine. Photograph courtesy of Earle G. Shettleworth, Jr., Maine State Historian

Maj. Raymond wrote to me that he saw you recently and conveyed war remembrances. I will be glad to see you if ever you come this way and will endeavor to call on you whenever I come to Providence. It is possible that I may come to the area for a few months to consult a volume in the John Carter Brown library.[13]

Always truly y[our]s,
Henry S. Burrage

Portland, Me.   Dec. 10, 1897.

My dear Maj. Bliss:

Your letter of yesterday has awakened a flood of memories. No, I did not recall that experience in the Libby yesterday. But if I had been sent down into that miserable rat-hole into which you were thrust I should have remembered it as distinctly as you I am sure. Now that your letter has stirred my memory I recall it all. I can see Maj. Turner in his office as he appeared when Maj. Phillips and the other officer whose name I forget were brought before him with myself. He made us his little speech expressing regret that he was obliged to put us in the cells in consequence of Gen Burnside's order, &c. When I suggested that on account of the capture of Pryor in retaliation for my capture, I did not see how he could do with me as he proposed. He replied, "No I cant," and then running his eyes over his lists of prisoners, he added, "I will take Capt. Bliss, First Rhode Island Cavalry." This was an announcement I had not anticipated, and I remember with what a heavy heart I mounted the stairs. You were the only prisoner I knew before I entered the prison, and we had had only a day or two together as you had just left the hospital. It was a great relief to me to learn later that you got out of the Confederacy before I did.

Your resolute bearing under such tyring [*sic*] circumstances I well remember. You showed the stuff you were made of. I can still see you as you collected your effects – it did not take you long– and then answered the call of the sergeant and descended the stairs. A day or two afterward I was sent to Danville.

In those days we could hardly have expected to review these things after a generation had passed away. But life has been graciously lengthened out, and both of us are glad we had a part in putting down the Rebellion. I hope a goodly number of years are still in store for both of us. I have many things yet which I wish to do, and I have no doubt that it is so with you.

You speak very kindly of Tom. I have heard from him and from Champlin the best things of your own boys and of the whole Bliss family. The reports the boys bring always stir my memory, and the old days of college and prison life come back. May it be so on to the end, and I love to think that the friendships of life do not end then but reach on into the blessed life beyond.

I thank you for your letter. If at any time any other memories come to you send them on.

Always truly yours,
Henry S. Burrage.

CHAPTER EIGHT
Biography of George N. Bliss

George N. Bliss was born in Tiverton, Rhode Island, on July 22, 1837, in a northern portion of the town called Eagleville. Tiverton was a fishing and farming community; its population in 1840 was just under twenty-two hundred. George Bliss was the first child of James Leonard Bliss (1812-1882) and Sarah Ann (Stafford) Bliss (1811-1908). James Bliss had been born in Seekonk, Massachusetts; George's grandfather, James Bliss, Jr. (1782-1832), also born in Seekonk, had been a lawyer and constable of the town. George Bliss's paternal great-grandfather, Dr. James Bliss (1757-1834), was a veteran of the Revolutionary War. At the age of nineteen, he had served as a surgeon's mate in Col. Thomas Carpenter's regiment of militia and was present at the Battle of White Plains. In 1646, A pioneer relative, Thomas Bliss, was among those who accompanied Reverend Samuel Newman from Weymouth, Mass., to Rehoboth, Mass., when he established his foundational Congregational Church. (In 1886 the name of the church was changed to Newman Congregational Church of East Providence and Seekonk. As an adult, George Bliss was a long-time member of the church). This connection may explain how Bliss received his middle name. The maiden name of George Bliss's paternal grandmother Nancy, was also Bliss (1784-1822). Her father, Captain Jonathan Bliss (1739-1800), had served under Captain Samuel Bliss (relationship unknown), who commanded a company at the "Lexington Alarm" in the Revolutionary War.[1]

Only a few details are known about the early lives of George Bliss's parents. When he was six years old, James Bliss's family moved to Marietta, Ohio, where his mother Nancy had been born. Nancy Bliss died there in 1822, when James was nine years old. Ten years later, his father, James Bliss, Jr., died of cholera in Marietta. With both parents deceased, nineteen-year-old James Bliss returned East in 1832. It was noted that Bliss's cousin brought him "the entire distance in a sleigh." While there is no information about his education, James Bliss was a skilled writer and had a good command of the English language; these skills are illustrated by a letter he sent his son in 1858 (see Appendix).

Bliss's mother, Sarah Stafford, was born in Tiverton. R.I. in 1811. She and James Bliss were living in Fall River, Mass. in 1835, when they were married. Both of George Bliss's maternal grandparents had also been born in Tiverton and lived out most of their lives there. Stephen Stafford (1756-1823), had fought in the Revolutionary War, rising from private to sergeant in "Toplian's regiment, of the R.I. State Troops." George Bliss's grandparents would have had little impact on his life. All but his maternal grandmother, Abigail Durfee Stafford (1765-1839), died before he was born, and she passed away when he was two years old.[2]

In 1839, the year Abigail Stafford died, the Bliss family left Tiverton and moved three miles north to Fall River, Massachusetts. The move afforded James Bliss considerable business opportunities. Fall River had recently become a center for industry (it was incorporated as a city in 1854). By 1840, it was a bustling metropolis of twelve thousand citizens and was well on its way to becoming the largest cotton manufacturing center in the United States. Fall River had numerous mills, an iron works, and many supporting industries. Located on the eastern shore of Mount Hope Bay at the mouth of Taunton River, local commerce greatly benefited from its busy port and easy access to Narragansett Bay and the Atlantic Ocean. James Bliss began a thriving tailoring enterprise in Fall River, centrally located at the southwest corner of Main and Central streets in "5 Granite Block." Bliss's home was located at 5 ferry Street, near the Taunton River and less than a mile from his business. During the twelve years the family lived in Fall River, the Bliss's added three more boys; James L. Jr. (1839-1906), Charles C. (1841-1896), and Jerome D. (1843-1919), followed by three girls, Caroline L., (1846-1932), Mary E. (1848-1928), and Joanne M. (1852-1942).[3]

The move to Fall River was fortuitous for George Bliss, as the town had significant educational opportunities. At that time, few communities provided comprehensive education, and high school graduates were rare. Fall River was one of the earliest towns in the region to establish a high school, doing so in 1849. Still, many children worked in the factories and had little schooling. Years after Bliss left the town, fourteen hundred children under fifteen years of age were working and did not attend school. Some working children were under ten years of age. As late as 1907, child labor was standard in Rhode Island. That year, more than six thousand children under sixteen were employed in mills and factories in the state. Bliss was fortunate to have had the opportunity and means to go to school. He attended public schools in Fall River, including three years at the high school, beginning there in 1851. At first, high school classes were temporarily held in a private school building that stood on the south side of Franklin Street, east of Oak. For his first year, Bliss would have attended this temporary school. In 1852, a new building was erected at the corner of Locust and June streets. It was first known simply as "the High School," but was later called the Foster Hooper school. Bliss attended this school his last two year in high school. There were relatively few students enrolled. In 1853-54, Bliss's last year, eighty-one students ("37 males, 44 females") attended the high school. Only a single room on the second floor was used for classes. Bliss graduated in 1854, at the age of seventeen.[4]

Little is known of George Bliss's boyhood. But with Fall River's proximate access to vast stretches of navigable water, George Bliss's lifelong love of fishing, boating, and sailing probably got its start there. Then, as now, the ground rose swiftly from the shoreline, providing scenic views of the bay and river. In the summer of 1854, the year Bliss graduated from high school in Fall River, his family moved twenty miles to what is today, Pawtucket, Rhode Island. (At the time, the town was part of Massachusetts. It became part of Rhode Island in 1862, the result of a long simmering border dispute between Rhode Island and Massachusetts, resolved by the United States Supreme Court.) Like Fall River, Pawtucket was an important industrial center. The first cotton-mill in the country had been established there in 1790, and it had many such factories and supporting industries. Pawtucket, with an 1850 population of about thirty-seven hundred, was smaller than Fall River. Nevertheless, it was a thriving, bustling community. James Bliss opened a merchant tailoring store in the Tyler building near the center of town. Located on the corner of Main

Street and Pleasant Street (where Main Street and East Avenue now meet), it was one of ten such businesses in the town. The family lived nearby on High Street, near Main. It is not known how long the Bliss family lived on High Street. By 1865 they had moved to 33 Cottage Street, on the east side of the Pawtucket River (now the Seekonk), which divided the city north to south. In the 1860s, the area immediately east of the river was not included in the town, but was part of Seekonk, Massachusetts. (This "twin sister" to the east was incorporated into the town in 1874.)[5]

James Bliss's house on Cottage Street was in a quiet residential area of two-story homes. (James and Sarah Bliss lived on Cottage Street the rest of their lives.) The Bliss's lived near the intersection of Cottage St. with Broadway Ave. and Summit Street. (Today, an interstate highway through Pawtucket occupies the portion of Cottage Street where the Bliss home once stood.) The house was a half mile from the center of Pawtucket and James Bliss often walked to and from his store, probably crossing the river via the Main Street Bridge. (One evening in the 1860s, while walking home from his store, he was "savagely assaulted and robbed by two ruffians, and for a long time his life was despaired of.") Near the Main Street Bridge was a waterfall, and below that the river was navigable to the sea. With such proximity to the water, George Bliss likely continued his fishing, boating, and sailing activities. (In a wartime letter dated June 20, 1862, he expressed his love of sailing in the area. He wrote, "I would give $10 for a day's cruise on the waters of the Narragansett, . . . in my eyes nothing can ever equal the attractions of my native bay.")[6]

James Bliss's financial condition was good, and he provided well for his family. Census records show that by 1860 he had real estate valued at twenty-five thousand dollars and personal property of one thousand dollars. By comparison, many of his neighbors reported significantly less wealth. The family also employed a twenty-eight-year-old live-in "servant" from Scotland, Joanna McDermaid.[7]

The family's move to Pawtucket helped launch another significant step in George Bliss's education. In September 1854, he began two years of study at University Grammar School in Providence, a private college preparatory school. It was there that he developed an enduring friendship with another student, David V. Gerald (1841-1871), who would later be the recipient of Bliss's wartime letters. Gerald's family was from the western part of Seekonk, Massachusetts, which also was annexed by Rhode Island in 1862 and renamed East Providence. The school was located "[O]n College Hill, directly opposite the beautiful grounds of Brown University, and near the Centre of business." The mission of the school was "to furnish superior advantages to young men in preparing for . . . Brown University. At present the school affords unsurpassed facilities for those who wish to enter college or engage in business." University Grammar School was relatively expensive. Tuition was based on the age of the student. Some years after he was there, Bliss would have been charged $120 per year. (By comparison, total expenses at Brown, which Bliss soon entered, were $62.80 per year, including "Tuition," "room-rent," "servants' hire," and "Use of Library.") The school's daily sessions were from 9 o'clock A. M. to 2 o'clock P.M., affording Bliss ample time to commute from home. He likely traveled the five miles between Pawtucket and College Hill on an omnibus line operated by Wetherell & Bennett. These busses ran twice a day from the Pawtucket station on Main Street at Mill Street.[8]

Bliss's photograph from 1860 Union College yearbook.
(Courtesy Special Collections, Schaffer Library, Union College)

In 1856, Bliss and Gerald left University Grammar School and enrolled at Brown University. Bliss apparently enjoyed his classical language studies;

he often used Latin or Greek expressions in his wartime letters to Gerald. Neither man completed the course of studies at Brown; after two years, they left the school. Bliss later wrote, "Owing to some difficulty with the faculty as to the management of the college I left Brown and entered Union College, at Schenectady, N. Y., in September 1858 and graduated there with the degree of A. B. in June 1860." The nature of Bliss's "difficulty" with the Brown faculty is not known. A biographical sketch by L. E. Rogers, published later in Bliss's lifetime and likely authorized by him, stated, "His decision of character and courage in adhering to his convictions were manifested in his college course, leading to the change of colleges rather than to submit to what he deemed rigid discipline." A letter from his father sent in January 1858, some months before he left the school, suggests that Bliss's troubles at Brown may have been self-inflicted. The heartfelt, four-page letter was one of only two communications from his father ever found in Bliss's papers. The letter expressed genuine concern for Bliss's future: "None but a father can estimate a father's anxiety for the welfare of his children; and especially for his first born." The elder Bliss admonished his son about being over-zealous in his pursuit of recreation. Skills at "hunting," "shooting" and "sailing," were of "little consequence indeed to the man who has higher and worthier aims." Perhaps Bliss's withdrawal from Brown had more to do with poor study habits or other misdeeds than to "rigid discipline."[9]

Whatever the issue was at Brown, Bliss left the university after the spring term of 1858, upon completion of his sophomore year. That fall he, Gerald and two other friends from Brown entered Union College in Schenectady, N.Y. Schenectady is located 200 miles North- west of Pawtucket and had a population of just under ten thousand in 1860. Union College was close to the center of town and had a student population of about three hundred. (That number dropped to one hundred seventy-five during the war, as students "dropped the book to take up the sword in defense [*sic*] of the flag.")[10]

Following graduation in June 1860 (Bliss and Gerald received bachelor's degrees), both men continued their educations at nearby Albany Law School, founded in 1851. It is not known why Bliss chose law as his profession. Perhaps he wished to continue in the footsteps of his grandfather, James Bliss, Jr., also a lawyer. In mid-nineteenth century

America, the standard preparation for the bar was a legal clerkship. The school's principal professors—Amos Dean, Ira Harris and Amasa Parker—felt that "the mere learning of law, is not learning how to practice it," and set up a structured educational program. To meet the requirements to graduate, a student must be of "good moral character," "have attended three full terms of the Law School," and prepared a "10 to 15 page dissertation on some legal subject. . ." The topics of Bliss's and Gerald's dissertations are not known, but they graduated in May 1861, with Bachelor of Laws degrees. The diploma, by an act of the Legislature, "entitles the person upon whom it is conferred . . . to Practice as Attorney and Counsellor at Law in all the Courts" in New York State.[11] Apparently, there was no reciprocity with Rhode Island, so neither man could immediately practice law in that state.

Although Bliss had a fine education, it appears his younger brothers and sisters received only spotty formal training. None attended University Grammar School, and no records can be found at nearby colleges or universities that show any of Bliss's siblings in attendance. Only one letter by a sibling is known to exist; it was from his brother Charles, four years younger than he. The letter appears in sharp contrast to the letters of George Bliss, reflecting an indifferent education together with poor writing and grammatical skills.

Bliss soon returned to Providence and continued the study of law in the office of forty-eight-year-old Samuel W. Peckham, at 41 Westminster Street, in an area known as Federal Hill.[12]

Bliss barely had a chance to get settled in Peckham's office before the national tragedy that was the Civil War swept him into a world apart from the practice of law in Rhode Island. Even as Bliss was taking his final exams in Albany, in the spring of 1861, the national situation had reached a crisis. Beginning with South Carolina in December 1860, southern states had begun seceding from the Union. War was declared when South Carolina troops fired upon Fort Sumter on April 12, 1861. Most in the country thought the war would be short, and regiments were signing up volunteers for just three-month enlistments. Bliss apparently did not believe he was needed and stayed employed with Peckham. The devastating Union defeat at Bull Run in July put an end to hopes of a short war. Only just starting out in his chosen profession, Bliss, like many northern men of his age, was swept up in the call to arms. The twenty-four-year-old was about to participate in his generations most cataclysmic event. With the interruption of the war, Bliss was not admitted to the Rhode Island Bar until March 1866, nearly a year after the conflict ended.

In September 1861, Rhode Island governor William Sprague began organizing New England's first cavalry regiment, with enlistments of three years. Bliss joined as a private that month. Shortly after enlisting, he was promoted to quartermaster sergeant, and then on October 4, 1861, to first lieutenant. Bliss served in that role for nearly a year. The regiment was composed of two battalions of recruits from Rhode Island, and one battalion from New Hampshire. Formed in Pawtucket, the regiment was initially called the First New England Cavalry. The name was changed the following April to the First Rhode Island Cavalry. The N.H. battalion was formed in Concord, N. H., and later joined the regiment in Rhode Island. Each of the three battalions contained four companies (also called "troops") of about eighty enlisted men each; with officers included, the regiment numbered about one thousand men. (Over time, discharged veterans, fatalities, and sickness dramatically lowered the effective strength of the regiment.)[13]

In early October, training operations began at Camp Hallett, located in a field along the Cranston Road in Cranston, R. I. The camp was named in honor of the regiment's first colonel, George W. Hallett, of the Providence Horse Guards, and Chief of Cavalry of Rhode Island. In December, the regiment was moved to newly erected barracks in a riding park near Pawtucket, named Camp Arnold, in honor of Lieutenant-Governor Samuel G. Arnold.[14]

According to stories passed down through Bliss's family, James Bliss had been against his eldest son joining the army. When it became clear he was determined to fight, his father prevailed on him to join the Masonic Order. The Masons were a worldwide fraternal organization "having in view the welfare of the race and the development of the intellect." It included many notable members; George Washington had once been a Mason. The organization carefully avoided taking political positions and its great tenet was "brotherly love." Freemasonry lodges were spread throughout both northern and southern states. Bliss was a member of Masonic Union Lodge #10 in his hometown of Pawtucket. On December

16, 1861, while organization and training of the regiment was underway, the lodge presented him with a "sword, sash and belt." Bliss accepted the gift with a patriotic speech before "a large gathering of the public."[15]

Toward the end of January 1862, the New Hampshire battalion joined the others in Pawtucket, and the formation of the regiment was completed. In March 1862, after months of winter training, the regiment left Providence for Washington, D.C., travelling in groups of several hundred. Bliss's unit paraded through Providence before proceeding south by steamship to New York City. They then traveled by train and stopped in Philadelphia and Baltimore before reaching the capital on the evening of March 14th. Most of the Union army was assembling there to protect the capital from Confederate attack and to prepare for offensive operations in Virginia, just across the Potomac River.[16]

The George Bliss that went off to war was an intelligent, well-educated man. He loved poetry, literature, and humor. He possessed a natural self-confidence, perhaps reinforced by his position as the eldest child in a family with doting parents. He was quick-thinking, decisive, and not easily flustered. These attributes had proven useful sailing some tricky waters in Narragansett Bay; they would prove even more important in battle. He had an athletic build, was tough and rugged and easily endured hardships. He stood less than five feet six inches tall, shorter than many men of the time, and in 1862 weighed one hundred and sixty-six pounds. (In later life his weight increased to over two hundred and fifty pounds. A uniform Bliss occasionally wore in parades decades after the war, now in the possession of his descendants, shows unmistakable signs of being let out repeatedly to contain his ever-expanding girth.)[17]

Bliss did not travel extensively in his youth and the regiments' journey from Providence was undoubtedly his first trip to the nation's capital, a city that had been taken over by the war. Thousands of troops were streaming into the city every day, and soldiers were garrisoned wherever space could be found, including the grounds of government buildings. The regiment drilled twice a day during its stay in Washington. Bliss did not like Washington. The army did not properly dispose of the massive amounts of human and animal waste. Bliss described the terrible odor of human waste that had been spread on grass fields near the camp. Prostitution was thriving, undoubtedly sustained by the vast numbers of young men away from home for the first time. Bliss wrote about being openly solicited on the streets of the capital by these ladies. He complained that dust raised by horses choked his lungs and made it difficult to see. He acknowledged the beautiful government buildings but referred to the rest of the city as a "dung pile."[18]

The regiment left Washington on April 4, 1862, on its first advance into Virginia. Accompanied by a slow-moving, mile-long wagon-train, they passed ". . . the Capitol, and through Pennsylvania avenue, and over Long Bridge..." Their destination was Warrenton Junction, "neither town nor village, but simply the point of connection of the Warrenton road with the Orange and Alexandria" railroad. Initially, they had little contact with the enemy, but endured miserable weather. Bliss wrote, "it rains with a disgusting perseverance," and four days later, "Still it rains, have had but one fair day for a week." The ground was so saturated with rain that the regiment's first encampment was long remembered as "Camp Mud." Traveling without tents and often without forage for the horses, the regiment began to deal with the daily indignities of life as soldiers. Bliss and the others were in Virginia until mid-September, during which time they often fought the Confederates in minor skirmishes. Bliss was soon able to write, "Don't tell father I have been shot at."[19]

George N. Bliss in June 1862. This is the only wartime image of him that has been found. (Photograph in the possession of Bliss descendants)

Before real battles were to test Bliss's mettle, the regiment faced a crisis of a different sort. In July 1862, Governor William Sprague appointed Alfred Duffié, a Frenchman, to the command of the First R. I. Cavalry, hitherto led by Col. Robert Lawton of Newport. Many officers were outraged by Sprague's appointment of an outsider and a highly emotional near mutiny occurred. Many officers resigned and angry letters were published in Rhode Island newspapers. Bliss wisely remained above the fray. The issue was soon resolved, and although Duffié led the regiment for only a single year, he became its most beloved commander.[20]

At about this time, First Lieutenant Bliss's letters reflect a young man supremely confident in his abilities. He was certain he had the skill and temperament to lead a company of troops, and actively sought promotion to the rank of captain. He worried that army procedures and politics might keep him from being promoted quickly. Bliss asked family members and friends to approach Col. Tristam Burges, an influential acquaintance (and father of college friend Arnold Burges), as well as others, to advocate for his promotion. In July 1862, Bliss got the promotion he sought, becoming captain of Troop C. He never advocated for further promotions and remained a Captain for the duration of the war.

A biographical sketch lists twenty-seven engagements in which Bliss participated.[21] While soldiers often faced the dangers of shot and shell, by far the most deaths in the Civil War occurred due to disease. Within a month of arriving in Virginia, Bliss was stricken with "severe dysentery." Carried to an infirmary after fainting, he was hospitalized for a day. Afterwards, Bliss had weeks of intestinal distress. While medical issues reappeared several times during his three years in the field, Bliss was proud to assert that he rarely missed any assigned duties, and he was uniformly matter of fact in describing the effects of illness.

In March 1863, the regiment was involved in the Battle of Kelly's Ford. Up to that time, the Confederate cavalry had consistently beaten its Union counterpart in battle. Kelly's Ford was considered a decisive Union victory and a turning point in cavalry operations. Bliss, who did not participate in the battle, was asked by his comrades to write an account, and submit it for publication in a Providence newspaper. He did so, the first of a series of occasional dispatches by Bliss, who eventually wrote under the nom-de-plum, "Ulysses."

Bliss served on "detached duty" several times in his military career. By far the longest was from August 1863 to May 1864, when he served in New Haven, Connecticut. There, he assisted in recruiting and training new soldiers and re-enlisting veterans who had served their three-year enlistments. Bliss also visited various parts of the army front in Virginia, and Union-held territory along the coasts of South Carolina, Georgia, and Florida. During his time in New Haven, Bliss was appointed to court-martial duty. He served on three courts-martial, in one of which he was Judge Advocate. The findings in all his cases were approved.[22]

In his wartime letters, Bliss only occasionally mentioned politics. Of the elections in Rhode Island in April 1864, he wrote, "I see that the Republicans have made a pretty clean sweep of R.I. I am glad of it, because I think they mean war to the death without any mental reservation or equivocation whatever. . ." As the presidential election of 1864 loomed, he remarked about the candidates and stated the results of straw-votes taken by soldiers. Bliss planned to vote for whomever would best bring about his priority of winning the war. For him, the clear choice was the Republican candidate, Abraham Lincoln. His heart, however, was with the Democrats. He wrote, "I am still a Douglas Democrat. . . When this war is over and our government has asserted its dominion over every foot of our territory, if then I am in the land of the living I hope to fight under the old Democratic banner."

In May 1864, soon after returning to the field from New Haven, Bliss's regiment was incorporated into General Philip Sheridan's army in the Shenandoah Valley. In August, with a superior force, Sheridan began inflicting a series of battle losses upon Jubal Early's army in the valley. Sheridan eventually forced Early out of the valley altogether. As part of this force, Bliss was placed in charge of his brigade's provost guard. He and his men were responsible for processing the many prisoners of the Shenandoah campaign. In September 1864, Bliss was carrying out an order in Waynesboro, Virginia, when a superior force of Confederates surprised Union forces there and began pushing them back through the town. Bliss led a saber charge to stop the Confederate advance, but the men, hastily assembled and not from his regiment, followed only a short distance before turning away. As he dashed among the troops of the Confederate Black Horse Cavalry, Bliss soon discovered he was alone in the attack. He managed to wound four of his foes and was about to escape down a side-street when his horse was shot and collapsed under him. Before he could rise, two enemy cavalrymen galloped up; one struck at Bliss with a carbine, the other with a saber. With his own saber he parried the blow of the carbine, which gouged the edge of his weapon. He could not stop the saber blow from the other man and was struck over his right eye. He jumped to his feet and promptly surrendered. After he gave up his weapons, he received a saber thrust to his back, injuring his left lung. Despite his surrender, Bliss could see a Confederate soldier deliberately taking aim with a pistol. In desperation, he called for protection as a Freemason. A nearby Confederate officer, Captain Henry C. Lee, himself a Mason, immediately stepped in and protected Bliss. After his wounds were dressed, he was taken to a hospital on the grounds of the University of Virginia in Charlottesville, where he was given excellent care by the chief of surgery, Dr. John Staige Davis.

With his wounds partially healed, Bliss was incarcerated for a period of four months at Libby Prison in Richmond, Virginia. At Libby, Bliss was held as a hostage for a period of forty-seven days, his life contingent on the safe release of Confederates held elsewhere under a death sentence. In February 1865, an exchange was worked out and Bliss was paroled. At Annapolis, Maryland, still recovering his health, Bliss was given a thirty-day leave of absence.[23] After his leave, he was placed on "light duty," where he again served on court-martial duty, this time as president.

In his letters, Bliss often mentioned friends and acquaintances, including young women. None of Bliss's female friendships seems to have been serious, however, until the spring of 1865. In a wartime letter to Gerald in May, Bliss revealed his affection for their friend Mattie Barstow, with the words, "I love Mattie and hope yet to marry her; I have no arguments to offer upon the subject; reason utterly fails to account for love affairs." It is not known what became of the relationship, but Mattie Barstow soon disappeared from Bliss's life. Bliss also flirted with the idea of substantially changing the direction of his life after he left the army. He contemplated giving up the practice of law and joining another veteran in a canned oyster business. These changes did not occur. By mid-May 1865, the war was over, and the twenty-seven-year-old Bliss was mustered out of the army. He returned to Pawtucket shortly thereafter. Census records show that by June 1 he was living in Pawtucket with his family.[24]

The George Bliss who returned to Providence was a well-known war hero. He soon restarted his legal profession by joining Gerald in the firm "[Frank W.] Miner and Gerald," located at 9 Weybosset St. In March 1866 he was admitted to the R.I. bar. In a pattern that would be repeated many times, he began filling his life with a host of activities. In addition to his law practice, he was editor of the Providence *Morning Herald*, a daily newspaper. He held this position for two years.[25] In late-1865, Bliss moved the five or so miles from Pawtucket to East Providence,[26] and soon began to delve into politics. (While the location of this initial East Providence residence has not been determined, Bliss would live out the rest of his life in the town.)

In March 1866, Bliss was selected as an officer at the Rhode Island Democratic Convention held in Providence. For the next seven years, he was the Democratic nominee for Rhode Island attorney general (1867-1873). At this time in Rhode Island, terms for state offices were one year and elections were held each April. Rhode Island was a strongly Republican state, and the Democratic candidates for state-wide office, including Bliss, lost every election during this period.[27] In 1868, thirty-year-old Bliss was elected to the Rhode Island General Assembly as the representative for East Providence. Bliss held the seat for five consecutive years.[28] In October 1868, he was a delegate to the Rhode Island Democratic Convention, held in Providence. A newspaper reported that "Resolutions were adopted . . . condemning the financial policy of the party in power, criticizing the reconstruction doings of Congress, and declaring it to be hypocritical and ungrateful to favor the giving the ballot to the ignorant negro while it is refused to the naturalized citizen." That same month, Bliss also participated in "The Democratic Flag Raising . . . [A] good many people . . . assembled at the corner of Main and Mill streets [Providence] to witness the raising there of a new and handsome Seymour and Blair flag [Democratic Party candidates for U. S. President/Vice President] . . . Gen. Olney Arnold presided, and he and Capt. George N. Bliss and Col. Thomas Steere addressed the crowd in an acceptable manner."[29]

Bliss became involved in civic activities soon after his move to East Providence. Thereafter, politics and civic activities were a large part of his life. In 1866, Bliss was chosen a member of the School Committee of East Providence. He served on the committee for twenty-five years and was superintendent of schools for thirteen years. In 1923, when Bliss was eighty-five, a new elementary school was named in his honor. The eight-room Bliss School was on Orlo Avenue in East Providence, just a few blocks from his residence on Taunton Avenue. The superintendent of Schools wrote that the school had been named "by unanimous vote . ., the Bliss school, in honor of yourself. . ."[30]

By 1867, Bliss and Gerald had opened a law office together. The *City Directory* listed "Gerald and Bliss" at 31 Market Square in Providence.[31] In 1868, Gerald moved to San Francisco with his new wife, the former Eliza A. Bishop. In February 1871, news arrived in Rhode Island that David Gerald had died in California at the age of thirty-one.

There is no record of the impact that Gerald's death had on Bliss, but it must have been profound. Gerald had been Bliss's closest confident and during the war their friendship was "the strongest tie that binds [me] to life now."[32] Still, Gerald's death at such a young age may not have been a complete shock. The wartime letters Bliss wrote from the field give a hint that Gerald's health was poor; he may have suffered from tuberculosis. In a somewhat transparent attempt to discourage Gerald from joining the army in 1862, Bliss had written that he did not think Gerald "would live three months if you joined the army, . . unless a man is strong and healthy, he is an incumbrance on his comrades this would be to me sufficient reason why you should not enlist. . . you should dismiss all thoughts of drawing the sword personally." A few days later Bliss wrote, "If I had the slightest suspicion that you would be guilty of the rashness of throwing your life away in the army, I would say more but I do not deem it necessary."[33] Gerald never joined the army.

In 1869 Bliss was unanimously elected by the General Assembly to a five-year-term as Commissioner of Shell Fisheries, and in 1874 was unanimously re-elected to a second term. Starting in 1884, having changed parties, he was elected to three one-year terms in the State Senate as a Republican. The party switch was apparently permanent.[34]

After the war, Bliss resumed activities with the Pawtucket Royal Arch Masonic Chapter, and soon became an officer. By 1868 he had moved to East Providence but was still associated with Union Lodge #10 in

Pawtucket. In 1874 he helped establish a new Masonic Lodge in East Providence, Rising Sun Lodge #30. He became member #1 and was named Master of the lodge (while under dispensation) that year. He was named master again in 1875 (after bylaws had been established). When the cornerstone of a new temple was laid in 1924, Bliss was featured prominently in several newspaper columns. The resulting structure, at Taunton Ave. and Alice Street in East Providence, is still an active Masonic lodge today.[35]

In January 1872, thirty-four-year-old Bliss married Frances A. Carpenter (1850-1930), who was not yet twenty-two years old. She was the daughter of William A. Carpenter (1813-1879) and Mary French Carpenter (1812-1910) of East Providence. "Fannie" Carpenter studied one year at Mount Holyoke Female Seminary (now Mount Holyoke College). She then taught school for a year (1869-1870) before marrying Bliss. Fannie was a member of the Newman Congregational Church in Rumford, East Providence, having joined in 1867. Bliss also joined the church, some eleven months after his marriage to Fannie. Eventually, George and Fannie Bliss joined the United Congregational Church, which was located within a half mile of their home on Taunton Avenue. In her obituary, Fannie Bliss was listed as a "charter member" of the United Congregational Church.[36]

Bliss and Fannie's father William Carpenter may have met in 1868 when they were both East Providence candidates for Representative in the Rhode Island General Assembly (Bliss at the time a Democrat, Carpenter a Republican). Bliss won the race against his future father-in-law.[37] William Carpenter was a farmer who owned two large parcels of land totaling more than forty acres. The land was situated on either side of Taunton Avenue immediately west of Pawtucket Avenue; this intersection is still known as Carpenter Corners. Bliss acquired 2.4 acres of Carpenter's land on its western edge and built a house at 490 Taunton Avenue, where he and Fannie lived the rest of their lives.[38] He and his wife had six children, five of whom survived infancy. Their first child, Gerald Morton (1873-1922), was named for David Gerald. Like his namesake, he died of tuberculosis. William Carpenter (1874-1965), lived into old age; George Miles (1876-1908) died of typhoid fever; Helen Louise (1877-1967), died in her ninetieth year; Carlton S. (1880-1881), died in infancy of pneumonia; Rose Danielson (1883-1959) also lived into old age.[39]

At one time Bliss was "Town Solicitor" for East Providence. In 1872, the year he turned thirty-five, the Town Council elected Bliss trial justice of East Providence District Court, and he served until 1886 when the General Assembly created the District Court system. He then was appointed presiding justice of the Seventh District Court, East Providence. Bliss presided over the Seventh District Court until he retired in December 1922, at age eighty-five. He estimated that he had heard over twenty-four thousand cases. His daughter Helen mentioned his pride in having had none of his court rulings overturned on appeal during his fifty years "on the bench."[40]

In the years following the war, Bliss joined several veterans' associations, including the Cavalry Veteran Association and the Soldiers' and Sailors' Historical Society of Rhode Island, which was organized in 1875. He served as Chairman of the Publication Committee for the latter organization. The group's goal was to place printed narratives of soldier's personal experiences in public libraries in Rhode Island and elsewhere. One hundred accounts were ultimately published by the society. Bliss presented papers before the group and published histories about the wartime exploits of his old regiment, the First Rhode Island Cavalry. He wrote *Cavalry Service with General Sheridan and Life in Libby Prison*, *Reminiscences of Service in the First Rhode Island Cavalry*, and *The First Rhode Island Cavalry at Middleburg, Va.*, among other titles. He also published an article about the beloved former commander of the regiment, General Alfred Duffié.[41]

For ten years after the war, Bliss did not know the names of the Confederates he encountered in Waynesboro at the time of his capture. That changed in 1875, when he met briefly with a Virginia Masonic group, the Richmond Commandery of Knights Templars, then visiting in Providence. Bliss told members of the group of his experiences in Waynesboro. With the help of these Masons, he soon learned the names of two of the Confederate participants, Captains Henry C. Lee and William A. Moss. Bliss began corresponding with Lee and Moss and in what must have been rare among soldiers of his day, developing lasting friendships with his former enemies. These friendships lasted until the deaths of Lee and Moss.

In August 1879, at age forty-two, Bliss was commissioned Major of Cavalry in the Rhode Island Militia. As there was only one battalion of cavalry in the militia, a biographical sketch of Bliss by Rogers correctly noted that Bliss "commands in the State militia the entire cavalry force of Rhode Island." He commanded the unit for four years. Bliss was afterwards referred to as "Major," rather than as "Captain," the highest rank he had attained during the war. Today, the Militia is known as the National Guard. In December 1880, in his position as Major of Cavalry, Bliss and his men received an invitation to "take part in the parade incident to the inauguration of General James A. Garfield as President of the United States." Apparently, Bliss's unit never took part in the inauguration.[42]

In May 1880, Bliss made a trip south that included a visit to his Virginia friends, William Moss, and Henry Lee. He wrote a series of travelogues about the trip that were published in the *Providence Journal* that month. While in Richmond, Bliss visited Libby Prison. He wrote, "I penetrated its cellar to the place I once occupied for forty-seven days, as a hostage for a private in the Confederate army. . . It seemed now far more repulsive than in the days when I was hardened by the rough life of a soldier, and in less than forty-seven seconds after I had found the spot, I gladly sought the free air of heaven outside of its walls. Libby is now occupied by the Southern Fertilizing Company and if the product is as powerful in its effect upon the soil as it is in the air, no farmer can afford to go without it." Bliss further wrote, "I met Capt. William A. Moss, who had come one hundred miles from Buckingham Court House to Richmond for the express purpose of welcoming to his native State, a man he had not seen for sixteen years, and who upon that former occasion had cut him down with a sabre, and to whom he spoke for the first time, as together, with bleeding wounds, we rode in an ambulance towards the Confederate Hospital in the Blue Ridge mountain, east of Waynesborough. Here also I met Capt. Henry C. Lee, a brother of Fitzhugh Lee, who, when all seemed lost, came to my assistance and saved the life of his enemy." In Charlottesville, he visited the University of Virginia and wrote, "On the 29th day of September 1864, I came to Charlottesville wounded and a prisoner, and falling into the hands of one of its professors, J. S. Davis, M. D., then a surgeon in a Confederate hospital, a friendship began which death alone can end." Bliss visited Richmond and Charlottesville for a second time in 1882, again visiting Libby Prison and Dr. Davis.[43]

Bliss was a member of "Farragut Post No. 8," a local chapter of the Grand Army of the Republic (GAR), located in East Providence. The GAR was a national organization of Union veterans with some three-hundred-thousand members. Bliss participated in numerous local GAR events. Each year the local posts conducted an "Annual Encampment" which included a day-long Memorial Day celebration. Bliss played a key role in many of these events. In 1885, for instance, he gave a public address, was in the lead carriage in the parade, and "conducted the exercises." The following year, he was the event "Marshal," and led sixty Civil War veterans as they marched up Taunton Avenue. As late as 1908, Bliss was judge advocate of the Post.[44]

Sometime in the 1870s Bliss became acquainted with and befriended an African American artist named Edward M. Bannister (1828-1901). Bannister, born in Nova Scotia, was the son of a West Indian father and African American mother. He lost his parents when he was very young. In the early 1850s Bannister moved to Boston, and then to Providence in 1869 or 1870. The two men likely met about 1875, when both had office space in the Woods building at 2 College Street. Bliss had his law office there; Bannister had a painting studio, equipped with a skylight, on the top floor. Bannister became a leading artist in Providence in the 1870s and 1880s. He received national attention after winning a first prize medal at the 1876 Philadelphia Centennial Exposition. When the judges discovered that the winner was a black man, they attempted to withdraw the prize from Bannister, but the other artists threatened to boycott the event and Bannister got his prize.

By 1878, Bannister was an original board member of the newly established Rhode Island School of Design and was a founder of the Providence Art Club, which was begun in his studio. A few months after Bannister's sudden death in Providence in 1901, his friends at the Providence Art Club organized a memorial exhibition of his work. One hundred and one Bannister paintings were displayed, including some works owned by Bliss. Bliss's daughter Helen remembered that on occasion her father would have former Confederate soldiers visiting at his home. He would ask these visitors what they thought about a particular oil painting hung over the fireplace mantel. After they unanimously admired it, Bliss would happily inform them that the painting was created by Bannister, a black man.[45]

In the 1880s, Bannister owned a two-masted sailboat named *Fanchon*. By 1891, Bliss had purchased Bannister's sailboat.[46] Bliss owned *Fanchon*, a gaff rigged yawl of about thirty feet in length, for at least the next twenty-three years. With a wide hull and equipped with sleeping quarters and a galley, it was well suited for long sailing trips. Bliss kept logbooks which show he often sailed from Providence, through Narragansett Bay and into the stretch of the Atlantic Ocean between Sag Harbor, on Long Island, and Martha's Vineyard, Massachusetts. He mentioned trips through Buzzards Bay, Vineyard Bay and Block Island Sound. He recorded many details of his voyages: the names of his passengers, the weather, which sails were set, what ships and people were observed, and the kind and number of fish caught by each person aboard. In later years Bliss apparently employed a crew to attend to the sailing chores; by then he seems to have preferred to concentrate on fishing.[47]

Bliss (left) and man believed to be Bannister aboard *Fanchon*.
Photo ca. 1895, in possession of Bliss's descendants.

A 1914 newspaper article presented a photograph of Bliss aboard *Fanchon* with the headline, "Closes Court to Go Fishing- Judge Must Have Yearly Trip." A cartoon showed someone whispering to the judge that "The tide and wind is right and the squid is runnin' fine." A nimble Judge Bliss is leaping over his bench yelling, "Court's Adjourned, Wow!" The accompanying article stated, "Attorneys arguing for and against a speedy trial of an alleged assault cas[e] had the following opinion handed down: 'I am going on my vacation the first of the week and the wind and tides make it inconvenient for me to hear this case after Monday.'"

Cartoon in 1914 Newspaper article. [48]

Bliss was a very busy man with many responsibilities. For example, in 1892, when he was fifty-five years old, he was Superintendent of Schools in East Providence and one of five members of the School Committee; Chaplain of the Rising Sun Masonic Lodge; Moderator of the East Providence Town Government; and Judge of the Seventh Judicial District Court, which convened in the "New Town building." In addition, he maintained a law practice in the city of Providence and was father to his five children. [49]

In 1897, long after the war ended, Bliss received the Medal of Honor for the action at Waynesboro; his was one of twenty-two such medals awarded to Rhode Island Civil War soldiers and sailors. The official document read, "While in command of the provost guard in the village, he saw the Union lines returning before the attack of a greatly superior force of the enemy, mustered his guard, and, without orders, joined in the defense and charged the enemy without support. He received three saber wounds, his horse was shot, and he was taken prisoner." Bliss proudly wore the medal when he participated in home-town parades.[50]

While Bliss had known the names of two Confederates at Waynesboro, Henry Lee, who had saved his life, and William Moss, whom he had wounded, it was not until much later that he learned the names of the three other men he wounded that day. In March 1902, he received a letter from Robert L. Baber. Baber had "seen in the *Richmond Dispatch* a very interesting war incident, speaking of your wounding at Waynesborough, Virginia, four men with a sabre, and as I received three sabre wounds on my head and believing that you were the man that wounded me, I respectfully request you to send me your photograph." From Baber, Bliss learned the names of the other men he wounded, Hugh Hamilton and Thomas W. Garnett.

Bliss had surrendered his saber when captured. In correspondence with Garnett, who lived in Curdsville, Virginia, he learned what happened to the weapon. "I got your sabre from Thad Sheppard, and carried it the balance of the war, and buried it on my return home after the surrender." Bliss must have asked Garnett to attempt to locate the saber, because in follow-up letters Garnett wrote, "I sent out a scout for the sabre. He reported last night that he had found it. . . I had been advised to get rid of my side-arms, else I might be taken for one of Mosby's scouts. Ten miles from here I hid the sabre under the bottom rail of a fence, near a large white oak tree, thinking at the time that I would go after it after things got quiet, but never did. When Mr. Sheppard moved his fence, his son tells me he found the sabre." "[Sheppard] said I was welcome to the sabre, but if sent to you $5 must be paid for it. I put the sabre under the fence April 11, 1865, and Sheppard found it in 1874. Nine years under the fence had left their marks. The leather on the hilt had rotted off, and the scabbard was nearly eaten up by rust. Sheppard put a wooden hilt on in place of the leather, and used it to kill rats, and cut off a part of the guard to make it handy. There is but one thing about it I can recognize and that is the dent place in the edge, which was in it when I got it." Bliss wrote that "this dent was made by the parrying of the carbine at the time [I] was wounded." The sabre was returned to Bliss thirty-eight years after he lost it, in 1902. He displayed the saber at his home for the rest of his life.[51]

In July 1913, Bliss joined thousands of veterans at the Great Reunion in Gettysburg, Pennsylvania, to celebrate the fiftieth anniversary of the major Civil War battle fought there. He slept, as hundreds did at that event, on a cot in one of the dozens of large tents on the site. He wrote to his wife, "It has been a magnificent time. It was expected there would be many deaths [at the Gettysburg reunion] and 500 coffins had been provided, but only 8 died out of the 53,000 old soldiers who assembled on the old battlefield. There were many flies in Gettysburg but the sanitary arrangements for the old soldiers were perfect and neither flies nor mosquitoes troubled us at all. . . Everybody is happy and satisfied. There never was a better pleasure excursion. I talked for 2 hours July 3[d] with General Munford. . ."[52]

Bliss was proud of his military service and proud too that all his brothers and some of his own sons had served in the military. On the leaf of a book of his exploits he wrote a note to his only grandson, then one year old: "My father had four sons and all bore arms for the Union in our great civil war. In the war with Spain in 1898 two of my sons served in the United States Navy."

Bliss died in August 1928. The front page of the August 30, 1928, *Providence Journal* announced, "Judge Bliss Dead, on Bench 50 Years." A photograph presented a rotund elderly man with a white mustache and beard, with the words, "Judge G. N. Bliss, Hero of Civil War, Half Century Judge of Seventh District Court, Dead in 92nd year." Additional headlines, in ever decreasing type font, cited Bliss's political career, his charge into the Confederates at Waynesboro, Virginia, and his Medal of Honor. The article listed highlights of his life, his membership in the General Assembly "for eight terms," and mentioned his death the evening before "at his home 490 Taunton Avenue, East Providence." He had been in "failing health for several months." The *Journal* highlighted the Revolutionary War role of his great-grandfather, Dr. James Bliss, and Thomas Bliss's part in founding the Newman church in Rehoboth. Bliss's survivors were mentioned; his wife Fannie, his son William, and his daughters, Helen Bliss Emerson, together with her two children, and Rose, who never married. George Bliss was buried at Lakeside Cemetery in East Providence. His wife of fifty-seven years, Fannie, died two years later, in March 1930, at age eighty.[53]

Bliss's Medal of Honor, now in the possession of his descendants.

Appendix

James Bliss's 1858 letter to son George, A sophomore in college

Pawtucket R.I.   Jan. 10, 1858

My Dear George

None but a father can estimate a father's anxiety for the welfare of his children; and especially for his first born. You have now reached a point both in your age and your education which naturally tends to increase this anxiety. I have therefore after much careful thought determined to speak to you in writing in order that I may more fully and concisely express my views and feelings; and that you may be able to understand and consider them more fully than if they were given in conversation.

I need not spent time nor space in telling you of the amount of care, labor and expense which I have undergone that you might enjoy your present position and advantages; and thereby attain a respectable and honorable position in life; your own experience the memories of your whole life render it unnecessary.

You will therefore take what I have to say upon the following important subjects as a proof that my regard for your welfare is in no sense diminished, but rather increased, by the lapse of time.

I shall graduate the points on which I wish to advise you in accordance with the order in which they stand morally.

Let me then ask you to consider first of all, the subject of <u>Recreation</u>. You resolved well, when you determined to preserve as far as possible the tone of your physical health, amidst the dangers of a student's life. But I want you to remember at the same time, that there are dangers and extremes on the other hand. Much, therefore, will depend on the choise [*sic*] which you make with respect to the character of your physical exercise inasmuch as the same end may be reached by different means. Walking, the ordinary sports of the college grounds and such Gymnastic exercises as you may be able to perform constantly and systematically attended to will secure to you that vigorous health which is desirable; at least so far as exercise can secure it.

Hunting and other field sports may be occasionally added with rowing and sailing; but these must all be indulged with great care. They are all of them exercises which have a tendency to develop a passion or love for them without regard to the object for which they are at first admitted, and generally when indulged in demoralize to a greater or less extent the minds and hearts of their full votaries. Shooting and hunting may be well enough even if followed until the practitioner becomes an expert, to a <u>backwoods</u> man a <u>trapper</u> or mountainer but to a professional man, nay to an intellectual man, their value is small indeed. So rowing and the management of a boat may all be well enough for a fisherman or sailor but is of little consequence indeed to the man who has higher and worthier aims. They all of them, also, have a tendency to produce low tastes, loose habits and vulgarity. They are also fruitful sources of temptation to negligence and indifference.

Recreation is sometimes sought in other ways. In books, in conversation and social intercourse and in amusements. Of these you will anticipate my preference for the first three. And if time and space would allow I could give you good reasons for my preference. In a well selected course of recreative reading you will not only be enabled to releive [*sic*] the mind from the effects of the dry and tiresome studies which constitute your college course but you will be enabled to store the mind with knowledge which will please while it profits. An ill read graduate is an educated ignoramus and there are many such. I am exceedingly anxious that you should not swell the number.

<u>Conversation</u> gives polish and power to the educated man who cultivates it to an extent which not every young man is aware. It is also a grand means of obtaining knowledge. <u>Social</u> <u>intercourse</u> not only relieves the mind from the effects of energetic action but softens and refines while it relieves.

Avoid all games of chance as amusements. The influence of the excitement which they produce, is too much like the wear of the mind by study, to make them a means of recreation. And then like the exercises to which I referred as injurious unless guarded, play is apt to engender a passion for play and hence the danger. The attainment of skill in the game, though you play for nothing and therefore think it innocent, will lay you under temptation to gambling which otherwise would never affect you. Let us suppose a case. A young man while at college [h]as become skilled at cards, or Black Gammon, or Billiards; up to this time he has merely played for amusement, but now he is traveling and the time hangs heavy on his hands, he witnesses the games that are being played by professional players or gamblers, he is satisfied he has greater skill than they, and the temptation comes upon him with fearful weight. Or he fails for a short time in realizing profits in his profession, and his consciousness of skill gives him fearful momentum to the temptation. Touch not the dangerous, often wicked, ruinous implements.

Reference to your studies you will of course expect. And what I have to say with respect to your prosecution of them will be condensed into a brief space. I would advise you first of all to consider them as a means not as an end: to explain as a means to the future acquisition of knowledge, and of power in whatever profession you may hereafter engage. This will cloth them with an importance and a dignity which they will not otherwise possess, and will stimulate you to greater earnestness and courage in their pursuit. When you study do it with a will. Be determined to do always, your best. If you cannot be number one in your class get as near to it as possible and all will be well.

Be very careful of your <u>reputation</u>. Multitudes of young men in your present position have made the "mistake of a life time" at this point. Make up your mind that it shall be as perfect as possible in every department and then consider it more valuable to you than life.

There is only one thing which out strips the last in importance and that is <u>Religion</u>. Of this last and most important of human possession I would speak with the carefulness and earnestness which its sacredness and value demand. I fear that though you may at some time have been impressed with a conviction of its importence [*sic*] and may even have cherished a desire for its blessings, you have stopped short of its attainment and are therefore a stranger to its consolations and advantages.

Some of those by whom you are surrounded may affect to dispise [*sic*] it esteeming themselves wiser than ten men who can render a re[a]son and they will perhaps endeavor to influence you in the same direction, but let me advise you to give no heed to their counsels. Their hostility to religion has generally its foundation in their ignorance or their wickedness, and they are generally the men whose example and enjoyments we would be least disposed to follow or share. Distinguish between name and the fact. Between the form and the power, the shadow and the substance. That you may see the importence [*sic*] of this matter let me ask these questions. What is health? What is learning? What is reputation without religion? We need this to make the rest valuable, useful, attractive blessed to ourselves and others.

And now my dear George hoping the importence of the matter will justify the length of this letter, asking you to read it carefully to think upon it seariously [*sic*] I submitted it as the last and highest proof of regard from your affectionate Father.

James L. Bliss
To George N. Bliss

Bliss's Patriotic Speech
December 16, 1861

A few months after joining the army, the twenty-four-year-old Bliss was presented with "a sword, sash and belt" by Masons in his hometown of Pawtucket. The presentation, "to a worthy brother of the Fraternity," was at the Masonic Temple, before "a very large and brilliant gathering of our citizens." The saber was presented by Reverend George Taft, after which Bliss gave the following address:

"Ladies, Gentlemen and Brethren:–To the able and eloquent words of the one so fitly chosen to consummate the wishes of my generous friends, I can reply but feebly and briefly. At a time when the wisdom and experience of years fail, a young man may well shrink from public speaking. Deeds, not words, the ear attentive to command, and the strong right arm to execute, alone recommend him to the consideration of his fellow-men. I need not tell you for what purpose this blade is to be drawn. From earliest times the sword has been the dread sceptre of sovereignty, and the last stern tribunal to decide the fate of nations. But never did the flashing steel leap from its scabbard in a more righteous cause than that which now gives it to the sunlight of truth.

"A government which has within the lifetime of many who still survive, raised us from a few feeble colonies to one of the most powerful nations of the globe–a government under whose auspices the material wealth of the country has more than doubled in the last ten years–a government which has raised the masses of the people to a level of intelligence and education; which may well excite the envy and amazement of Europe; this government so replete with this and other advantages, which, should I here attempt to enumerate, the morning sun would light this hall before I should have finished,–this government a few ambitious and unprincipled men wish to destroy.

"They thought the sons of sires who fought at Lexington, at Bunker Hill and at Yorktown, would offer them no resistance. They fondly dreamed that a race of cowards lived among the bleak hills, and along the rocky shores of New England. Ah! that was a fearful mistake! Could they have foreseen the rushing of thousands, pressing forward to maintain the Constitution and the laws, treason, appalled, would have shrunk back upon herself, and this infamous conspiracy never have seen the light of day. But now, despair gives them courage, and they fight on with the absolute certainty of ultimate defeat, knowing full well that the history of our times will consign them to an immortality of infamy far surpassing that of the wretch who fired the most beautiful Temple of all Greece; for he destroyed only the Temple of a heathen Goddess, but these attempt the destruction of the fair Temple of Liberty, whose lofty dome has long been a shelter to the nations. And, lifted high above these traitors, glowing with increasing lustre as the years roll on, Abraham Lincoln and his illustrious compeers shall live enshrined in the hearts of a grateful people, while history shall record their names among those who, in the hour of peril, did not despair of the Republic. That this sword may in some slight degree aid to accomplish such a result, is the best return I can make my kind friends, and while the blood courses through the channels of life, I pledge this sword to the service of our common country. That country still remains.

"'By that dread name we wave the sword on high,

And swear with her to live, for her to die.'

"But words better become him who taketh his armor off than he who putteth it on. Henceforth this sword must speak for me, and when, amid the sulphurous clouds and red glare of battle, our regiment rushes on the foe, may the inscription on this blade–'Onward to Victory'–be prophetic."[54]

Chapter Notes

Introduction

1   Emerson/Stevens, eds., *"Don't tell father,"* 20.
2   Gallagher, *Civil War*, 153, 184.
3   Lee *Pocket Diary.*
4   Gallagher, *Civil War*, 153, 161, 184.
5   Henry C. Lee to Bliss, January 15th, 1885.

Chapter One

1   Find-a-Grave for Alexander Dixon Payne; Bliss, *Cavalry Service*, 30-32; Stiles, *4th Virginia Cavalry*, 129-30; U.S. Census records for Warrenton, in Fauquier County, Virginia, for 1850-1920.
2   *Annals of the War*, 590-613; obituaries in the *Richmond Times* of March 9, 1893, and the *Richmond Dispatch* of March 9 and 11, 1893.
3   Hopewell, *Black Horse Cavalry*, 477-479, 821-22.
4   Ibid, 477-479.
5   Ibid, 821-22.
6   Find-a-Grave for Alexander Dixon Payne; The *Savannah Republican* of April 29, 1863.
7   The "gallantry at Waynesboro" was Bliss's charge into the Confederate Black Horse Cavalry in September 1864. At the time of the "Hartwood adventure," Bliss described in a letter what happened when he saw the larger Confederate force approaching:

"I had 12 men with me these I formed in single rank across the road facing the enemy (it was a road through woods) soon the head of the column appeared in sight and halted they seemed a little taken aback. Conversation: reb "what regiment is that" U[nion] "advance one" Reb "what regiment is that." U "what regiment is that" Reb. "I ask you that question." U "Advance one," Reb "are you rebels or union," to this last question I answered "Union" with all the vim I could put in my voice and the rebs instantly disappeared; about 5 minutes afterwards 3 soldiers of our Brigade who escaped from the aforesaid column when they went to the right about came down the road to me and told me that the rebs. had driven our men back so I took my 12 men about a mile to a safer location. I sent a Corpl to call in a part of my picket but it was too late and 1 Lt (Lieut [Lothrop B.] Shurtleff), 1 Corpl and 14 of my men were taken prisoners (5 of them from my troop) their names will be published in the Press. I put out just in time to save the remainder of my command. The last man of my little column had scarcely got 50 yards past a double picket I left behind me when the rebels made their appearance, the two men on this post fired their carbines then drew their revolvers and put in two shots apeice [*sic*] more when the rebs disappeared *magna celeritate* ["with great speed"], I guess they thought they had stumbled on a fort. About half an hour later this same post was again attacked and exchanged shots with the enemy, I then drew in three more posts and saw nothing more of the rebs." (Emerson/Stevens, eds., *"Don't tell father,"* 323)

8 Col. Scott's account was like Bliss's, except as to the outcome. Scott wrote that when the Confederates returned with a significant force, the Union commander at once surrendered. Payne was said to have inquired of the commander why he did not attempt to rescue Payne's Union prisoners. The officer replied, "I was only waiting to surrender, for we were all too much excited to see that the greater part of your force were prisoners." *Annals of the War*, 603-604. Only a few of Bliss's men had been captured.

9 In this letter, Bliss learned that his ruse may not have worked, and that he faced a weak force. Interestingly, his daughter, Helen Louise Bliss Emerson, may never have been told of Payne's version of the encounter. She often told her grandchildren about her father's quick thinking that day.

10 John Scott had also written in glowing terms about Bliss's charge into the ranks of the Confederates at Waynesboro (*Annals of the War*, 611). In a newspaper article titled "What is Fame?" undoubtedly written by himself, Bliss related a portion of Scott's article and noted, "[T]his is in accordance with the idea of Byron, that fame is being killed in battle and having your name spelled wrong in the *Gazette*." (Providence *Daily Journal*, March 20, 1879) Bliss had found it amusing that in his article, Scott had incorrectly referred to him as J. A. Bliss.

11 Hugh Hamilton was one of the four Confederates Bliss wounded at Waynesboro. See his letters in Chapter Five.

Chapter Two

1   Emerson/Stevens, eds., *"Don't tell father,"* 121.

2   Ibid, 260-61.

3   Ibid, 145, 246.

4   *Providence Magazine* 29 [August 1917]: 503; clipping from an unknown Providence newspaper ca. March 17, 1915.

5   Farrington was probably referring to *Sabres and Spurs*, a book published in 1876 by the regiment's chaplain, Frederic Denison. On page 208, the author described how the First Cavalry Brigade, commanded by Colonel Duffié, with the second, commanded by Colonel McIntosh, and eight hundred men of the First and Fifth Regulars, and one battery, four days rations and one day's forage, left Morrisville early on March 17, 1863, arriving near the ford at daylight. The advanced guard, consisting of forty men of the Fourth New York and one platoon of the First Rhode Island, under Major Chamberlain, of the First Massachusetts (chief of General Averill's staff), were then ordered to cross the river.

6   Lieut. Simeon A. Brown, a "mechanic," was born in Burrillville, but at the time he enlisted, was living in Douglas, Mass., just over the border of northwestern Rhode Island. Brown was mustered into Company C of the First R.I. Cavalry as a sergeant in the fall of 1861 and was promoted to lieutenant in January 1863. (DMR, Troop C, R.I. State Archives; Emerson, *Town of Douglas*, 118; *Annual Report of Adjutant General 1865*, 375) In the engagement at Kelly's Ford, Brown was selected by Maj. Samuel Chamberlain, the commanding officer, to lead a group of twenty men across the Rappahannock River. Of Brown, Bliss wrote, "Capt. [Lieut.] Brown's horse received two bullets, and three passed through the Lieutenant's clothing." (Bliss, *"Don't Tell Father,"* 122) In his history of the First Massachusetts Cavalry, Benjamin Crowninshield noted that "Almost all the Confederates guarding the ford were killed, wounded, or captured," under Brown's leadership. (Crowninshield, *First Massachusetts Cavalry*, 111) Bliss later asserted, "General Hooker, commander of the Army of the Potomac at that time, sent no thanks to Averell for his services, but he sent a message to Lieut. Brown . . . and thanked him personally for the gallant manner in which he charged across the river at Kelly's Ford and recommended him to be promoted to the rank of Captain. Brown died shortly afterward [i.e., after the war] from disease contracted in the service." (Bliss "Comment" in Meyer, "The Sailor on Horseback," 66-67) Brown was injured at the battle of Middleburg, Virginia the following June.

Second lieutenant Simeon A. Brown (n.d., MOLLUS Mass. Civil War Collection, U.S Army Heritage and Education Center, Carlisle, Penn.)

7   Lieut. James M. Fales, from Warren, R. I., again distinguished himself three months later. He was captured at Middleburg on the morning of June 18 when his saddle came loose as his horse jumped a stone wall and he was thrown to the ground. Fales, sent to Libby Prison, arrived in Richmond on June 23rd; he was not released from captivity until February 1865. In a gripping and vivid account of his imprisonment which was written by George N. Bliss in the first person, as though by Fales alone, Bliss described Fales's "one year, eight months and four days" of captivity in the Confederate South. Fales was one of the prisoners who managed to escape from Libby Prison in February 1864 after some captive Union officers, led by Col. A. D. Straight, dug a tunnel under the prison with makeshift tools. Fales went free for a few days but was re-captured and sent to the "stockade" at Danville, Virginia and then, in June 1864, was selected as one of the Union prisoners to be "put under fire" in Charleston where the Union army was shelling the city. After yellow fever broke out in Charleston, Fales and his fellow prisoners were moved to Columbia, S.C.

Fales also managed to escape from imprisonment at Columbia, with his comrade from the First Rhode Island Cavalry, Edward E. Chase. Although they were aided by African American residents in the area where they escaped, Fales and Chase, who almost died of starvation, wandered about the woods in western N.C. and Tennessee, and were eventually re-captured and returned to a facility in Salisbury, N.C. and then sent to Danville, Va. At Danville, Fales was reunited with his old cammander, Gen. Duffié, who had been taken prisoner at Winchester, Virginia. According to this Bliss/Fales account, the first words that Duffié uttered when he saw Lieut. Fales arrive in Danville, were, "Fale [*sic*] I want to get out of this." In this narrative, Bliss/Fales claim that Fales and his former colonel, "had many talks and planned different ways of escape." On February 16, 1865, Fales and about three hundred other prisoners were sent by "box-cars to Richmond." On the morning of February 22, the Union prisoners were marched to a "rebel steamer," which took them to a landing at "Butler's Dutch Gap Canal," where they spied a "flag-of-truce steamer, with the grand old flag streaming in the breeze," and "a brass band struck up with 'Home Sweet Home.'" Bliss/Fales described that day: "The effect was wonderful; some of the prisoners shouted like lunatics, some cried, some laughed, some lay down and rolled over and over in the dirt." About five men who were exchanged with Fales "had become helpless idiots from their suffering," and though they reached Annapolis the next morning, "six of our comrades had died on the passage." This account ended with these words: "Since my release, I have been a constant sufferer from diseases caused by hardships of prison life, yet, never, in the darkest hours of pain and despair have I for an instant regretted that, in war time, I wore the uniform and discharged as best I could, the duties of a soldier in defence [*sic*] of our common country." (Bliss, *Prison Life of Lieut. James M. Fales*) In a complete printed listing of all six series of "Narratives," George N. Bliss noted, "Lieutenant James M. Fales and I were together when this paper was written. As Comrade Fales told the story of his prison life, I wrote it down as nearly as possible in his own words and then condensed the narrative as much as possible—G. N. Bliss"

8   Charles H. Thayer, born in Franklin, Mass. in 1840, joined Burnside's 1st Rhode Island Regiment in the spring of 1861 and served at the battle of First Bull Run. He enlisted in the First Rhode Island Cavalry in the fall of 1861 and was "put in charge of the training camp [i.e., Camp Hallett] in Cranston, R.I." Thayer was promoted to first lieutenant of Company C in 1862, serving under Bliss; he was promoted to captain of Troop B in February 1863. He was wounded and taken prisoner at the Battle of Kelly's Ford and was sent to Libby Prison; he was exchanged and "honorably discharged" in December 1864. Following the war, Thayer became a dentist and settled in Chicago. (Blake, *History of Franklin*, 187-88; Denison, *Sabres and Spurs*, 497; Andreas, *History of Chicago*, 3:544)

Charles H. Thayer became captain of Troop B in February 1863. When a 1st lieutenant, Thayer was in Bliss's Troop C. (Carte de visite image ca. spring 1863, courtesy of Leo Kennedy)

9   The 6th Regiment Cavalry, Ohio Volunteers was formed in ten counties of northeast and north-central Ohio in 1861. In addition to the action at Kelly's Ford, the regiment participated in the Gettysburg Campaign three months later, fighting at the battles of Brandy Station, Aldie, Middleburg, and Upperville.

10 William W. Averell graduated from West Point in 1855 and had a successful career as a cavalry officer. A natural horseman and leader, for two years starting in the fall of 1862, Averell conducted raids that succeeded in disrupting Confederate communications and supply lines. (Heidler and Heidler, *Encyclopedia*, 149)

11 Colonel (later Brigadier General) Alfred Napoleon Duffié (1833-1880), commanded the First Rhode Island Calvary for a single year but was the regiment's most beloved commander. Born in Paris, Duffié (pronounced Doof-yea) studied at military schools from the age of ten. Commissioned a lieutenant in the French army, he fought in the Crimea, Russia, and Austria and was wounded several times. Duffié came to the United States in 1859 and at the outbreak of the Civil War accepted a captain's commission in the Second New York Cavalry (also known as the Harris Light Cavalry). In July 1862, Governor William Sprague IV appointed Duffié colonel of the First R.I. Cavalry. An inspirational leader, his finest talents were in organization and training of cavalry. Those skills served him well in an army that entered the war with few leaders who possessed them. Duffié's appearance was described as follows: "He is of medium stature, erect form, light frame, nervous temperament, dark complexion, full hazel eyes, black hair, athletic in action, humorous in manner, exact in routine, firm in discipline, and thoroughly accomplished in his profession" (Bliss, *Duffié and the Monument*, 8) Duffié skillfully commanded and trained the cavalrymen of the First Rhode Island, who had suffered from poor leadership since the unit's inception in December, 1861. In addition to his skills as a veteran army officer, Duffié brought endearing personal qualities to his position. While "almost entirely ignorant of the English language," Duffié was inspiring, as shown in a "Special Order" addressed to the regiment on September 27, 1862, which read: "As the character of a nation always depends upon the individual virtues of her citizens, and not upon the splendor of her court or her wealth; so the efficiency of her army depends entirely upon the individual virtue of its soldiers and their constant attention to the minutiae and drill of daily and hourly life, and not upon the splendor of its appointments or its numbers." (Denison, *Sabres and Spurs*, 162; the Special Order was probably translated into fluent English by a clerk or aide.)

Despite his reputation as a strict drillmaster, the new colonel was friendly and approachable. After he undertook the job of Duffié's private secretary in March 1863, Henry A. Cleveland observed, "Col. Duffié, in the selection of his staff officers, fortunately picked as fine and splendid set of fellows as one could wish to be with—jovial, good natured and sociable; but then who could help being jovial, near the lively, jolly little Colonel, who is a host of company in himself." It would be "fun" for his readers to be in camp for a few days, Cleveland penned, "and listen to some of [Duffié's] drolleries—ever ready to see fun going on when professional business is not interfered with." (*Pawtucket Gazette and Chronicle,* April 10, 1863)

In June 1863, Duffié was promoted to brigadier-general and never again commanded the First Rhode Island Cavalry. Reading his final address to his command, one can understand why Duffié was so well regarded by his men: "In bidding farewell to my old regiment, I do so with sentiments of unfeigned pain and grief at being obliged to sever a connection which has been at once my pride and honor to have held from its commencement to this moment, bearing, as it does, no personal unkindness to forgive, no private grief to be assuaged, on my part; and may I be allowed to pleasurable hope of the same immunity from yourselves." Duffié was captured by his nemesis, John Mosby, in late October 1864. He was sent to Libby Prison, and was there at the same time as Bliss, but the two did not meet. Bliss explained why: "[A]n unhealed wound had sent me to the hospital [so] I did not have the pleasure of meeting my old commander." Duffié was soon transferred to Danville, Va., "where he suffered hunger, cold and the nameless evils of a prisoner's life in the Confederacy." While at Danville, Duffié led other prisoners in a desperate effort to escape. The attempt was thwarted after "several brave men" were killed. Duffié was paroled in February 1865. (Bliss, *Duffié and the Monument,* 24, 29-30; Bartlett, *Memoirs of R.I. Officers,* 209-19; Heidler and Heidler, *Encyclopedia,* 623-24)

In 1869, Duffié was appointed American Consul to Cadiz, Spain, at the time an important naval base. Duffié died in November 1880, of "consumption," at the age of forty-seven. Letters reveal that Bliss corresponded with Duffié's widow, Mary A. Duffié, about a plan to construct of a monument in his former commander's honor. In 1889, Mary Duffié and her son Daniel participated in the dedication of the monument in Providence's North Burial Ground. Bliss also assisted Mary Duffié in obtaining a pension for her husband's military service. Bliss later published an affectionate remembrance, *Duffié and the Monument to his Memory.*

**Colonel (later General) Alfred Duffié, commander of the
First Rhode Island Cavalry. Photograph taken in July 1862,
by Timothy H. O'Sullivan. (Library of Congress Prints and
Photographs Division, LC-B811- 644 [P&P] LOT 4191)**

12 In a deposition associated with Bliss's effort to obtain for Farrington a medal of
honor, Farrington wrote, "After my wound was dressed I wrapped a handkerchief
around my neck, went back and took command of the 1st Rhode Island Cavalry
and lead my Regiment in two successful charges against the Rebels on the
afternoon of the same day I was wounded."

13 Nathaniel Bowditch (1836-1863), a captain in the First Massachusetts Cavalry,
was the son of Henry Ingersoll Bowditch, a prominent physician and abolitionist
in Boston. Nathaniel Bowditch grew up in Boston and attended the Lawrence
Scientific School at Harvard where he studied natural science under famed
scientist Louis Agassiz. Bowditch had just embarked on medical studies in
the fall of 1861 when he was commissioned Second Lieutenant in the First
Massachusetts Cavalry. He was promoted to First Lieutenant in October 1862,
and in December 1862, appointed adjutant. He became aide-de-camp to Col.
Duffié the following February. In a memorial volume published in 1865,
Bowditch's father quoted "one of Duffié's staff and also a lieutenant in the
Rhode-Island forces" as proclaiming after Bowditch's death, "[N]othing could
have been more splendid and heart-stirring than the appearance of the Adjutant
[i.e., Nathaniel Bowditch], when the order was given. He was, at that moment,
in advance of our forces. . . . Raising himself erect in his saddle, throwing aloft
his glittering sabre, he called on us to follow, and immediately dashed forward
without a look behind. The speed of the horse, and his own energy, carried
him to the front faster than any of us could follow. In vain did I try to keep

near him; it was impossible. He was seen to unhorse two rebels. I heard one of the privates cry out to his comrades, 'See how Adjutant Bowditch is fighting!'" When Confederates outflanked the Union forces, Bowditch apparently fought on, rather than retreat. His father summarized his son's actions: "It seems that he threw himself fearlessly and resolutely, far in advance of the command he was leading into the enemy's ranks, and found, too late, that there were none to support him. Perceiving himself surrounded, he attempted to cut his way back. At that moment, he received a sabre blow to the head; and he was dragged to the ground by his dying horse, which had been shot under him. He also received a shot in the shoulder. . ." While lying helpless, Bowditch received a "fatal shot through the abdomen." He was examined by two surgeons on the field and told that he was "mortally wounded"; he is said to have responded, "'I have done my duty; I am content.' According to his father's account, after waiting some time alone, lying on the battlefield gravely wounded, Bowditch was rescued by a Union soldier who put him on a horse. He was evacuated to Morrisville in an ambulance, arriving at between ten and eleven o'clock that night. Bowditch spent the night in "the only farmhouse in the place," which had been turned into a field hospital; it was "crowded with the wounded." The next day, he was "carried" back to camp, about twenty miles, in an ambulance. There he was tended by "his faithful mulatto servant, Lewis" and at 11 P.M. Bowditch died. Bowditch was reportedly conscious throughout the day and a half between receiving his fatal wounds and dying. In an extract from a letter to Dr. Bowditch, Capt. Thomas Sherwin lamented: "It is hard, indeed, that, in the first fight [in which] the cavalry has ever been engaged, so glorious a fellow as he should fall." His father's memorial volume has a detailed account of Nathaniel Bowditch's military actions at Kelly's Ford and his death. It also includes letters from Nathaniel Bowditch's military associates, including his colonel ("I send to you the remains of your son. . ."), many condolence letters from noted abolitionists like Harriet Beecher Stowe and Lydia Maria Child, as well as a number of newspaper accounts of the battle of Kelly's Ford, including an account of Bliss's that was published in the *Providence Journal* on March 26, 1863. (Bowditch, *Memorial of Nathaniel Bowditch*; Bowditch's death is also discussed in Faust, *The Republic of Suffering*, 89-90,167-170, 181-82, and 266)

14 Pages 211-12 of Denison's book described the charges led by Major Farrington and Captain John Rogers. "The two forces came together at full speed horse to horse man to man sabre to sabre. What a sight! The conflict was short, determined, deadly. The enemy the famed [J.E.B.] Stuart and his boasted Virginia Cavalry was broken, rolled back, utterly repulsed, with very severe loss. Suitable exultation ran through our ranks; and this charge was pronounced by the general commanding to be one of the most splendid ever made. . . . the victory was complete. . . . The field of battle was an open one, favorable for

cavalry maneuvers; and this is believed to be the first instance in the war when any considerable cavalry force met sabre to sabre in an open field fight."

15 Letter, Bliss to Secretary of War Henry L. Stimson, February 6, 1911, found in Bliss's papers.

16 Affidavit of Leverett C. Stevens, February 14, 1911, found in his Bliss's papers.

17 Letter, Bliss to R.I. Senator George Peabody Wetmore, June 13, 1912, found in Bliss's papers.

18 Farrington to Bliss, June 16, 1912, found in Bliss's papers.

19 Denison, *Sabres and Spurs*, 296-304; obituary of Guild from an unknown Attleboro newspaper found in Bliss's papers.

20 The envelope of this letter was postmarked "Lexington, Ky, Feb 20 7PM [18]85." The written date of 1884 is apparently in error.

21 Sergeant Jeremiah Fitzgerald was from Ireland.

22 U.S. Census records of 1850 and 1860 for District 1, Buckingham County, Virginia, pages 28 and 66, respectively. U.S. Census records of 1870 for Maysville Township, Buckingham County, Virginia, 22.

23 U.S. Census records of 1880 for Maysville Magisterial District, Buckingham County, Virginia, 7; War Department Application for Headstone, O. Q. M. G. Form No. 623, approved April 12, 1933.

24 In an article, Bliss wrote, "Lieut. [Simeon A.] Brown . . . was the first to leap his horse over the abattis, and gallantly did his command follow, but such was the severity of the rebel fire that only three men succeeded in reaching the opposite shore with the gallant Lieutenant." The article continued, "Many horses were shot down in the water, and many a brave rider wounded. The rebels soon left their pits and ran toward the woods, but our boys charged upon them, capturing twenty-five, with their horses and arms." Moss was undoubtedly firing at Lieut. Brown, whose horse received two bullets; Brown had three shots pass through his clothing. (Correspondence of the Journal [G. N. Bliss], "The First Rhode Island Cavalry at the Battle of Kelly's Ford," *Providence Journal*, March 26, 1863)

25 The book Moss mentioned likely was Frederic Denison's, *Sabres and Spurs*, a history of the First Rhode Island Cavalry. Bliss had assisted Denison in writing the book and authored the ten-page chapter, "The Battle of Kelly's Ford." The "paper" Moss mentioned was probably "Reminiscences of Service in the First Rhode Island Cavalry." In its thirty-two pages Bliss detailed the Union version of the battle at Kelly's Ford.

26 Captain James Breckinridge (1837-1865) was a brother of two other Confederate soldiers, Cary and Peachy G. Breckinridge, and nephew to John C. Breckinridge, who had been James Buchannan's vice president from 1856-1860.

27 The battle of Five Forks took place on April 1, 1865. The Union victory there forced the Confederate Army and government to abandon Richmond. Within days, the war came to an end.

28 Marquis, ed., *Who's Who in New England*, 199.

29 Meyer, "The Sailor on Horseback," 28, 30; Crowninshield, *First Massachusetts Cavalry*, 116.

30 See biography of Chamberlain at https://tshaonline.org/handbook/online/articles/fchah (accessed 7/31/21).

31 This was written on stationary with the seal of Massachusetts printed in the top left corner, and the words, "Massachusetts State Prison, Warden's Office." The "book" was likely *Sabres and Spurs*, by Frederic Denison, the 1st R.I. Cavalry's chaplain; the paper was likely Bliss's article, *Reminiscences of Service*, 15-16, which was published the previous year. In it, Bliss described the battle of Kelly's Ford, and mentioned Chamberlain.

32 Chamberlain had been ordered to supervise the crossing of Kelly's Ford. The first attempt to cross was quickly driven back. At that point, Bliss later wrote, "Major Chamberlain of the First Massachusetts Cavalry, a staff officer, came to the First Rhode Island Cavalry and said, 'I want a platoon of men who will go where I tell them.' He was given a platoon of eighteen men, commanded by Lieutenant Simeon Brown, and started with them for the ford. The Major told Lieutenant Brown he wished him to charge across the river and drive the enemy out of the rifle pits, but just as he finished his instructions by saying, 'If you do that it will be a good thing for you,' the Major was himself hit by two rifle bullets, one cutting off the tip of his nose and the other entering his mouth, and taking such a course as finally led to its extraction from between his shoulders." The charge, without the major, was a spectacular success. (Bliss, *Reminiscences of Services*, 15-16)

33 Chamberlain was referring to the cover of Denison's book with crossed sabers pointing down.

34 Just prior to this parenthetical line, Chamberlain had lost control of his pen, making an awkward mark down the page. Apparently, the bullet Chamberlain received at Kelly's Ford had not been removed from near his spine as Bliss had supposed.

Chapter Three

1 1850-1880 U.S. Federal Census materials for Pawtucket, R.I.; Denison, Sabres and Spurs, 519. On the Invalid Reserve Corps, see https://en.wikipedia.org/wiki/Veteran_Reserve_Corps (accessed 7/31/21)

2 This letter is from the George N. Bliss Collection (MSS 298) in the Mary Elizabeth Robinson Research Center at the Rhode Island Historical Society.

3   Surgeon Wilbur was from Westerly, R. I. (Denison, *Sabres and Spurs*, 479). No information on Solomon Yagers has been found.

4   Thomas J. "Stonewall" Jackson was shot accidentally by his own men on May 2, 1863 and died of his wounds on May 10, 1863. Heidler and Heidler, *Encyclopedia of Civil War*, 1065.

5   In a letter to Gerald during the war, Bliss wrote of the incident related here. He remarked, humorously, that the watch that stopped the bullet "ought to have been a bible." (Bliss, *"Don't Tell Father,"* 128)

Chapter Four

1   H. B. McClellan, *The Campaign of Stuart's Cavalry,* 303.

2   Bliss, *"Don't Tell Father,"* 121.

3   Heidler and Heidler, *Encyclopedia*, 623-24); Emerson/Stevens, eds., *"Don't tell tell father,"* 136-41.

4   *A Memorial of John Leverett Thompson of Chicago* (Chicago: The Craig Press, 1890); A.T. Andreas, *History of Chicago*, 2:468-69; Waite, *New Hampshire in the Rebellion*, 545-46; Denison, *Sabres and Spurs*, 33, 101, 273, 337, 475.

5   Ayling, *Register of the Soldiers and Sailors*, 843, 885; *The Maine Bugle*, "A Review of Aldie," by George N. Bliss, April 1894, 130.

6   Ayling, *Register of the Soldiers and Sailors*, 885.

7   Thompson was probably referring to Bliss's planned publication about the battle, published in 1889; it included this letter. Bliss wrote, "I expected to have had the revised paper to which allusion is made in the foregoing letter, but the sudden death of General Thompson, early this year, obliges me to publish this; which, in my opinion, is a graphic picture of what is sometimes called secret history. This gallant officer was, after leaving our regiment, Colonel of the First New Hampshire Cavalry, and Brevet-Brigadier General. G. N. B." (*Bliss, The First Rhode Island Cavalry at Middleburg*, 48-51.)

8   Early on June 17, 1863, orders were received from the Second Brigade, Second Cavalry Division: "Colonel A. N. Duffié, First Rhode Island Cavalry: You will proceed with your regiment from Manassas Junction, by way of Thoroughfare Gap, to Middleburg; there you will camp for the night, and communicate with the headquarters of the Second Cavalry Brigade. From Middleburg you will proceed to Union; thence to Snickersville; from Snickersville to Percyville; thence to Wheatland, and, passing through Waterford, to Nolan's Ferry, where you will join your brigade." Denison, *Sabres and Spurs*, 232.

9   Apparently, it was Frank Allen's advance guard that nearly captured J.E.B. Stuart and staff. Later that evening, Duffie sent Allen to Aldie in a vain attempt to garner reinforcements.

Allen, a clerk, mustered into Troop J of the regiment in October 1861 with a rank of private. He was from Chelsea, Vermont. Allen received a 2nd Lieutenant commission in December 1861 and was eventually named captain of Troop K in January 1863. (DMR, Troop J, R.I. State Archives; Appendix, *R.I. Adjutant General's Report for 1866,* 32) Allen joined the New Hampshire Cavalry in the winter of 1864. (Waite, *New Hampshire in the Rebellion,* 545-46 832)

10 Duffié's report to Joseph Hooker was well received; he was immediately promoted to brigadier general, from the date of the Middleburg affair. Duffié later said, "I get licked like hell and they make me Brig Gen'l." Emerson/Stevens, eds., *"Don't tell father,"* 146.

11 While Robert E. Lee was not in Middleburg at this time, General J.E.B. Stuart was present and was surprised by the unexpected appearance of the 1st R.I. Cavalry.

12 In Chaplain Denison's book, *Sabres and Spurs,* details of the death and destruction at the stone wall that night are given on the pages Farrington indicated.

13 Arnold Wyman, a "Mechanic" from Manchester, N.H., joined the First R.I. Cavalry in October 1861, and was commissioned first lieutenant by the governor of New Hampshire. Wyman was thirty-five at the time of his enlistment. (DMR, Troop L, R.I. State Archives) At the time of the battle at Middleburg, Wyman was a captain. He became major in the First New Hampshire Cavalry when it was formed in January 1864. He was wounded in November 1864, in Middletown, Va., and mustered out of service in July 1865. (Ayling, *Register of the Soldiers and Sailors,* 845)

Captain Arnold Wyman from a carte de visite found in Bliss's papers. Wyman's signature is on the reverse side with the words, "1st N. H. Cavalry, March 1864." By that date, the First R. I. Cavalry's New Hampshire battalion had been detached to form the First New Hampshire Cavalry regiment, and Wyman was appointed major.

14   Edward E. Chase was an 1857 graduate of Providence High School. He was mustered into the First Rhode Island Cavalry as a sergeant-major on December 14, 1861. Chase was promoted to First Lieutenant of Troop E on August 4, 1862, and to captain of Troop H on February 4, 1863. (Spicer, *The High School Boys*, 73) Chase was captain of Troop H when he and some of his men were taken prisoner at Middleburg the night of June 17, 1863. Bliss later noted, "[Major] Farrington mounted his men . . . and attempted to join the regiment; but at this time a mounted force of rebel cavalry had entered the woods, and Captain Chase, after joining his men to a Confederate column, supposing it to be the First Rhode Island Cavalry, did not discover his mistake until called upon to surrender." (Bliss, *First Rhode Island at Middlebury*, 13) Chase was sent to Libby Prison in Richmond, Virginia, and later to Columbia, S.C. where he eventually met up with James Fales, also of the 1st R.I. Cavalry. Both men escaped from imprisonment at Columbia and were eventually re-captured. Chase was exchanged in early 1865, and discharged March 1 of that year. (Dyer, *Annual Report for 1865*, 2:34)

15   Capt. Joseph J. Gould (b. 1840) was from Middletown, R.I. (Rogers, *Representative Men of Rhode Island*, 2: 1395) In May 1861, Gould, who went by his initials "J. J.", enlisted as a private in Company F of the First Rhode Island Volunteers. He was mustered out in August and joined the First Rhode Island Cavalry in December 1861; Gould is recorded as having signed up every man in the original Troop A in which he served as captain until August 27, 1864, when he resigned due to "continued ill health." When Gould left the cavalry unit, Bliss hailed him as the "senior captain" in the regiment, praising Gould's "true patriotism and ardent zeal to perform his whole duty" which had kept him in service "long after he should have been in hospital." (See September 9, 1864, Ulysses report, in Emerson/Stevens, eds., *"Don't tell father,"* 197.) Gould later moved to Philadelphia. (Woodbury, *First Rhode Island Regiment*, 204; DMR, Troop A, R.I. State Archives; Crandall, *Annual Report for 1865*, 391)

16   "Secesh" was a commonly used slang term for "secessionist," referring to the Confederate army, a southern soldier, or a Confederate sympathizer.

17   Otis C. Wyatt, from New Hampshire, was mustered in as a second lieutenant in Company G in August 1862. He was promoted to first lieutenant in January 1963. He resigned in April 1864. (Denison, *Sabers and Spurs*, 526, 533)

18   Farrington brought two officers and twenty-three men through Confederate lines to safety. (*The Maine Bugle*, "A Review of Aldie," by George N. Bliss, April 1894, 130)

19   1913 VMI yearbook, *The Bomb*, 101; Thomas T. Munford to E. W. Nichols, July 23, 1911, Munford Papers, VM.I., as reported in Akers, "Colonel Thomas T. Munford," (hereafter referenced as "Akers"), 2-3, 8-14; 1860 U.S. Census for Northern District, Bedford County, Virginia, 105.

20   Akers, 14-15.

21   https://en.wikipedia.org/wiki/Thomas_T._Munford

22   Akers, 40.

23   Ibid, 115-16; https://en.wikipedia.org/wiki/Thomas_T._Munford

24   Bliss, *Sabre Lost and Found*, 35. Munford's grave marker in Springhill Cemetery, Lynchburg, Virginia.

25   The first five paragraphs of this letter refer to the battle in Waynesboro, Va. in Sept. 1864 (see Chapter Five). These paragraphs were similar to a Munford letter about that battle and have been omitted.

26   Other reports indicate that Gen. Fitz Lee had been stricken with "inflammatory rheumatism." (Akers, 23)

27   The "very inferior force" Munford mentioned was Bliss's 1st R.I. Cavalry, which appeared unexpectedly before Middleburg on June 17.

28   See McClellan, *The Campaign of Stuart's Cavalry*, published in 1885.

29   Throughout his four years of service in the Confederate army, Munford was repeatedly passed over for promotion. Even when the likes of Robert E. Lee and J.E.B. Stuart recommended him for advancement, he was passed over. He believed the army was biased in favor of West Point graduates. (Akers, 21-22)

30   The booklet titled *Prison Life of Lt. James Fales* was written by Bliss. He explained, "Lieut. James M. Fales and I were together when this paper was written. As Comrade Fales told the story of his prison life I wrote it down as nearly as possible in his own words, and then condensed the narrative as much as possible."

31   Munford was clearly miffed by the Wickham situation. He mentioned it again in an 1899 letter. "Gen. Wm. C. Wickham was Colonel of the 4th Virginia Cavalry of the 2nd Brigade Cavalry. I was Senior Colonel. Wickham was elected to Congress. Stuart had endorsed and recommended me to command the Brigade and I was commanding it, but Wickham, being a Congressman-Elect got himself made Brigadier and held both offices and drew the pay of both. I did his work . . ." (Munford to James Longstreet, Feb. 1899, Glen Irving Tucker Papers, Southern Historical Collection, University of North Carolina, as reported in Akers).

32   Krick, *9th Virginia Cavalry*; *The Norfolk Virginian*, Dec. 8, 1895; *The Richmond Times Dispatch*, June 23, 1905.

33   Ibid.

34   This letter was written on stationary with the words, "Wholesale Dealers and Packers of Oysters," printed in large letters across the top of the page, "McCullough's Pier," written in smaller letters immediately below, and the names, "J. J. Phillips, E. M. Henry, W. J. Phillips" along the left side of the page.

35   Henry's captain was Thomas Towson. Before the war Towson was a farmer. He entered service as a lieutenant in April 1861, when the 9th Va. Cavalry was

formed. He was promoted to captain in October 1862. Records indicate that Towson was present at every rollcall until his death at Brandy Station on June 9, 1863.

36   Thomas W. Haynes (1827-1877) was from King & Queen County. He attended the University of Virginia and was a lawyer before the war. Haynes enlisted as a sergeant in Company H of the 9th Va. Cavalry, known as Lee's Rangers, in June 1861. In June of the following year, he was appointed captain of the company. Haynes was wounded at Upperville, Virginia, on June 21, a few days after the Middleburg fight. But according to regiment records, the wound he received that day was not the serious wound Henry mentioned. In October 1863, three months later, Haynes was shot through the body at Manassas, and was disabled for life.

37   At the time of the Middleburg battle, Bliss held the rank of captain. The "major" may have been John L. Thompson. See his letter, above, in this chapter.

Chapter Five

1   Bliss, *Cavalry Service*, 20, 204-10.

2   From *"Don't tell father I have been shot at": The Civil War Letters of Captain George N. Bliss, First Rhode Island Cavalry* © 2018 George N. Bliss. *Edited by* William C. Emerson *with* Elizabeth C. Stevens by permission of McFarland & Company, Inc., Box 611, Jefferson NC 28640. www.mcfarlandbooks.com.

3   Weyer's Cave is about thirteen miles northwest of Waynesboro, Virginia.

4   William B. Wooldridge (ca 1828-1881) joined the Confederate Army as first lieutenant in April 1861, spending his entire four years in the 4th Virginia Cavalry. He received promotion to captain in January 1863, and to major the following fall. At Spotsylvania, May 1864, he was badly wounded, and his left leg was amputated above the knee. Wooldridge survived the ordeal, returned to his unit, was promoted to lieut. colonel and then colonel before the year was out. He then took command of the 4th Va. Cavalry until the war ended. (R. A. Brock, Southern Historical Society Papers, Volume XXXVII, 325-26)

5   On Henry C. Lee, see biography below in this chapter. The letters following his name stood for "Assistant Adjutant and Inspector General."

6   The "ranking officer ordering the charge" was Col Lowell of the 2nd Mass. Cavalry.

7   Despite seeing a great deal of fighting during the Civil War, Thomas T. Munford seemed to genuinely admire Bliss. In a letter not included here, he wrote, "Few men have <u>ever</u> experienced your "fate"! think of it! going through four years of war! In a personal encounter, wounding four men & then visiting their homes! America and Americans! Ours was a <u>Civil</u> War, indeed, but when brave men meet they are ever ready to accend [*sic*] to theirs the same high motives which

govern their own motives, and when a matter is settled it means that it is at an end." (Munford to Bliss, May 8th 1903)

8   Although his letter did not mention it, Munford apparently wished to interrogate Bliss after the battle. Bliss later wrote, "In the forenoon of September 29th, a mounted courier came to the hospital [in the Blue Ridge Mountains] and said he had orders to take me to the headquarters of Gen. Thomas T. Munford, commanding the Confederate force that had attacked us on the preceding day, and that he had a horse for me at the door. I was very weak from loss of blood and told him it would be impossible for me to sit in a saddle, so the messenger returned without me." (Bliss, *Sabre Lost and Found*, 17)

9   U.S. Census records for Buckingham County, Virginia for 1850-1860.

10 Certificate of Death, Commonwealth of Virginia, for Robert Lindsey Baber, dated October 20, 1917; 1938 *Application for Headstone* for Baber; Baber's *Application of Disabled Solder, Sailor or Marine of the late Confederacy*, after 1910 [date obscured] at Virginia State Library and Archives; *Confederate Pension Application*; *1870 U. S. Census for Slate River Township, Buckingham County, Virginia*, 18; U.S. Census records for Buckingham County, Virginia for 1870-1910; Table of Tracts of Land for the Year 1887 for Slate River District, Buckingham, Va.

11 Rock Island is no longer on the Virginia map, but in 1900 Baber was living in Slate River Township, Buckingham County, Virginia, about seventy-five miles west of Richmond. 1900 *U. S. Census for Slate River Township, Buckingham County, Virginia*, 9.

12 Bliss lived in East Providence, R.I. This address, in the neighboring city of Providence, would have found him at his law office at 19 College Street.

13 See William A. Moss's letters in this chapter, below.

14 See Thomas Garnett's letters to Bliss in this chapter, below.

15 Photograph not found. This photograph of Baber, taken from Find-a-Grave, shows him perhaps in his early sixties.

Robert Baber

16 Garnett's *Application of Disabled Solder, Sailor or Marine of the late Confederacy,* April 1916, from Virginia State Library and Archives; *Form 5, Application of a Widow of a Soldier...* pension application by his widow, Ann Garnett, May 1928; 1870 *U. S. Census for Curdsville Township, Buckingham County, Virginia,* 34.

17 Arcanum, Virginia no longer exists as a community. It was in Buckingham County, in the Piedmont region of the state, and was likely near Farmville, a town from which Garnett mentioned mailing a package.

18 See William Moss's letters to Bliss in this chapter and Chapter 3. For Robert Baber, see his letters in this Chapter.

19 Thaddeus D. Sheppard (circa 1846-1881) was from Buckingham County, Virginia. (*Virginia Deaths and Burials, 1853–1912* Index. Family Search, Salt Lake City, Utah, 2010). His listed occupation before and after the war was "farmer." (1860 *U. S. Census for District N. 2, Buckingham County, Virginia,* 73; 1870 *U. S. Census for Curdsville Township, Buckingham County, Virginia,* 13) Sheppard had enlisted in Company K of the 4th Virginia Cavalry in March 1862, at about sixteen years of age. He had been captured at the battle at Kelly's Ford in March 1863 and exchanged the same month. (Stiles, *4th Virginia Cavalry,* 92)

20 See Hugh Hamilton's biography in this chapter, below. Garnett was wrong about Baber's death. He lived another fifteen years.

21 This letter, the first Bliss received from Garnett, was transcribed from Bliss's publication, *How I Lost My Sabre in War and Found it in Peace,* pages 37-38.

22 This is one of only a few letters Bliss wrote to his southern friends that was found in his papers. Baber returned it to Bliss with a note written on the back.

23 This was written on letterhead as follows: "Public School Department, Superintendent's, Office., Town Hall, Taunton Ave., East Providence, R. I." George Bliss's civic activities began in 1866 when he was elected a member of the School Committee of East Providence. He served on the committee for twenty-five years. He was superintendent of schools for thirteen years.

24 At the outbreak of the Spanish-American war in 1898, Bliss's sons William C., age 23, and George M., 21, joined the navy reserves; both served briefly aboard the sailing sloop U.S.S. *Constellation.* George later served on both the *Ajax* and the *Manhattan.* Both were ironclad monitors built during the Civil War.

The USS *Ajax* as she looked in 1898. She was commissioned immediately after the Spanish-American war ended, at which time Bliss's son, George M. Bliss, served aboard.

25 On the back of Bliss's July 21, 1902 letter was a handwritten note, "Mr. Garnett, I don't intend to give the sabre up for less than five dollars July 26th. B F Shepherd"

26 "Capt Moss" was William A. Moss, at the time of the Waynesboro fight a lieutenant in the Confederate cavalry. Bliss wounded Moss before he was captured, and they rode together in a wagon to a field hospital after Bliss, too, was wounded. See Moss's letters to Bliss below in this chapter.

27 Morgan Strother was a farmer before and after the war. He was about forty-two years old at Waynesboro. (1860 and 1870 *U.S. Census for Madison County, Virginia*)

28 On Henry C. Lee, see below in this chapter.

29 Ann and Thomas Garnett resided at 815 Maple Avenue in Waynesboro, a few blocks south of Main Street, where Bliss's charge took place. They lived with their daughter Ann Garnett. (Pension application of Ann E. Garnett upon the death of her husband, Form No. 5, dated 28 May 1928)

30 The Union captain with Bliss was very likely Captain Daniel R. Boice, of Piscataway, N. J., a captain in the Third New Jersey Cavalry. His regiment was often referred to as the "Butterflies," because of their distinctive and very colorful uniforms. (Peter T. Lubrecht, *New Jersey butterfly boys in the Civil War: The Hussars of the Union Army* [Charleston, South Carolina: The History Press, 2011], 130) Boice had been captured later that night and was in Libby Prison when Bliss met him again. Bliss later wrote, "Captain Boice told me that he was

in command of the squadron of the Third New Jersey Cavalry I had led to the charge at Waynesborough; that he wheeled the squadron about and retreated because of a body of the enemy's cavalry on his left." (Bliss, *Sabre Lost and Found*, 28)

31 Per U.S. Census records for Fauquier County, Virginia, 1850-1920.

32 Stiles, *4th Virginia Cavalry*, 114

33 U.S. Census records for Fauquier County, Virginia, 1850-1920.

34 Certificate of Death, Registration District No. 302, Commonwealth of Virginia, 3176

35 Apparently, Bliss had written to check details of his encounter with Moss at Waynesboro. Four years after this letter, Bliss published a paper describing his moments with Moss. He wrote, "Later in the evening [of Sept. 28, 1864] I was put into an ambulance with Captain William A. Moss, (at that time a lieutenant,) and rode several miles to a small house in the mountains. I found Captain Moss to be a brother mason, who did everything possible for my comfort. He had received a bullet-wound from some other soldier in addition to a sabre-cut from me, but happily recovered from his wounds and now lives at Buckingham Court House, Virginia." (Bliss, *Cavalry Service*, 29)

36 At this time, Bliss had three sons, Gerald (1873-1922), William (1874-1965), and George (1876-1908), and one daughter, Helen (1877-1967). It was likely the birth of Helen to which Moss referred.

37 See Henry Lee's letters below in this Chapter. Lee was never a major, his highest rank was captain.

38 Wm. T. Allen of the 1st National Bank of Richmond could not be further identified.

39 Atlantic, Mississippi and Ohio Railroad (AM&O) was formed in 1870 in Virginia from three east-west railroads which traversed across the southern portion of the state. Organized and led by former Confederate general William Mahone (1826-1895), the 428-mile line linked Norfolk with Bristol, Virginia by way of Suffolk, Petersburg, Lynchburg, and Salem.

40 The papers sent were not found.

41 This letter was addressed to Bliss, in care of "Prof. Davis, University of Va." In May 1880, Bliss had taken a trip south to visit his newly acquired southern friends. In Charlottesville, Bliss visited John S. Davis, a doctor who had treated him at the University of Virginia after his capture. He also visited Richmond, and toured Libby Prison, site of his four-month incarceration during the war and met with Henry Lee.

42 Although Bliss obviously did not visit Moss at his home while in the south, Moss did meet up with Bliss. Bliss later wrote that [Moss] had come "one hundred miles from Buckingham Court House to Richmond" to see him.

43 Moss is referring to "apple brandy" he had given Bliss while sharing an ambulance after both were wounded in Waynesboro. See letter Moss's letter of June 21, 1884, below.

44 In 1881, George and Fannie Bliss lost their infant son Carlton to pneumonia.

45 *The Youth's Companion* was an illustrated weekly newspaper, published by the Perry Mason Company in Boston, Massachusetts, from 1827 to 1927. It was the first American publication written for children but evolved into a paper for the whole family, and by 1900 had over 500,000 subscribers. It included short stories (often in installments), poems, and articles on a wide variety of topics. (https://vintageamericanways.com/youths-companion/)

46 About this time, the name of the town was changing from "Waynesborough," to "Waynesboro." In this letter, Moss uses both spellings.

47 Moss's description, together with other sources, identifies the likely location today as in front of 330 West Main Street in the center of Waynesboro.

48 See Henry C. Lee's letters below in this Chapter.

49 The paper lost was likely Bliss's ninety-nine-page booklet, *"Cavalry Service with General Sheridan, and Life in Libby Prison"* In it, Bliss had detailed his charge into the 4th Virginia Cavalry and recounted his interactions with Moss.

50 John Paul (born 1839) was judge of the United States District Court for the Western District of Virginia. Appointed by President Chester Arthur, he served from 1883 until his death in 1901. During the war, Paul had been a captain in the 1st Virginia Cavalry, which, like Moss's 4th Virginia Cavalry, had been part of General Williams C. Wickham's brigade at the time of Bliss's encounter with Moss.

51 The enclosure was an invitation, dated Aug. 30th, 1887, written "To the Survivors of the Fourth Regt. Va. Cavalry," to join a large celebration on Oct. 27, 1887, in Richmond. The event was the laying of the cornerstone for a monument to Robert E. Lee. Generals Joseph E. Johnston, Jubal Early, and Wade Hampton were featured in parades, as were many members of the Lee family, including Bliss's friend, Henry Lee, and his brother Fitzhugh, then governor of the state. Countless representatives from Confederate regiments all over the south, including the Fourth Regt. Va. Cavalry in the invite Bliss received, were present. An oration by Col. Charles Marshall, of Baltimore, was expected, on the subject, "What mean ye by this monument to an enemy of the Union which you teach us to cherish and defend?" John P. Sousa led the Marine Band as it played an arrangement composed for the occasion. (*Richmond Dispatch* of October 27 & 28, 1887) It is not known if Bliss attended the event in Richmond.

52 Moss died of "inflammation of stomach and bowels" at age fifty, two months after this letter was written.

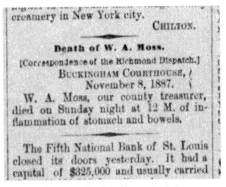

Obituary for William A. Moss

53   By this time, Bliss was no longer involved in state politics in Rhode Island. He was, however, the presiding justice of the Seventh District Court in East Providence.

54   https://en.wikipedia.org/wiki/Fitzhugh_Lee

55   Henry C. Lee Obituary, *Richmond Dispatch*, June 8, 1889

56   Lee *Pocket Diary*

57   By chance, one of these brothers, Daniel Murray Lee, indirectly impacted Bliss's life. Murray Lee served in the Confederate Navy for the entire war, and among other adventures, had participated in a successful night attack upon the USS *Underwriter*. The *Underwriter*, a 325-ton side wheel steamer, measured 186 feet long and thirty-five feet wide, boasted an 800-horsepower engine, two 8-inch guns, a 12-pounder howitzer, and a 30-pounder rifle. On board were twelve officers and seventy-two men, commanded by Acting Master Jacob Westervelt. In the raid, led by John Taylor Wood, grandson of President Zachary Taylor and nephew of President Jefferson Davis, more than three-hundred Confederates in fourteen boats silently approached the ship, rushed aboard, and overwhelmed the crew. By chance, Bliss's close friend, Capt. Edward H. Sears was on the ship. Sears, after having served in the army, had joined the navy and was assistant paymaster on the *Underwriter*. He, along with the rest of the crew, was captured. The Confederates were unable to fire up the boilers of the *Underwriter* before the batteries of Fort Stephenson, a federal fort on the riverbank, opened fire on the vessel. Unable to move the vessel upriver, Wood was forced to burn it. Once away, most of the captured crew were quickly paroled, but not Sears. During the incident, he had thrown the key to the *Underwriter's* safe overboard. As reprisal, the Confederates confined him in Libby Prison, in Richmond. Bliss met with Sears the night he entered Libby Prison in December 1864, ten months after Sears's capture. Sears was to be paroled the next day and agreed to carry letters for Bliss should he wish it. Bliss wrote several that Sears carried out in his boot.

(http://northcarolinahistory.org/encyclopedia/uss-underwriter; Bliss, *Cavalry Service with Sheridan*, 38)

58   *1880 U. S. Federal Census for Abingdon District, Washington County, Virginia,* 29; In the nineteenth century, the C&O railroad employed coal agents to assist mine owners in selling their coal; Lee was a go-between from mine to market. This was advantageous for the C&O because the coal thus sold would be shipped via the railroad and thus revenue generated. Lee was likely located in Richmond because that was the C&O's headquarters city with all its main offices there. He would have been handling coal contracts all over the country, but mainly in the Northeastern and Midwestern portions of the nation, where most C&O coal ended up. After about the turn of the twentieth century, the C&O no longer employed agents, as the business was then large and self-sustaining. (From letter, Thomas W. Dixon, Jr., Chairman & President Emeritus & Chief Historian, C&O Historical Society, to William Emerson, August 25, 2014)

59   Henry C. Lee Obituary, *Richmond Dispatch*, June 8, 1889. See other obits below:

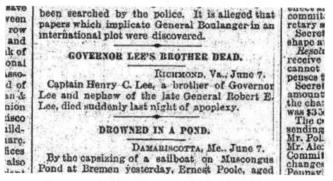

Henry C. Lee's death notice in the
***Richmond Examiner* of June 8, 1889**

ATURDAY, JUNE 8, 1889.

HENRY CARTER LEE.

Sudden Death in This City of a Brother of the Governor.

Captain Henry Carter Lee, brother of Governor Fitzhugh Lee, died suddenly Thursday night at his residence, 318 north Fifth street, of a stroke of apoplexy.

Apparently he was in good health on Wednesday. Thursday morning he was somewhat complaining and took to his bed. No fears as to his condition were entertained, however, until late in the evening, when he became suddenly worse.

Drs. George Ben. Johnston and W. Augustus Lee were called in, and found the patient beyond the reach of medical assistance. Captain Lee continued to sink rapidly, and at 10:30 o'clock expired.

THE DECEASED.

Deceased was forty-seven years of age, and was a son of the late Commodore Sydney Smith Lee. His aged mother lives with the Governor.

Captain Lee leaves four brothers—Governor Fitzhugh Lee; Major John M. Lee, of Richland, Stafford county; Daniel M. Lee, of Fredericksburg; and Robert C. Lee, of Alexandria, now in Scott county.

HIS FAMILY.

Deceased married Miss Sallie B. Johnston, daughter of the late Hon. John W. Johnston, ex-United States senator, and a sister of Dr. George Ben. Johnston. He leaves four children, as follows: Johnston, Sydney Smith, William, and Nannie Mason Lee—the oldest being nineteen and the youngest twelve years of age.

PURSUITS IN LIFE.

Soon after his marriage Captain Lee moved to Fulton, Ga., and engaged in farming, but later returned to Virginia and located at Abingdon, the birthplace of his wife, and followed agricultural pursuits, and subsequently formed an insurance agency in partnership with General Dabney H. Maury. Captain Lee moved to Richmond several years ago, and was for eight years coal agent for the Chesapeake and Ohio railway.

WAR RECORD.

Early in the war the deceased enlisted with the Richmond Howitzers, and was subsequently promoted to a place on General Wickham's staff. He was a brave soldier, and enjoyed the fullest confidence of his commander and associates. In private life he was of a modest and retiring disposition. He had a wide acquaintance throughout the State, and his sudden death will be sad news to his many friends.

THE GOVERNOR INFORMED.

Governor Lee was in Norfolk Thursday, but when his brother was found to be dangerously ill he was telegraphed for and reached the city with Mrs. Lee at 11 o'clock yesterday morning.

MRS. LEE IN MARYLAND.

Captain Lee's wife was in Maryland at the time of her husband's death, having gone there on a visit a little over a week ago. She has been informed by wire and is expected to reach the city at 9 o'clock this morning. The details of the funeral will not be arranged until she arrives, but the interment will take place in Alexandria, probably tomorrow morning.

PALL-BEARERS.

The following gentlemen have been chosen to act as pall-bearers: Messrs. J. C. Dame, Richard E. Frayser, Richard F. Bourne, R. Travers Daniel, Frank D. Hill, Page McCarty, R. D. Corr, and Dr. W. A. Lee,

Brooklyn [N.Y.] *Daily Eagle* of June 7, 1889

60 Lee's Jan. 25, 1879 and Jan. 15, 1885 letters are from the George N. Bliss Collection (MSS 298) in the Mary Elizabeth Robinson Research Center at the Rhode Island Historical Society. All others herein were found among George N. Bliss's papers.

61 Written on "Chesapeake and Ohio Railway" stationary, the names and positions of important officers of the railroad were printed at the top, including "W. C. Wickham, Second Vice-President" and "Henry C. Lee, Special Agent." "Richmond" was lined out and "Abingdon" was written in its place. On page five, Lee had drawn an arrow to Wickham's name writing, "Our general, then in C.S. Congress."

62 On the first page of this stationary, Richmond was crossed out and Abingdon was substituted.

63 This letter was written on stationary of Ford's Hotel, Richmond, Virginia.

64 In the spring of 1880, Bliss journeyed to Virginia and met with many of his ex-Confederate friends. At the time this letter was written, he was visiting Dr. John Staige Davis in Charlottesville, accounting for the address shown.

65 In a memoir published after the war, Bliss identified the "Butterflies" as the Third New Jersey Cavalry; they were "known in the army as the 'Butterflies,' on account of their gay uniforms." He also described how it was he who led the charge of those men. "Colonel [Charles Russell] Lowell said to the officer in command, 'Major, let your first squadron sling their carbines and draw their sabres and charge.' The order was given, 'Forward;' but not a man moved, they were completely disheartened by having seen the other troops driven back. The captain in command of the squadron said, 'Corporal Jones, are you afraid' and the corporal made no reply. The men wavered and Colonel Lowell said, 'Give a cheer boys, and go at them,' and at once, suiting the action to the words, spurred his horse at the gallop towards the enemy, followed by myself, both waving our sabres. The squadron at once cheered and followed. After going a short distance, Colonel Lowell drew out to one side to be ready to send other troops to the support of the squadron, and I was left to lead the charge." (Bliss, *Sabre Lost and Found*, 11)

66 Lee was wounded again later in the war. In an unpublished diary, he noted soon after the April 1, 1865 battle of Five Forks, "I suffered a good deal from the wound recd at Five forks." Details of Lee's wound are not known. (Lee *Pocket Diary*)

67 In Lee's unpublished diary kept near the end of the war, he penned details of the harrowing days during and after the retreat from Richmond, Robert E. Lee's surrender at Appomattox, and the loss of his beloved horse "Pip." "April 8th [1865] About 2 a.m. moved in rear of infantry to Appomattox, C. H. not pressed much. March[ed] all day, & until very late at night. Gnr Lee joined me-I was extremely fatigued, & nearly starved. April 9th moved through the C. H. flanked the enemy, got no [on] the Lynchburg Road, followed Rosser['s] div[ision]. Rest of the Army entirely surrounded, surrendered. Withdrew before the flag of truce came in, our skirmish line I expect was captured, as they could not withdraw in time. Met Bob Lee at Concord Depot. Went to Lynchburg and camped about nine P. M. April 10th Went to gen Munford[']s- slept nearly all day- Returned very early. April 11th Left gen Munford passed through Liberty & there heard of the destruction of the wagon train, the loss of Danville [Jefferson Davis had temporarily moved the Confederate capitol to Danville on April 3rd], the impressment of 'Pip' by the artillery at Appomattox C. H. the loss of my boy Wilson." (Lee *Pocket Diary*)

68 Bliss included this letter, with numerous minor alterations, in a story published after the war. (Bliss, *Sabre Lost and Found*, 58-65)

69 The initials "A. A. & I. G. - P. A. C. S." stand for "Assistant Adjutant and Inspector General Provisional Army of the Confederate States." The Provisional Army of the Confederate States served as the "regular" army, compared to "volunteers." (Per correspondence with Michael Shaffer, Assistant Director/ Lecturer at The Civil War Center, Kennesaw State University, Department of History and Philosophy.)

70 This letter was written on Chesapeake and Ohio Railway stationary.

71 The "book" may be the booklet Bliss published in 1884 entitled, *Cavalry Service with General Sheridan and Life in Libby Prison*. In an Appendix Bliss had included Lee's letter dated July 20, 1884, the letter Lee thought might have been "shorter."

72 The booklet had the following note: "Edition limited to two hundred and fifty copies."

73 In his booklet, Bliss described the abuse he received after he surrendered to the Confederates, which nearly led to his death. He also described being robbed by several of the enemy while in captivity. These passages may be what Lee was complaining of in his comment, "You give a pretty bad account of your treatment."

74 "Capt. Addiman" is likely Bliss friend and law partner, Joshua M. Addeman, who apparently made a visit south. Addeman was born in 1840 in New Zealand to Australian parents. They made a six-month voyage on a whaling vessel and arrived in Providence, Rhode Island, in 1843. Addeman attended Providence public schools and was an 1862 graduate of Brown University. At the end of his senior year, he enlisted as a private in the 10th Rhode Island Infantry, Co. B., for three months service in Maryland and Virginia. He later joined the 14th Rhode Island Heavy Artillery, the state's only regiment of African American soldiers, and was soon promoted to captain.

After the war Addeman took up the profession of law. Also involved in government, he was Rhode Island's Secretary of State from 1872-1887. For at least fifteen years (1869-1884), he and Bliss were law partners. Their firm, Bliss & Addeman, was in the Woods' New Building, at No. 2 College Street, in Providence.

75 Letter written on stationary with the logo of the state of Virginia, and the words, "Commonwealth of Virginia, OFFICE OF THE AUDITOR OF PUBLIC ACCOUNTS." It is not known if Lee ever worked for the Commonwealth of Virginia.

76 Lee is referring to the *Richmond Whig*, and to Senator William Mahone, whose name he spelled "Mahane" and also correctly. One newspaper referred to the *Richmond Whig* as "Senator Mahone's personal organ . . ." (*Shenandoah Herald*,

April 19, 1882) Mahone (1832-1895) had a spectacular career in railroads, both before and after the Civil War. As a general in the Confederate army, his counterattack during the Battle of the Crater, in July 1864, turned near defeat to a spectacular Confederate victory. After the war, he entered politics, and was representing Virginia in the U. S. Senate when this letter was written. His willingness to caucus with Republicans cost him support from the white electorate, as did his relatively lenient treatment of African Americans. His legacy has largely been erased from Virginia history. (https://www.encyclopediavirginia. org/Mahone_William_1826-1895#start_entry, accessed April 2019)

77 The financial difficulties Lee and Bliss apparently were enduring were likely what is referred to as the "Panic of 1884," a major economic event during the long recession of 1882 to 1885. The panic created a credit shortage that led to a significant economic decline in the United States. The shortage turned a recession into a depression, with a nearly 33 percent decline in economic activity. (https://en.wikipedia.org/wiki/Depression_of_1882%E2%80%9385; https://en.wikipedia.org/wiki/Panic_of_1884, both accessed April, 2019)

78 The article Bliss apparently sent Lee has not been discovered. When found in Bliss's papers, the envelope of this letter contained the following enclosure:

EDITOR McCLURE of the Philadelphia Times finds a good many more colored officials in the South than in the North. He finds colored Democratic members of the South Carolina Legislature, "nominated and elected mainly by white votes," and colored policemen in Mobile and New Orleans. We have also seen them in Charleston. He moralizes thus: "Pennsylvania and Philadelphia, where the black voters hold the balance of power in both city and state, could not elect a colored man to the Legislature, or to any other honorable or lucrative office, in the strongest Republican district; but South Carolina Democrats elect him to office, with all the lingering prejudices of the relation of master and slave."

79 An article by ex-Confederate General Thomas T. Munford appeared in the *Southern Historical Society Papers* of 1884. It was titled "Reminiscences of Cavalry Operations," with sub-title, "Battle of Winchester, September 19th, '64." Late in his article, Munford described Bliss's charge into the Confederate cavalry and noted, "[A] Federal officer, who fell into my hands, behaved with such conspicuous gallantry . . . I take pleasure in making a note of it." Bliss later rectified errors in Munford's account; his note, titled "A Correction of General

Munford," appeared in issue XIII of the publication. (Jones, *Southern Historical Society Papers*, 427-430, 447-459, 575)

80 Several articles were published in Richmond papers discussing a proposal to dismantle Libby Prison and reconstruct it as a tourist attraction in Chicago. For instance, an article titled "Libby Prison Sale" appeared in the January 15, 1888 edition of the *Richmond Dispatch*. Included in the article was a letter from a former Union officer who had been a prisoner there. "I must confess the proposition startled me, particularly when it was stated that the building was to be used for a 'curiosity-shop'—a public show. The proposition is too monstrous, the purpose too base and sordid, to be calmly considered." In 1889, the building was dismantled and reconstructed in Chicago and was called the Libby Prison War Museum. Its doors were open until 1899. (Reprint of Official Publication #12, Richmond Civil War Centennial Committee, 1961- 1965, no copyright claimed; original compiled by R. W. Wiatt, Jr.)

81 This was the last known communication between Lee and Bliss. Henry C. Lee died suddenly sixteen months after he sent this letter. Lee's death notice appeared in the *Richmond Examiner* of June 8, 1889. His passing was noted in newspapers around the country, including the *Brooklyn NY Daily Eagle* of June 7, 1889.

82 Bliss rewrote Payne's document, with minor corrections of fact, clarified several sentences, and apparently sent it back to Payne for his approval. Someone, probably Payne, also added the first names of some individuals. Bliss published the rewritten version in his 1903 paper, "*How I lost my Sabre in War and Found it in Peace.*" Payne's letter and two handwritten versions of his "narrative" were found in Bliss's papers.

Chapter Six

1 Jordan, *Charlottesville in the Civil War*, 46; Bliss, *Sabre Lost and Found*, 17-18

2 Ibid.

3 Jordan, *Charlottesville in the Civil War*; Discussion with John Staige Davis IV, at his home in Charlottesville, October 27, 2006; Catalogue of Students, for the Thirty-seventh Session–1860-61, University of Virginia, 5; Editorial Committee, *Alumni Bulletin of the University of Virginia*, (Charlottesville, Va.: University of Virginia Press, Volume 7, Issues 1-5, 1914), 35-37; 84

4 Two obituaries for Davis's son, John S. Davis Jr., from unknown newspapers, found in Bliss's papers; Find-a-Grave; Catalogue of Students, for the Thirty-seventh Session–1860-61, University of Virginia, 5. See detailed biography at https://www.encyclopediavirginia.org/entries/ Davis_John_Staige_1824-1885 (accessed 1/22/22).

5   Despite being a prisoner, Confederate personnel at the hospital in Charlottesville apparently had a high opinion of Bliss. He wrote a friend, "I was very kindly treated in the hospital and found myself on exhibition as 'the bravest Yank you ever saw,' I began to think myself one of the most remarkable heroes of modern times, but have now so far recovered as to look on the ground occasionally and talk with my fellow victims as though I was an ordinary mortal." (Emerson/Stevens, eds., *"Don't tell father,"* 209)

6   Davis was apparently referring to his brother, Eugene (1822-1894), a Confederate officer who had graduated from the University of Virginia. Davis was a lawyer and farmer in Charlottesville. He had been captain of Company K, 2nd Virginia Cavalry. He was captured late in the war, likely at the battle of Yellow Tavern, which occurred in May 1864. After the war, he was mayor of Charlottesville. (National Park Service, *Soldiers and Sailors Database.* Accessed Feb. 2018)

7   Samuel D. Moses had studied under Davis at the University of Virginia in the 1862-63 session. Three months before this letter, Bliss had received a letter from Moses. Writing from Exeter, New Hampshire, Moses wrote, "[I]t has occurred to me that a few lines would be gladly received by you from one, for whom, I had every reason to believe, you formed some attachment during your stay in Charlottesville, Va." Moses noted the "very different circumstances . . . surrounding us both now, but such are the fortunes of war."

Chapter Seven

1   Bliss, *Cavalry Service*, 30-32

2   Emerson/Stevens, eds., *"Don't tell father,"* 212-13

3   Ibid, 212-13; Bliss, *Sabre Lost and Found*, 22-23

4   Emerson/Stevens, eds., *"Don't tell father,"* 216, 285

5   https://en.wikipedia.org/wiki/Henry_Sweetser_Burrage; Committee of the Regiment, *History of the Thirty-Sixth Regiment, Massachusetts Volunteers, 1862-1865* (Boston: Press of Rockwell and Churchill, 1884), 194-95, 256; "Henry S. Burrage," in Burrage, *Brown in the Civil War*, 248-49

6   Ibid, 274-75

7   Ibid, 322

8   https://en.wikipedia.org/wiki/Henry_Sweetser_Burrage

9   In 1884, Bliss published an account of his time in Libby Prison and his selection as a hostage. It was entitled, *Cavalry Service with Sheridan and Life in Libby Prison.*

10   Major Thomas P. Turner was the "commandant" of Libby Prison. He was a rigid disciplinarian and intensely disliked by the prisoners. After the war, unlike most soldiers, Confederate jailers were barred from seeking amnesty. Turner was imprisoned for more than a year, much of the time in basement cells in Libby,

undoubtedly the same cells that Bliss and the other hostages had occupied. He was eventually released due to lack of sufficient evidence. (Byrne, "Libby Prison," *Journal of Southern History*, 24 [1958]: 430–443; Official Records, ser. 2, vol. VIII, 28–29, 26)

11 Robert Ould was Confederate commissioner for exchange of prisoners (Bliss, *Sabre Lost*, 55)

12 Bliss undoubtedly had sent Burrage his newly published booklet titled, "*Cavalry Service with General Sheridan and Life in Libby Prison.*"

13 The John Carter Brown Library is an independently administered and funded center for advanced research in history and the humanities, founded in 1846 and located at Brown University since 1901.

Chapter Eight

1 Bliss, *Sabre Lost*, 5; Adams, *Fall River* Directory; Bliss's obituary, *Providence Journal*, August 30, 1928; James L. and Sarah A. Bliss grave markers in Walnut Hill Cemetery, Pawtucket, R.I,; James Bliss obituaries in circa May 1, 1882 Providence newspapers, found in Bliss's papers; James Bliss, in J. Homer Bliss, *Genealogy of the Bliss Family*, 33. Dr. James Bliss and Capt. Jonathan Bliss in Johnston, *Daughters of American Revolution*, 100, 101, 106.

2 Stephen Stafford U. S. Census records at Tiverton, R. I. for 1790 (page 370), 1800 (63), 1810 (176), and 1820 (213); Military record and life dates for Stephen Stafford are from *U.S., Headstone Applications for Military Veterans, 1925-1963*, for descendant Robert T. Scott, Oct. 21, 1953; Abigail Stafford in Application to *Sons of the American Revolution* for David Lee Farnum, National number 97316, Sept. 18, 1968.

3 Tax records for thirty-eight-year-old James Bliss show a well-established tailor in Fall River. In 1850 he had $2200 in business real estate, with "Cloth Silk & Linen" valued at $5500. The business generated $8800 a year in "Annual Product" of "Pants & Vests," and "Coats." (*Schedule 5, Products of Industry in Fall River, in the County of Bristol, State of Massachusetts, for the year ending June 1, 1850*, 311.) James Bliss is listed in the first directory for the city as "merchant tailor," and was one of nine "Clothing and Furnishing Goods" merchants listed. (1853 *Fall River Directory*, 39, 103). Fenner, *History of Fall River*, 1, 3, 5, 22, 68, 76, 80, 96-98; Life dates for Charles, James, Jr., Caroline, and Mary Bliss are located in the James L. Bliss family plot at Walnut Hill Cemetery, Pawtucket, R. I. Life dates for Jerome Bliss in North Burial Ground Cemetery, Providence, R. I.; for Joanne (Bliss) Estes, life dates are at Oak Grove Cemetery, Fall River, Mass., plot OG5157; 1853 *Fall River Directory*, 110. Sarah Bliss's older sister, Patience Stafford (1792-1880), fifty-four years old, was living with the James Bliss family in 1850. She resided with the Bliss's much of the remainder of her

life, and is buried in the James Bliss plot in Walnut Hill Cemetery, in Pawtucket, R. I.

4   Hudson, *Factory Inspection* 7-8; City Council, *City of Fall River*: 258-263.

5   *Sabre Lost and Found*, 5; Robert Grieve, *An Illustrated History of Pawtucket, Central Falls and Vicinity, A Narrative of the Growth and Evolution of the Community* (Pawtuckel, R. I.: *Pawtucket Gazette and Chronicle*, 1897), 126; Pawtucket, *Past and Present* (Boston, Mass.: Walton Advertising & Printing, Co., 1917), 12.

6   Over the decades, James Bliss's house number on Cottage Street changed (at various times it was 33, 38 and 110). It is not clear if the family moved, or the house numbers were changed. Details regarding Pawtucket streets and buildings from a map by O. H. Bailey and J. C. Hazen, *Bird's Eye View of Pawtucket, & Central Falls, R. I.* (Boston: J. K. Nauber & Co., 1877). House numbers on Cottage Street are from Harold H. Richards, *Richards Standard Atlas of the Providence Metropolitan District* (Springfield, Mass.: Richards Map Co., 1917), Bol. 2: *Plate 21*. Population figures from 1850 *U. S. Census for Pawtucket*, 740. On the attack on James Bliss, see his obituary, *Pawtucket Chronicle and Gazette*, May 5, 1882.

7   James Bliss's financial condition and household occupants are from the 1860 *U. S. Census for the Town of Pawtucket, Mass.*, 83. McDermaid must have become an integral part of the Bliss family, staying in the household until her death in 1894. She is buried in the family plot at nearby Walnut Hill Cemetery, and her headstone is similar to that of other family members.

8   For University Grammar School, see *Catalogue University Grammar School*, 16, 22, 38; and Anonymous, *History of the State* 253 - 83. On early Pawtucket transportation, see Grieve, *An Illustrated History*, 120.

9   On Brown University, see Bates, *Historical Catalogue*, 115, 466; *Officers and Students of Brown, 1856-57*, 15-18, 21; *Officers and Students of Brown, 1857-58*, 13-14; and *Providence Directory for 1860*, 203. On Bliss's departure from Brown, see Bliss, *Sabre Lost and Found*, 6; Rogers, *Representative Men*, 556; and letter from James L. Bliss found in Bliss's papers, dated January 10, 1858, in the Appendix.

10 See *Union College, A Record*, 48, 59.

11 Both Bliss and Gerald are listed as graduates in Union University in its *Centennial Catalog*. For details on Bliss's and Gerald's class at Albany Law School, see *Circular and Catalogue*, 6- 7, 10, 11, 15-16.

12 On Peckham, see 1860 *U. S. Census for 2nd Ward Providence City*, 90, and 1861 *Providence Directory* (Providence: Adams, Sampson & Co., 1861), 119.

13 Bliss described his early days in the regiment in Bliss, *Sabre Lost and Found*, 6. The date of his promotion to second lieutenant is from his commissioning document, found in his papers. On the New Hampshire battalion, see Waite,

New Hampshire in the Rebellion, 545-46; Rogers, *Biographical Cyclopedia*, 556; and Denison, *Sabres and Spurs*, 26, 30-32. Following the end of the war, the regiment mustered out (disbanded) on August 3, 1865. At that time, the regiment numbered just thirteen officers and three hundred sixty-five men (Denison *Sabres and Spurs*, 463).

14 Details of the training operations are in Denison, *Sabres and Spurs*, 29-32.

15 On the Masonic Order, see Roberts, *House Undivided*, 9. Perhaps James, himself a Mason, understood what his son would later relate in a wartime letter (Sept. 27, 1864), "Dave, this Masonic tie is the strongest thing between man and man in this whole world, the most bitter rebel when I make the Masonic sign is at once my friend and will protect me even at the risk of his own life." (Emerson/ Stevens, eds., *"Don't tell father,"* 202) James Bliss's wisdom proved sound; at one point in the war, the Masonic connection undoubtedly saved George Bliss's life. Bliss's speech was published in the *Providence Evening Press* of December 17. A copy of the article was found in Bliss's papers. The full speech is presented in the Appendix.

16 Details of the trip to Washington are in Denison, *Sabres and Spurs,* 30-31, 40-42.

17 Bliss gave his weight in his Oct. 6, 1862, wartime letter to Gerald (Emerson/ Stevens, eds., *"Don't tell father,"* 90). His height and weight in later years were recorded on a form dated in 1913. He had a close-cropped beard and moustache and an unusual physical oddity of which he was proud, now known as "syndactyly." The separation between his second and third toes, on at least one of his feet, was not complete. While the joints worked properly, flesh connected these toes nearly to the last joint. An inherited trait, it was known in his family as "Bliss toes," and has been passed down through three Bliss generations. Both his great-grandchildren Sandy King and Bill Emerson have "Bliss toes."

18 Bliss's description of Washington in his March 18,1862, wartime letter. (Emerson/Stevens, eds., *"Don't tell father,"* 13-14)

19 The movement into Virginia is discussed in Denison, *Sabres and Spurs,* 54-61. He mentioned being shot at in his wartime letter of June 11, 1862 (Emerson/ Stevens, eds., *"Don't tell father,"* 52-53).

20 The arrival of Duffié is detailed in Denison, *Sabres and Spurs,* 99-111. On Duffié, see Note 11 in Chapter Two. Bliss later memorialized Duffié in a booklet called, *Duffié and the Monument to his Memory.*

21 For a list of Bliss's engagements, see Rogers, *Biographical Cyclopedia,* 556-57.

22 See Rogers, *Biographical Cyclopedia,* 556-57.

23 Bliss's leave is documented in his military records, now in the National Archives. "Special Orders, No. 75," from the War Department, was dated February 15, 1865. It stated, "Leave of absence is hereby granted the following officers: Captain George N. Bliss, 1st Rhode Island Cavalry, a paroled Prisoner of War,

for thirty Days." The order was signed by E. D. Townsend, Assistant Adjutant General.

24 See Bliss's wartime letter of May 14, 1865 (Emerson/Stevens, eds., *"Don't tell father,"* 227-28), and Bliss, *Sabre Lost and Found*, 33. Also see 1865 *Rhode Island Census for Pawtucket Rhode Island*, 162-63.

25 An article titled "Judge Bliss Retires," appeared in an unknown Providence newspaper on December 22, 1922. It incorrectly stated that the law firm Bliss joined immediately after the war as "Miner and Roelker." By 1865, Miner's law firm was "Miner and Gerald," and no Roelker was listed in the Directory. (1865 *Providence City Directory* [Providence: Adams, Simpson & Co., 1865], 114, 137.) The law firm Bliss joined was undoubtedly "Miner and Gerald." Bliss mentioned the editorial job in a letter written April 24, 1880, to R. W. Bettersby, Esq., local editor of the Virginia newspaper *Farmville Mercury*, who published it (article found in Bliss papers). Bliss had written, "Among my youthful indiscretions I discharged, for two years after the war, the duties of local editor of a daily newspaper. . ." Another source wrote that George Bliss "was for several years editor of the *Morning Herald*, a daily paper published at Providence." (Bliss, *Genealogy of the Bliss Family* 3:1147)

26 Although the 1868 *Providence Directory* listed Bliss as still living in Pawtucket, he had surely moved to East Providence by then. Bliss addressed a letter from East Providence on Oct. 8, 1865, and he was chosen for the East Providence School Committee in 1866, indicating that by that year he would have been a resident of the town. Bliss ran for state office in 1868 representing East Providence, (Providence: Simpson, Davenport & Co., 1868) 30, 309. The 1869 *Providence Directory* (Providence: Simpson, Davenport & Co., 1869), 31, lists Bliss's residence as "East Providence."

27 Three men were named as officers at the Rhode Island Democratic Convention. Bliss was one of two "Secretaries." (*Philadelphia Inquirer*, March 22, 1866) His seven nominations for state attorney general, running as a Democrat, were reported widely. See, for instance, *New York Tribune*, March 15, 1867; *New York Herald*, March 12, 1868, March 25, 1869, and March 19, 1873; *Troy (N. Y.) Daily Times*, March 18, 1870; *Troy (N. Y.) Daily Whig*, April 8, 1871; *Syracuse (N. Y.) Daily Standard*, March 21, 1872. In the 1872 election, Bliss ran against Willard Sayles, a Republican, who had once been lieutenant colonel of Bliss's regiment. The vote count was, "Sayles.....7918; Bliss.....5357." J. F. Cleveland, compiler, *The (N. Y.) Tribune Almanac and Political Register for 1872* (New York, N. Y.: The Tribune Association, 1872), 57.

28 Information from Bliss's obituary in the *Providence Journal* of Aug. 30, 1928.

29 From the *Pawtucket Chronicle and Gazette*, Oct. 16, 1868, and Oct. 23, 1868.

30 Bliss was invited to the "Public Opening and Inspection" of the new Bliss School in a letter from J. R. D. Oldham, Superintendent of Public Schools in East Providence, dated January 23, 1923. This letter was found among Bliss's papers.

31 1867 *Providence City Directory* (Providence: Simpson, Davenport & Co., 1867), 30.

32 Per letter from Mrs. E. R. Ledford to Bliss, October 25, 1862 (George N. Bliss Collection [MSS 298], Mary Elizabeth Robinson Research Center at the Rhode Island Historical Society)

33 George Bliss to Gerald, August 21 and 25, 1862 (Emerson/Stevens, eds., *"Don't tell father,"* 78-82)

34 Rogers, ed., *Biographical Cyclopedia,* 556; Buffalo *Courier & Republic* newspaper, March 21, 1870; 1870 *Providence Directory* (Providence: Simpson, Davenport & Co., 1870), 363. The party change is reflected in a November 1922 article from an unknown newspaper, titled, "Judge Bliss Retires," found in Bliss's papers. "Judge Bliss's attitude toward resigning his post has been causing the Republican leaders of this State some concern during the past several months. Had he not offered his resignation to the Governor before Jan. 2, it would have to be tendered to Gov.-elect William S. Flynn, a Democrat, who would then have an opportunity to appoint a Democrat to the post. . ."

35 In its October 30, 1868 edition, the *Pawtucket Gazette and Chronicle* reported, "Masonic.–The annual meeting of Pawtucket Royal Arch Chapter for the election of officers was held on Wednesday evening last, when the following named gentlemen were chosen and installed...King–George N. Bliss." Information on the laying of the temple cornerstone is from the Providence, R. I. *Sunday Tribune* of Oct. 26, 1924. History of the Masonic Lodge in East Providence was obtained by William Emerson in personal communications with John Lawson III, Secretary of Rising Sun Lodge #30, in May 2013.

36 Life details for "Mrs. Fannie Bliss" are from an obituary in the *Evening Bulletin,* Providence, March 26, 1930. In January 31, 1919, Fannie Bliss filled out a Mount Holyoke alumnus questionnaire. In it she wrote, "Although in Mt. Holyoke female Seminary but a year its influence has followed me through all my life. May God bless the college abundantly in the years to come." Five years later, January 6, 1924, she wrote, "George Bliss, 86, has dropped out of various clubs. Was District Judge of East Providence for over 40 years. Retired a year ago. Is in fairly good health for a man of his years. Does not use glasses to read or write." (Per researcher Helen Tuttle's report to Mary Emerson Sweet, Bliss's granddaughter, in 1992. In her report, Tuttle added a personal recollection as well; "I remember [when about eight years old] calling on Cousin Fanny with my mother and grandmother. [I was] a bit afraid or in awe of your grandfather.") George Bliss's obituary, in the *Providence Journal* of Aug. 30, 1928, refers to his church as the "Union Congregational Church." This was undoubtedly a

misprint. The minister who presided at Bliss's funeral was from the United Congregational Church, which was also the church Bliss's wife attended. This church was located at "North Broadway, near Broadway, Six Corners" in East Providence. (1892-93 *East Providence City Directory*, 118).

37 Carpenter's party affiliation was mentioned in his obituary in the *Providence Journal*, July 21, 1879. A newspaper for April 1, 1868, reported, "[T]he official count disclosed the following result: For Governor–Lymon Pierce 186; Burnside 70. . . For Representative–George N. Bliss 152; William A. Carpenter 59; Henry H. Ide 48. Edward Pearce and George N. Bliss were officially declared to be elected." The news clipping, from an unknown Providence paper was found in Bliss's papers. David V. Gerald was mentioned as having assisted Bliss in correcting an irregularity with the ballots.

38 The "Carpenter Estate and Bliss acreage" is found in *Atlas of the Providence Metropolitan District Volume 2* (Springfield Mass.: Richards Map Co., 1917), plate 10. Family anecdotes described Bliss's house as first being lighted with kerosene lanterns. Bliss's daughter Helen remembered that as a young girl one of her chores was having to "trim" the wicks. Bliss converted to gas lights, perhaps in the 1890's, with the piping visible along the walls within the house. Eventually he shifted to electric lighting, about 1910, and the wiring was fitted into the existing gas pipes. According to Bliss's granddaughter, Mary Emerson Sweet, who lived at 490 Taunton Ave. in 1920, her mother remembered using an outhouse as a young girl. Eventually Bliss added a "tank room" in the attic. Water was pumped up by hand to provide water pressure for toilets. Sweet indicated that William Carpenter's property was part of a very large parcel of "Carpenter" property from the 1600s. Carpenter had acquired the property from his father, Otis Carpenter, who had divided the property among his sons. Otis Carpenter's house was just east of William Carpenter's, on Taunton Ave. at the corner of Pawtucket Ave.

39 Life dates for most people mentioned are from William A. Carpenter's family grave marker (lots 379 & 390) in Lakeside Cemetery in East Providence. Life dates for Carlton are from 1880 *U. S. Census for the Town of East Providence*, 8, information from Bliss's granddaughter, Mary Emerson Sweet, and the *Providence Journal* of August 30, 1928.

40 Information regarding Bliss is from a November 1922 newspaper article titled, "Judge Bliss Retires," found in Bliss's papers, and William Emerson's personal discussions, circa 1955, with Helen L. Bliss Emerson. In August 1917, a newspaper reported on what may have been a typical case in Bliss's courtroom. A man accused of driving while intoxicated pleaded guilty and was fined $200 and costs. Boston *Christian Science Monitor*, August 17, 1917.

41 As Chairman of the Publication Committee, Bliss was involved in many of the papers being prepared for publication. Two manuscripts were found in Bliss's

papers. One of these was published by the society (see Charles O. Green's, *An Incident in the Battle of Middleburg*). The other manuscript found, which apparently was never published, was from George Earle (see Chapter 3).

42 Rogers, ed., *Biographical Cyclopedia*, 556-57; *Providence Journal*, August 30, 1928; invitation from "Executive Committee on Inaugural Ceremonies," dated Dec. 15, 1880, found in Bliss's papers; the *National Republican*, March 2, 1881.

43 The articles appeared in the Providence *Journal* throughout the month of May 1880. The portion of Bliss's piece about meeting with Moss and Lee was included in the June 30, 1880, Virginia newspaper the *Farmville Mercury*. It was titled, "A Romance in Real Life" and incorrectly referred to the writer as George W. Bliss. "The following extract from the Providence (Rhode Island) *Journal* will be interesting to many Virginia readers. The writer is evidently Judge George W. Bliss, of Providence; and the Capt. Wm. A. Moss referred to is our big-hearted and genial friend—late of the C. S. A. and now Treasurer of the county of Buckingham. There is a spice of the romance and chivalry that gathers around this incident so gently touched by Judge Bliss, calculated to warm every Virginian heart, and place the bloody shirts of all the Republican editors and orators of the North at half mast. What a blessing it would be to our torn and bleeding country if the cowardly bomb proof patriots, that from secure places during the 'reign of blood,' hissed on the dogs of war, could only appreciate the pure sentiments and manly generosity of those brave spirits that quailed not in the deadly shock of battle. If such knightly combatants as Captains Moss and Bliss, can cordially grasp each other's hands across the 'bloody chasm,' why should the malignant cowards who failed to follow either flag, now wave the bloody shirt and kindle anew the fires of hate, of malice and of strife." Bliss's "extract" was then presented. Bliss's second visit to Richmond was reported in another series of articles which appeared in the *Providence Journal* in May and June 1882. These articles were apparently written by a companion of "the Major." They reported on a visit Bliss had made ten years earlier to Henry W. Longfellow and included a letter from the famous author. Bliss also visited the White House and shook hands with President Chester A. Arthur. All these articles were found in a Bliss scrapbook among his papers.

44 On Farragut Post No. 8, see *Proceedings* of the Nineteenth, Twentieth and Forty-First Annual Encampment GAR, 12, 23; 41, 42; and 7, 29, respectively.

45 Bliss and Bannister were listed at 2 College St., Providence, in the 1875 *Providence City*, 40, 49. Information on Bannister was presented in a catalogue, Kenkeleba House, *Edward Mitchell Bannister 1828-1901* (New York; Harry N. Abrams, Inc., 1992). The catalogue was part of an exhibit of Bannister's work presented at the Kenkeleba Gallery and Whitney Museum of American Art in 1991-92. At the 1901 exhibit, three paintings owned by Bliss were displayed. "The Grove," n.d., and "Bath Road Cliff, Newport," 1889, were owned solely

by Bliss. A third painting displayed, "Dutch Cow and Girl," n.d., was owned by Bliss and an individual named Gardner. "Bath Road Cliff, Newport" is still in the possession of Bliss's descendants. The story of Bliss and visitors viewing Bannister's painting is from recollections by Frederick Emerson of discussions with his grandmother, Helen L. Bliss Emerson, circa 1955.

46 According to the Sept. 3, 1904, edition of *The Corrector*, a Sag Harbor, New York, newspaper, Bliss had sailed the *Fanchon* to Sag Harbor for thirteen consecutive years, suggesting that by 1891 he owned the "auxiliary yawl."

47 Several *Fanchon* logbooks were found in Bliss's papers.

48 The cartoon was part of an article from the *Boston American* newspaper of July 19, 1914. It was found in Bliss's papers; another copy of the cartoon is located in the Bliss folder of Special Collections at Union College, Schenectady, N. Y.

49 The 1892-93 *East Providence Directory*, 117, noted that George N. Bliss, judge of the Seventh Judicial District Court, "sits at 2:30 P.M., Fridays, and every day at 9 A.M." Bliss's court was the only one listed for the town.

50 Bliss's Medal of Honor, and a large "Certificate" associated with it and issued in 1927, are in the possession of Bliss's descendants. In a 1911 article, Bliss wrote, "There were, first and last, over 2,000 men in my regiment, and I am the only man who received the Congressional medal of honor." (Washington, D. C., *National Tribune*, April 20, 1911) In 1916, Bliss was notified by the adjutant general of the War Department that his name had been entered on the "Army and Navy Medal of Honor Roll." Established by congress that year, the Honor Roll came with a special pension of ten dollars a month. The War Department letter, dated Oct. 11, 1916, was found in Bliss's papers. Bliss's daughter, Helen Bliss Emerson, in discussions with William Emerson, circa 1955, spoke of her father displaying his medal at parades.

51 As with the other former Confederates that he encountered at Waynesboro, Bliss became friends with Baber, Hamilton, and Garnett. In postwar letters to Bliss, found in Bliss's papers, each of the three men mentioned visits to their homes by him. Under the header, "Enemies Meet as Friends," a Virginia newspaper reported Bliss's visit to Garnett's home in May 1903. "Captain George N. Bliss of East Providence, R. I. has been spending some days with Thomas W. Garnett, of Curdsville, their first meeting since September 28, 1864, when Captain Bliss met single-handed in a cavalry duel Mr. Garnett and a portion of the Fourth Virginia cavalry. . ." The article recounted Bliss's charge and capture, and Garnett's role in returning Bliss's saber to him. (Richmond Virginia *Times-Dispatch*, May 10, 1903)

52 Letter from Bliss to his wife Fannie, July 6, 1913. Bliss and Confederate General Thomas T. Munford had become friends after the war. They corresponded numerous times, and several Munford letters to Bliss are transcribed in this

volume. Munford visited Bliss at least once, in 1897 (Bliss, *Sabre Lost and Found*, 35).

53 Information is from Fannie Bliss's obituary in the Providence *Evening Bulletin* of March 26, 1930. Only three of Bliss's five children to reach adulthood survived him. Two sons, Gerald M. Bliss and George M. Bliss, had predeceased their father.

54 From news clipping in unknown paper found in Bliss's papers.

Bibliography

Published Works by George N. Bliss

Cavalry Service with General Sheridan and Life in Libby Prison. Providence, R.I.; The Rhode Island Soldiers and Sailors Historical Society, 1884.

Duffié and the Monument to his Memory. Providence, R.I.; The Providence Press, 1890.

The First Rhode Island Cavalry at Middleburg, Virginia June 17 and 18, 1863 Providence, R.I.; The Rhode Island Soldiers and Sailors Historical Society, 1889.

How I Lost My Sabre in War and Found It in Peace, "Personal Narratives of the Events in the War of the Rebellion, Papers Read Before the R. I. Soldiers and Sailors Historical Society," sixth ser., no. 2 (Providence: Published by the Society, 1903)

Prison Life of Lieut. James M. Fales. (Personal Narratives (Second Series, No. 15), iii. Providence, R.I.: N. Bangs Williams & Co., 1882.

Reminiscences of Service in the First Rhode Island Cavalry, Providence, R.I.; Sidney S. Rider, 1878.

Primary Sources

Ayling, Augustus D. *Revised Register of the Soldiers and Sailors of New Hampshire in the War of the Rebellion 1861-1866* (Concord: Ira C. Evans, 1895).

Bliss, Aaron T., compiler. *Genealogy of the Bliss Family in America* (Midland, Michigan, published by the author, 1982).

Bliss, J. Homer. *Genealogy of the Bliss Family of America* (Boston Mass.: Rockwell and Churchill, 1880).

Brandt, Henry Y. *1865 Schenectady Directory* (Schenectady: W. D. Davis, 1865).

Burrage, Henry S. *Brown in the Civil War: A Memorial* (Providence: Providence Press Co., 1868).

Catalogue of the Officers and Students of Brown University, 1856-57 & 1857-58 (Providence: Knowles, Anthony & Co., 1856, 1857).

Crowninshield, Benjamin W. *A History of the First Regiment of Massachusetts Cavalry Volunteers* (Boston and New York: Houghton, Mifflin and Co., 1891).

Denison, Frederick. *Sabres and Spurs: The First Regiment Rhode Island Cavalry in the Civil War, 1861-1865. Its Origin, Marches, Scouts, Skirmishing Raids, Battles, Sufferings, Victories and Appropriate Official Papers, with the Roll of Honor and the Roll of the Regiment.* Providence: The First Rhode Island Cavalry Veterans Association, 1876).

History of the State of Rhode Island with Illustrations (Philadelphia: Hong, Wade & Co., 1878).

Johnston, Sarah H., complier. *Lineage Book National Society of the Daughters of the American Revolution* (Harrisburg, Penn.: Telegraph Printing Co., 1913).

Lee, Henry C. *Pocket Diary*, American Civil War Museum, Richmond, Virginia.

Meyer, William E. "The Sailor on Horseback," Personal Narratives, 7th ser. No. 5 [Providence, Soldiers and Sailors Historical Society, 1912].

University Grammar School. *Catalogue of the Teachers and Students of the University Grammar School* (Providence: Hammond, Angell & Co., 1872).

Waite, Otis Frederick R. *New Hampshire in the Great Rebellion* (Claremont, N. H.: Tracy, Chase & Co., 1870).

Secondary Sources

Adams, George. 1853 *Fall River Directory, Embracing a Part of Tiverton* (Fall River: R. & J. Adams, 1853).

Akers, Anne Trice Thompson. "Colonel Thomas T. Munford and the Last Cavalry Operations of the Civil War in Virginia" (Virginia

Polytechnic Institute and State University, unpublished Master of Arts thesis: 1981).

Andreas, A. T. *History of Chicago from the Earliest Period to the Present Time* (Chicago: The A. T. Andreas Co., 1886).

Annals of the War (Philadelphia: The Philadelphia *Times*, 1879).

Annual Report of Adjutant General of the State of Rhode Island for the Year 1865 (Providence: Providence Press Co., 1866).

Anonymous. *History of the State of Rhode Island with Illustrations* (Philadelphia: Hong, Wade & Co., 1878).

Bailey, O. H. and Hazen, J. C. *Bird's Eye View of Pawtucket, & Central Falls, R. I.* (Boston: J. K. Nauber & Co., 1877).

Bates, Louise. *Historical Catalogue of Brown University,1764-1914* (Providence, R.I., Brown University, 1914).

Blake, Mortimer. *A History of the Town of Franklin, Massachusetts, from its Settlement to the Completion of Its First Century, 2ⁿᵈ March 1878; with Genealogical Notices of Its Earliest Families, Sketches of Its Professional Men, and a Report of the Centennial Celebration* (Franklin, Mass.: Published by the Committee of the Town, 1879).

Bowditch, *Memorial of Nathaniel Bowditch, Lieutenant, First Massachusetts Cavalry* (Boston: Privately Printed by John Wilson & Son, 1865).

Centennial Catalog of 1795 – 1895 of the Officers and Alumni of Union College in the City of Schenectady, N. Y. (Troy: Troy Times Printing House, 1895).

Circular and Catalogue of the Law School of the University of Albany for the year 1860-61 (Albany: Munsell & Rowland, 1861).

City Council. *City Charter and Revised Ordinances of the City of Fall River: With Appendix* (Fall River, Massachusetts; Almy, Milne & Co., 1879).

Descriptive Muster Rolls (DMR) for the First R.I. Regiment, R.I. State Archives.

Dyer, Elisha. *Annual Report of the Adjutant General of the State of Rhode Island and Providence Plantations for the Year 1865. Corrected Revised and Republished in Accordance with Provisions of Chapters 705 and 767 of the Public Laws.* 2 vols. (Providence, R.I.; E.L. Freeman & Son, 1893 and 1895).

Emerson, William A. *History of the Town of Douglas [Massachusetts] From the Earliest Period to the Close of 1878* (Boston: Frank W. Bird, 1879).

Emerson, William C. and Stevens, Elizabeth C., eds. *"Don't tell father I have been shot at," The Civil War Letters of Captain George N. Bliss, First Rhode Island Cavalry* (Jefferson, N.C.: McFarland Press, 2018).

Fall River Directory, 1853.

Faust, Drew Gilpin. *The Republic of Suffering: Death and the American Civil War* (New York: Alfred A. Knopf, 2008).

Fenner, Henry M. *History of Fall River Massachusetts* (Fall River: Monroe Press, 1911).

Gallagher, Gary W. *The American Civil War* (The Great Courses, Chantilly, Va., 2000).

Green, Charles O. *An Incident in the Battle of Middleburg*, in *Personal Narratives of Events in the War of the Rebellion, Seventh Series, No. 3* (Rhode Island Soldiers and Sailors Historical Society; 1911).

Grieve, Robert. *An Illustrated History of Pawtucket, Central Falls and Vicinity, A Narrative of the Growth and Evolution of the Community* (Pawtucket, R. I.: Pawtucket Gazette and Chronicle, 1897).

Heidler, David S. and Heidler, Jeanne T. *Encyclopedia of the American Civil War: A Political, Social and Military History*. (New York: W.W. Norton, 2000).

Hopewell, Lynn. *A Biographical Register of the Members of Fauquier County Virginia's "Black Horse Cavalry" 1859–1865, Company H, Fourth Virginia Cavalry* (unpublished manuscript: http://blackhorsecavalry. org/files/2007-06-18,%202006-07-30-1830%20FCPL%20 manuscript%20wo%20Natv%20Sns%20.pdf).

Hudson, M. Ellery. *Fourteenth Annual Report of Factory Inspection* (Providence, R. I.; E. L. Freeman Company, State Printers, 1908).

Johnston, Sarah H., complier. *Lineage Book National Society of the Daughters of American Revolution* (Harrisburg, Penn.: Telegraph Printing Co., 1913), XXXVII.

Jones, Rev. J. William, Secretary, *Southern Historical Society Papers*, Volumes XII & XIII (Richmond: Wm. Ellis Jones, Printer,1884).

Jordan, Ervin L., Jr. *Charlottesville and the University of Virginia in the Civil War* (Lynchburg: H. E. Howard, 1988).

Krick, Robert K. *9th Virginia Cavalry*, Virginia Regimental History Series, H. E. Howard Inc. http://9thvirginia.com/coa.html & http://9thvirginia.com/coh.html.

Marquis, Albert Nelson, ed., *Who's Who in New England: A Biographical Directory of Leading Living Men and Women of the States of Maine, New Hampshire, Vermont, Massachusetts, Rhode Island and Connecticut* (Chicago: A.N. Marquis & Co., 1909).

Pawtucket, Past and Present (Boston, Mass.: Walton Advertising & Printing, Co., 1917); *1857 Pawtucket and Woonsocket Directory* (New York, N. Y.: William H. Boyd, 1857).

Proceedings at the Nineteenth & Twentieth Annual Encampment of the Department of Rhode Island, Grand Army of the Republic.

Providence City Directories, 1857-1890.

Richards Harold H. *Standard Atlas of the Providence Metropolitan District, Volume 2,* (Springfield, Mass.: Richards Map Co., 1917).

Roberts, Allen E. *House Undivided, the Story of Freemasonry and the Civil War* (Richmond: Macoy Publishing and Masonic Supply Company, 1961).

Rogers, L. E., ed., *Biographical Cyclopedia of Representative Men of Rhode Island* (Providence: National Biographical Publishing Co., 1881).

Schenectady Directories, 1858-1890.

Spicer, William. *The High School Boys of the Tenth Rhode Island Regiment with a Roll of Teachers and Students of the Providence High School Who Served in the Army or Navy of the U.S. during the Rebellion,* Personal Narratives in the Events of the War of the Rebellion, Second Series, no. 13 (Providence: N. Bang Williams, 1882).

Stiles, Kenneth. *4th Virginia Cavalry,* 2nd Edition (Lynchburg, Virginia: H. E. Howard, Inc., 1985).

Union College, 1795-1895, A Record of the Commemoration of the One Hundredth Anniversary of the Founding of the Union College (New York, 1897).

U.S. War Department. *A Compilation of the Official Records of the Union and Confederate Armies.* 70 vols. (Washington, D.C.: Government Printing Office, 1880-1901).

Waite, Otis Frederick R. *New Hampshire in the Great Rebellion* (Claremont, N. H.: Tracy, Chase & Co., 1870).

Index

Numbers in *bold italics* indicate pages with illustrations